Don't let the title *PROOF* fool you; this is not a traditional book about apologetics. It is a book that works out how Christians themselves are the "proof" of God's grace. Instead of viewing robust biblical teaching as a deadening weight on vital Christian living, these two authors are busy finding freedom through the intoxicating joy of irresistible grace (as the subtitle puts it). The detailed endnotes will satisfy more intellectual readers ... prove a great help to the rest of us who w... of the central truths of the gospel transforn...

D. A. CARSON, Research Profe...

PROOF is one of the most well-reasoned and heart-engaging presentations of the Reformed Faith I have read since becoming a Christian in 1968. Rooted in the history of theology, faithful to the text of Scripture, and accessible to a contemporary audience, these brothers throw the curtains wide open on the contours and grandeur of the gospel.

SCOTTY SMITH, Teacher-in-Residence, West End Community Church

PROOF is biblical, forceful, winsome, and clear about who God is, how God works, and what God wants. Daniel and Timothy have given us a treasure!

DARRIN PATRICK, Pastor, The Journey

A book on the doctrines of grace that delights as much as it challenges? That exhilarates as much as it informs? That entertains as much as it enlightens? Be still my beating heart.... *PROOF* is a rare breed indeed. Get it, savor it, let it bowl you over with the spectacular grace of God.

JARED WILSON, author of *The Storytelling God*

This book demonstrates a wealth of reflection on both modern and ancient sources, helping us rediscover the scandal of the gospel,... the central fountain of the Christian life.

J. D. GREEAR, author of *Stop Asking Jesus into Your Heart*

Daniel and Timothy will take you on a journey of grace in a way that you've never lived it before!

GREGG R. ALLISON, Professor of Christian Theology,
The Southern Baptist Theological Seminary

PROOF is a fresh, new approach to the historical doctrines of grace. It will refresh and encourage the veteran learner and provide substance without the complicated jargon for the novice.

TRILLIA NEWBELL, author of *United: Captured by God's Vision for Diversity*

Sadly, the doctrines of grace have often been used to score theological points. But *PROOF* shows how grace changes lives and brings joy.

TIM CHESTER, Associate Director, Porterbrook Seminary

At the end of *PROOF* you will walk away with a comprehensive knowledge of grace, and even more importantly, with a heart of worship for the Grace-Giver.

FLAME, Grammy-nominated hip-hop artist, ClearSightMusic.com

Modern believers, who often unknowingly swing from license to legalism in their attempts to please God, need this joyous proclamation of the plan of salvation. This is a wonderful way of introducing the Canons of Dort to the heirs of the Me Generation.

ERIC REDMOND, Professor-in-Residence, New Canaan Baptist Church

If predestination has often felt stodgy and stifling, this book's for you. *PROOF* is not your standard portrayal of Reformed theology. It's unlike anything I've come across before. The style is engaging, the stories are captivating, the logic is compelling, and best of all the theology is rock solid and biblically faithful. Trust me, you'll love this book (even when you don't agree with it!).

SAM STORMS, Lead Pastor, Bridgeway Church

Pastorally wise and academically rigorous, ... *PROOF* will pull you into the conversation and press you to consider afresh the biblical text and your own experience of God's grace.

J. MICHAEL THIGPEN, Executive Director, Evangelical Theological Society

PROOF contrasts true grace with our typical perception of grace in a way that will drive souls to experience freedom, joy, and worship.

REBEKAH HANNAH, Columbia University Christian Union Ministry Fellow, editor of GospelTaboo.com

Daniel Montgomery doesn't just understand grace ... no, grace arrested him, then grace tutored him, and now grace compels him to help others stand amazed.

DAVE HARVEY, Pastor, Four Oaks Community Church

PROOF paints a powerful picture that the gospel is not a cheap bucket of grace that sits at the foot of the cross. Rather, the gospel is an ever-flowing, deep river of irresistible grace that flows from the foot of the cross.

BRIAN CROFT, Senior Pastor, Auburndale Baptist Church

Since Before Time Began

PROOF

FINDING FREEDOM *through the* INTOXICATING JOY *of* IRRESISTIBLE GRACE

DANIEL MONTGOMERY *and* TIMOTHY PAUL JONES

ZONDERVAN®
.com

ZONDERVAN

PROOF

Copyright © 2014 by Daniel Montgomery and Timothy Paul Jones

This title is also available as a Zondervan ebook.
Visit www.zondervan.com/ebooks.

This title is also available in a Zondervan audio edition.
Visit www.zondervan.fm.

Requests for information should be addressed to:

Zondervan, 3900 *Sparks Drive SE, Grand Rapids, Michigan 49546*

Library of Congress Cataloging-in-Publication Data

Montgomery, Daniel, 1974–
    Proof : finding freedom through the intoxicating joy of irresistible grace / Daniel
Montgomery and Timothy Paul Jones.
      pages cm
     ISBN 978-0-310-51389-6 (softcover)
     1. Grace (Theology) 2. Liberty--Religious aspects—Christianity. I. Title.
BT761.3.M663 2014
234–dc23
                                                 2013049565

This book is published in association with Nappaland Literary Agency, an independent agency dedicated to publishing works that are: Authentic. Relevant. Eternal. Visit us on the web at: *http://www.NappalandLiterary.com.*

Cover design: Curt Diepenhorst
Cover photography: Tomas Rodriguez/Corbis
Interior design and composition: Greg Johnson/Textbook Perfect

Printed in the United States of America

HB 11.14.2017

PROOF
is dedicated to our partners in the gospel,
the current and future pastors
of the Sojourn Network.

Truly, you are proof of God's grace.

Philippians 1:3-5

CONTENTS

Chapter 1

WAKE UP TO GRACE

I do not at all understand the mystery of grace — only that it meets us where we are but does not leave us where it found us.

ANNE LAMOTT

What left a mark
No longer stings
Because grace makes beauty
Out of ugly things.

U2, "Grace"

Have you ever had a dream … that you were so sure was real? What if you were unable to wake from that dream? How would you know the difference between the dreamworld and the real world?

MORPHEUS, *The Matrix*

WHAT IF WE TOLD YOU THAT YOU'RE LIVING IN A DREAMWORLD? The world that you think you know is an illusion — an alternate reality that makes the world of *The Matrix* look like child's play.

You've grown up thinking that your performance makes you who you are. You've been taught that it's true since you were a kid. You heard the message in chore charts, report cards, standardized tests, recitals, and athletic banquets. Then you grew up, and you heard the message again from your coworkers, your boss, your friends, and even your spouse.

Everything from Viagra to Pinterest tells us it's true. Performance matters. It's the message that dominates our view of reality: "If you do well, you will be rewarded. If you don't perform, you'll miss out, and you might even be punished." Performance — work and reward — is one of the basic structures of our lives. As a result, we grow up thinking, "I am what I am because of what I do ... or because of what I've failed to do."

But what if we told you that it's all a lie?

What if we proved to you that, when you stake your identity on your performance, you're delusional. Better yet, what if we told you a truth that can set you free from this lifelong delusion?

Here's how the apostle Paul expressed this truth: "By the grace of God I am what I am," and "What do you have that you did not receive?" (1 Corinthians 15:10; 4:7). In other words, "It's what God gives to you that makes you who you are." What matters most in life isn't anything that you have done or can do. It's what God chooses to do for you through Jesus Christ.

Waking Up from Our Delusions about God

Now, what if we told you that *God* isn't who you think he is?

Most people believe in a God who is inspiring but not particularly powerful. He may manage a miracle or two from time to time, but mostly he watches the world from a distance and shows up occasionally to remind us to make better choices. According to research from sociologist Christian Smith, the overwhelming majority of American teenagers and young adults assume that God is *not* involved in the day-by-day management of the universe. "God," in the words of one fifteen-year-old, "just kind of stays back and watches, like he's watching a play, like he's a producer."

"This God is not demanding," Smith observes. "He actually can't be, since his job is to solve our problems and make people feel good." He is little more than a Divine Butler who serves us or a Cosmic Therapist who comforts us.[1] This deity is, in the words of a popular song, "watching us from a distance," but "we are the instruments" and our destinies are up to us.[2]

The participants in Christian Smith's studies seldom used the word *grace* to describe God's workings in the world. In fact, the term "grace" was mentioned more frequently in reference to the TV show *Will and Grace* than in connection with God.[3] This should come as no surprise to us. After all, if people see God as a Divine Butler and Cosmic Therapist, there's little need for grace. Grace is an undeserved gift—not a passing sense of comfort provided by a personal problem-solver. No grace, no mystery, and no majesty marks the workings of such a deity. When life is going well, he fits nicely on the shelf. When trouble comes, he rarely *makes* anything better. Instead, he simply encourages people to put more effort into *doing* better. Even if he does happen to intervene, his assistance depends on our willingness to cooperate.

There's a problem with this God, though.

He isn't real.

The butler-and-therapist god is a lifeless and hopeless dream, a sham god who deserves no glory and gives no grace. But untold millions place their faith in this illusion of god, never realizing that what they're ultimately worshiping is themselves.

The true and living God, revealed to us in the Scriptures, is neither a butler nor a therapist, and he certainly is no dream. He is the gracious and holy King whose reign has erupted into human history in the person of Jesus Christ (Revelation 1:4 – 8). This God "does whatever pleases him, in the heavens and on the earth, in the seas and all their depths" (Psalm 135:6). Whatever he plans, he brings to pass; whatever he declares, he does (2 Kings 19:25; Isaiah 46:10 – 11). Through his word, he created all things. By his word, he holds everything together (John 1:1 – 3; Hebrews 1:2 – 3).

This God we meet in the Bible is no passive producer, encouraging people to perform better. He is a measureless mystery whose plans never fail, and his beauty enthralls the hearts of those who love him (Psalm 45:11). He swirls solar systems into existence out of empty space (Hebrews 11:3). He sets princes on thrones and flings kings down in the dust (Daniel 2:21). He has unleashed his kingdom on earth through a virgin's womb and crushed the power of the devil through his cross and empty tomb (Luke 2:26 – 52; John 1:14; Revelation 12:1 – 12).

And yet, paradoxically, this God of power and glory is also a God of grace.

When your soul is awakened to the serpent-crushing sovereign described in the Scriptures, it's difficult to get comfortable on the couch of a Cosmic Therapist. The true God is a wild and unpredict-

"Millions of people — inside the church as well as outside — think they love God when in fact they hate him. What they love is the tame 'God' they've made up in their heads based on what they want God to be like. They keep the real God out of their consciousness. If they did become conscious of him, in all his holiness and power, they would hate him."[4]

GREG FORSTER

able mystery. "The LORD is God; besides him there is no other," the ancient prophets declared and thus shelved the stories of every other god — including the Divine Butler and Cosmic Therapist — in the fiction section (Deuteronomy 4:35 – 40; Isaiah 45:5).[5]

In eternity past, God chose to save undeserving sinners "to the praise of his glorious grace" (Ephesians 1:5 – 6). Now he is on a global rescue mission, chasing down undeserving rebels and changing their hearts so that they turn to him and freely submit to his kingship (Isaiah 43:5 – 7; Acts 16:14; Ephesians 1:5; Revelation 5:9 – 10). By his grace, God transforms sinners into his beloved adopted children, filling the bank accounts of their identity with all the goodness of his Son, sealing their destiny by the power of his Spirit, and securing them on a journey that will not end until his splendor floods the earth like waters surging in the sea (Psalm 72:19; Habakkuk 2:14; Romans 4:24; 2 Corinthians 1:21 – 22; Ephesians 1:4 – 5, 13 – 14). The true and living God does all this for his own glory and for the praise of his grace (Isaiah 43:7; Ephesians 1:6; 1 Peter 5:10). When the apostle Paul described God's works of grace, he found himself facedown in worship, overwhelmed by a mystery he couldn't comprehend: "Oh, the depth of the riches of the wisdom and knowledge of God! How unsearchable his judgments, and his paths beyond tracing out! ... To him be the glory forever!" (Romans 11:33, 36).

Waking Up from the Delusion That Grace Depends on You

But the popularity of the butler-and-therapist deity shouldn't surprise us. "There is no doctrine more hated by worldlings," pastor

> "The gospel is not really the gospel unless it is a gospel of *grace*; in other words, the gospel is only good news if it announces what *God* has done to save sinners."[6]
>
> JAMES MONTGOMERY BOICE AND PHILIP RYKEN

One Gospel, Three Aspects

The gospel is the good news that God's kingdom power has entered human history through the life, death, and resurrection of Jesus Christ. When we repent and rely on his righteousness instead of our own, his kingdom power transforms us, and we become participants in the restoration of God's world. The three aspects of the gospel are the kingdom, the cross, and God's grace.

1. The gospel of the kingdom is life with God under God's rule.
2. The gospel of the cross is the life, death, and resurrection of Jesus by which God accomplishes our salvation, rescues us from his wrath, incorporates us into his people, and inaugurates his reign in the world.
3. The gospel of grace is the wonderful news that God accepts us, shares his life with us, and adopts us as heirs of his kingdom not because we have earned it or deserve it but because God chooses to give all of this freely at Christ's expense.

C. H. Spurgeon once pointed out, "as the great, stupendous, but yet most certain doctrine of [God's] sovereignty."[7] Ever since human sin plunged the world into darkness, people have been working to bury God's sovereignty and mystery beneath an ever-multiplying multitude of graceless counterfeits (Romans 1:23). As John Calvin once observed, "Human nature is, so to speak, a workshop that's continually crafting idols."[8]

The precise shape of these counterfeits may shift from one generation to the next, but the patterns of idolatry are as ancient as sin and as current as the last commercial you watched. Sometimes idols happen to be physical images of created beings, but not always. Idols are also found in less obvious locations — in the balance of your bank account, in the praises of your peers, in the delusion that you can control your destiny. God the Divine Butler and Cosmic Therapist is simply the latest expression of this long line of pretend gods, and his popularity isn't limited to people who sleep in on Sunday mornings. Even among those who list "Christian" on their social-media profiles, the distinction between the living God and the cultural counterfeit can sometimes be less than clear.[9]

One popular television preacher professes on his website that "a personal relationship with Jesus" is humanity's only hope. And yet, despite this tip of the hat to Jesus, his messages are dominated by talk of the butler-and-therapist deity. As he tells it, God is capable of improving our lives by releasing "more of his favor" — but, until we do our part, God can't do much of anything at all. "God is waiting on you," he proclaims. "You don't get the grace unless you step out. You have to make the first move."[10] In other words, whether or not you receive God's grace depends largely on you. God doesn't do his part until "you do everything you can do" and he "sees your resolve."[11]

This way of thinking about God is wildly popular — but it's simply not true. The grace of the sovereign God has never waited for us to make the first move. Forbidden fruit was still fresh on our first parents' lips when God stepped into the Garden of Eden and lavished undeserved favor on them. At the very moment when Adam and Eve deserved death that never ends, God clothed them with the skin of a beast and promised them a Son whose triumph would grind the serpent's skull into the ground (Genesis 3:15, 21).

God showed grace to the first two human beings, but it wasn't because he discerned good intentions buried somewhere deep inside their souls. When God found them hiding in the garden, they were clutching clumps of leaves against their groins and blaming everyone but themselves for their failure. God's sovereign grace blossomed in that new-fallen garden for the same reason grace fills people's lives today. The untamed God gives undeserved mercy to unresponsive sinners. God shows grace, not due to any human deed or desire, but because he has a merciful plan — a plan that began before time and requires no contribution from any of us (Romans 9:11 – 16; Ephesians 1:3 – 6; 2 Timothy 1:9).

Waking Up from the Delusion that Leads to Despair

Grace threatens the fleeting sense of self-centered comfort that our dreamworld provides — and that's why television preachers with Texas-sized smiles aren't the only people living under the delusion that we can do something to trigger God's grace. Deep inside, that's what we all want to think. At the root of every counterfeit deity and every human religion is the notion that our performance can achieve some sort of negotiated settlement with a holy God. The butler-and-therapist deity is simply the latest riff in a chorus that the whole world has been singing ever since our first parents left Eden. This isn't just the story of the ancient pagans and a few popular preachers today. It's your story and mine.

"Human nature," a German preacher named Martin Luther once pointed out, "is no longer able to imagine or conceive any way to be made right with God other than works."[12] We are willing to "buy any recipe for salvation as long as it leaves the responsibility for cooking up salvation firmly in human hands."[13] Only a message of grace can shatter the delusion that we're capable of cooking up our own salvation through schemes that barter human works for divine merit — and that's precisely why human religion will always attack and avoid every hint of authentic grace.

Human religion allows us to delude ourselves into believing that, somewhere in the inmost recesses of our souls, there is some minuscule outpost of goodness that kick-starts God's work in our lives — some prayer we can pray or righteous deed we can do. Even if we admit that we can't do anything to *start* God's work, human religion assures us that *surely* there's something we can do to keep it going. And so we work to manage our sins more effectively, to serve in more ministries at church, to multiply our theological knowledge, to keep artificial preservatives away from our family's dinner plates — whatever it is that we think might merit more favor from God and others. When that happens, the good news of grace has been eclipsed by a delusion that's not really good news at all (Galatians 1:7; 5:1 – 12).

If you're like us, you've spent some time trying to gain God's approval through pleasing and performing. Maybe you're still on that pathway right now. Perhaps you remember a time when you were profoundly aware of what it means to be unconditionally accepted by God. But now that sense of wonder has faded, buried beneath the burden of

"Christianity is not a religion; it is the proclamation of the end of religion. Religion is a human activity dedicated to the job of reconciling God to humanity and humanity to itself. The gospel, however — the good news of our Lord and Savior, Jesus Christ — is the astonishing announcement that God has done the whole work of reconciliation without a scrap of human assistance."[14]

ROBERT FARRAR CAPON

more expectations than you'll ever be able to manage. You still trust in Jesus, but the joy of his grace has gotten lost in the shuffle.

You say yes to far too many tasks, scrambling after the slightest hints of praise in the faces around you. When you fall short of others' expectations, you replay your failures again and again. On your better days, your successes almost seem to balance your screwups. On your darker days, you suspect that your shortcomings have forever skewed everyone's opinion of you — even God's — and you wonder what it will take to regain God's good favor. In the end, you're left with a calendar that's full but a soul that still feels empty, one more captive of the deadly delusion that your deeds determine your identity. The futility you feel is real, and it's far larger than you. The whole world groans beneath the weight of this vast gap between the way things are and the way we long for them to be (Romans 8:20 – 25).

Waking Up to Grace

The purpose of *PROOF* is to be an alarm clock that awakens you from the delusion that your destiny depends on you and frees you to discover the intoxicating joy of God's wild and free grace. "Salvation comes from the LORD," the wayward prophet Jonah whispered when he finally woke up to grace — and that's precisely the point of *PROOF* (Jonah 2:9). From beginning to end, everything in your salvation, even your faith, has been a gift that God single-handedly planned and secured (Ephesians 1:4 – 5; 2:1 – 8). When the triumph cry of Jesus thundered from the cross — "It is finished" — every human work that God demanded was fulfilled for everyone who would ever trust in him (Matthew 27:50; John 19:28 – 30).

The empty wisdom of human religion proclaims, "What goes around comes around. God helps those who help themselves. You get what you pay for" — but these are lies that lead only to bondage and despair. The gospel of grace speaks an entirely different word, a word that's filled with paradox and mystery. By God's grace, we get what someone else paid for. By grace, God helps those who not only *can't* help themselves, they don't even want to. By grace, what goes around stops at the foot of the cross, never to come around again.

What you need isn't a better purpose, another prayer, or one more plan for self-improvement. What you need is what we all need — to "wake up" to God's wonderful and undeserved love. You need to wake up to the freedom and joy of what God — on his own — has accomplished for us in Jesus. What you need is grace. To understand what this grace is like, let's first take a look at what this grace *isn't*.

Grace Is Not Approval

The grace that we're describing here doesn't tell us that we're already good enough for God. It's not a diluted sentimentalism that downplays sin and never calls for change. That's what German martyr Dietrich Bonhoeffer lampooned as "cheap grace" — grace without any growth or change.[15] Such "grace" fits well with the delusion of a butler-and-therapist deity, but it produces no lasting joy. Instead, it mocks the holiness of God and births a sense of entitlement that expects God to approve whatever we think will make us happy.

Grace Is Not Earned

And the grace we're describing is not simply a starting point that requires us to perform after we're "in." It's not a bait-and-switch system that starts with salvation by grace but then burdens people with a list of requirements that must be maintained if they want to remain right with God. That kind of system hides behind the label of grace, but it isn't grace at all. We cannot work hard enough to earn God's love (Ephesians 2:9). Bait-and-switch grace is just one more expression of human religion that tries to add effort and earning to God's finished work. It's grace with strings attached, and grace with strings attached isn't really grace at all (Romans 11:6; Galatians 2:15 – 21).

"Grace means God's love in action toward people who merited the opposite of love. Grace means God moving heaven and earth to save sinners who could not lift a finger to save themselves."[16]

J. I. PACKER

Grace Is God's Wonderful Acceptance Given Freely at Christ's Expense

What we're describing as "grace" is a breathtaking shot of divine love that leaves you slaphappy and staggering at the truth that God has accepted you fully and completely, not due to anything you could ever do, but solely through what Jesus Christ has already done. This grace is not a payout that God grants to winners. It's one-way love that's not based on anything we have done, can do, or might do.[17] It's not even a reward that God hands out to those who happen to choose him (Romans 9:16). It's *God's wonderful acceptance of us not because we have earned it or deserved it but because he gives it to us freely at Christ's expense.*

As long as we live under the delusion that God doles out favor according to our deeds, fear of punishment will always crowd out the freedom and joy of God's grace. It's this fear that drives us to try harder but then leaves us wondering: *What if I didn't really mean it when I asked Jesus into my heart? Does this sin mean I'm not saved anymore? Was that sickness God's punishment for something I did? What did we do that caused God not to let us have children? Did she die because God was angry with me?* Only grace can set us free from such fears. Grace alone enables us to trust that Jesus already took the punishment for every failure — past, present, and future — so that no condemnation remains for those who find their rest in him (Romans 8:1 – 4; 1 John 4:18).

Why Grace Matters

The reason these truths matter so deeply to the two of us is not because we get it perfectly. If you spent a few moments with our wives or children, you'd soon learn that we struggle day by day to live by grace. We need to wake up from the delusion that we can earn God's favor just as much as you. Grace matters to us because we've seen over and over how people's lives are changed when they drink deeply from this thirst-quenching well. Grace matters because we've tasted it — just a bit — and found that only grace satisfies.

When the church where we serve began, I [Daniel] was a twenty-five-year-old patriarch in a congregation where the average age was twenty. The fact that I had a wife, a college degree, and my own apartment set me apart from the core group of teenagers and twentysomethings who began to gather in rented space near Bardstown Road in Louisville. Before long, I was struggling to juggle the roles of church planter, leader, preacher, pastor, husband, father, and friend. God blessed Sojourn with numeric growth, but I was still living as if God's grace and the church's growth depended on how well I performed. It didn't take long before I was frustrated, confused, and terrified of failure. My first response was to devour the latest leadership and church-growth books, to attend all the most promising conferences, and even to host a few conferences — but none of these efforts cured my fear of failure. I was seriously considering turning Sojourn over to a better leader and planting another church — or perhaps even leaving pastoral ministry altogether.

Then something happened that I can't completely explain.

I was leading a community group in a small apartment. I asked the participants to meditate in pairs on Psalm 51 and to confess their sins genuinely and specifically. As I began confessing my sins, I felt the overwhelming weight of my inadequacies, and the cheap veneer of my efforts shattered. Then, in the depths of this crushing brokenness, I found myself even more overwhelmed by the beauty and sufficiency of God's grace in Christ. Frustrations faded as I embraced anew the truth that I no longer had anything to prove because, in Christ, everything was already proven and done. None of this was new information. Yet, in that moment, I received the truth in a new way. I experienced what one author has described as "gospel wakefulness."[18] I knew with renewed depth that God's grace in my life didn't depend on my performance.

New connections emerged from this new wakefulness. Before, I'd always seen gospel proclamation and the personal experience of God's grace as two disconnected categories. But that's not what I found when I read King David's cry of confession in Psalm 51. In this psalm, the experience of God's pardon is precisely what compelled David to call his people to seek the righteous King of kings (Psalm 51:10 – 13). The same grace that releases us from our guilt drives us to declare God's grace to the world.

What I needed that night when God spoke to me through a psalm was living proof of grace that's bigger than me. I still need that proof, and so do you. Since that night, Sojourn has outgrown two locations and multiplied into a multicampus community of four thousand. This community has birthed a church-planting network and a movement in the horn of Africa that has seen more than fifty thousand people turn to Christ. Yet none of us will ever outgrow the need to be reminded anew of the wonder of God's grace — grace so outrageous that it overwhelms the most rebellious, offends the most religious, and lavishes life-giving love on the likes of you and me.

What Is PROOF?

Whenever we talk about PROOF, we're referring to an acronym that summarizes five key facets of God's amazing grace. PROOF reminds us of five different ways in which we experience the grace of God at work in our lives:

P **Planned Grace** Before time began, God mapped out the plan of salvation from first to last. God planned to adopt particular people as his own children; Christ offered himself as a sacrifice for these people's sins and as a substitute who satisfied God's righteous requirements in their place (John 10:11 – 18; Ephesians 1:4 – 12).

R **Resurrecting Grace** Everyone is born spiritually dead. Left to ourselves, we will never choose God's way. God enables people to respond freely to his grace by giving them spiritual life through the power of Christ's resurrection (John 5:21; Ephesians 2:1 – 7).

O **Outrageous Grace** God chose people to be saved on the basis of his own sovereign will. He didn't base his choice to give us grace on anything that we did or might do (John 15:16; Ephesians 2:8 – 9).

O **Overcoming Grace** God works in the lives of his chosen people to transform their rebellion into surrender so that they freely repent and recognize Christ as the risen King (John 6:44, 65; Ephesians 2:4 – 10).

F **Forever Grace** God seals his people with his Holy Spirit so that they are preserved and persevere in faith until the final restoration of God's kingdom on the earth (John 10:27 – 29; Ephesians 1:13 – 14; 4:30).

The message that God saves us single-handedly by his grace sets us free from the unending treadmill of human effort and earning. And that's the point of this book.

Proof That Makes You Stand

The message of grace frees every believer to stand before God without fear (Romans 8:15 – 30; Hebrews 10:19 – 22; 1 John 4:15 – 18). This doesn't happen because our works have earned us a place in God's presence. It happens because our lives have been joined with Jesus through faith. Once we see that our salvation has *never* depended on anything we do, we have nothing to fear and nothing to prove. God in Christ has already provided every proof we need to be acquitted of every charge against us. This proof can never be earned, and it will never be deserved. It can only be received, and it's through this receiving that we find freedom and rest (Hebrews 4:3 – 11).

Proof That Makes You Stagger

But PROOF isn't only about evidence that enables you to stand before the bar of God's justice. It also points to a proof that causes you to stagger at the sheer strength of God's love. If you had been a British sailor in the days of pirates, part of your daily pay would have included a pint of rum.[19] In locations where water wasn't always drinkable and scurvy was a constant threat, these rations were vital for the sailors' health — but sometimes officers tried to slip some water into the rum. That's why sailors learned to "prove" their rations by mixing a bit of rum with gunpowder and igniting the concoction. If the gunpowder flashed, the sailors knew their rum was full proof.[20]

Like the pure rations that flashed in the tankards of eighteenth-century sailors, the undiluted message of grace is intoxicating — so strong that it leaves us slaphappy and singing for joy at the thought that God chose to love us precisely when there was nothing lovable about us.[21]

This joy is the fuel that drives Christian worship. When a church proclaims God's undiluted grace, the deadly delusions of human religion are drowned in a flood of gospel-fueled freedom and intoxicating joy. The response of the redeemed is to "sing and shout, teach and admonish, and experience the rich joy of God's indwelling Word. We sing with grace, and we sing because of grace."[22]

But don't take our word for it. Listen to the apostle Paul: "Do not get drunk on wine," Paul declared after describing God's gracious plan in exquisite detail. "Instead, be filled with the Spirit, speaking to one another with psalms, hymns, and songs from the Spirit" (Ephesians 5:18 – 19).[23] It's almost as if Paul was saying to the Ephesians, "You remember that fleeting sense of freedom you used to feel at parties when the wine was flowing a bit too freely and everyone joined together in a rollicking rendition of the same song? The freedom you were trying to find back then is precisely what God's grace now provides — but without the debauched choices in the night or the throbbing hangover when sunlight spills through your window the next morning. So sing like Christ has set you free, because he has! Overflow with his Spirit, and savor the intoxicating joy of God's wild and scandalous grace."

Nothing Left to Prove

It's time to wake up.

If you're a believer in Jesus Christ, your deeds no longer determine your destiny.

From the moment you first rest in Christ as your only hope, you have no failures to hide and no triumphs to hide behind. Your short-fallings no longer fall short. Your future is secure. You are forgiven, and you are free (Matthew 17:25 – 26; John 8:31 – 36). There is no greater favor for you to earn because God has already given you the greatest favor of all: "the gift of [being right with God] ... through the one man, Jesus Christ" (Romans 5:17). Nothing remains for you to prove. Your right standing is the right standing of Christ himself, given by grace through faith "from first to last" (Romans 1:17).

We realize that some of you may not be convinced. Maybe it sounds too good to be true — or too easy. Perhaps you've spent several years trying to earn your wings on the well-worn pathway of pleasing and performing. It started in your childhood with the adhesive stars on your Sunday school charts — each star signifying a visitor brought or a verse memorized — and the echoes of applause when you perfectly recited your part in the church play. Years later, the daily check boxes in your Bible reading plan have replaced those star-spangled charts, but the sense that there's *something* you can do to gain God's favor remains as strong as ever. The idea that there is no script to recite, no boxes to check, and no stars to collect seems too good to be true. And when you consider the appalling claim that your righteousness rates no higher than a sleazy pimp or a toothless meth addict who's just turned to Christ, your gut reaction is to blurt out, "But that isn't fair!"

And you're right.

It isn't fair.

It's better than fair.

It's grace.

PROOF FOR LIFE

Meditate on these Scriptures and song lyrics. Work with a friend or family member to memorize the catechism questions and answers.

What Is Grace?

God's wonderful acceptance of us not because we have earned it or deserved it but because he gives it to us freely at Christ's expense.

God's Grace in the Scriptures

"In love he predestined us for adoption to sonship through Jesus Christ, in accordance with his pleasure and will — to the praise of his glorious grace, which he has freely given us in the One he loves" (Ephesians 1:4 – 6).

"For it is by grace you have been saved, through faith — and this is not from yourselves, it is the gift of God — not by works, so that no one can boast" (Ephesians 2:8 – 9).

"He has saved us and called us to a holy life — not because of anything we have done but because of his own purpose and grace. This grace was given us in Christ Jesus before the beginning of time, but it has now been revealed through the appearing of our Savior" (2 Timothy 1:9 – 10).

God's Grace in Song

Lord, we confess our many faults
And how great our guilt has been
Foolish and vain were all of our thoughts
No good could come from within.

But by the mercy of our God
All our hopes begin
And by the water and the blood
Our souls are washed from sin.

It's not by works of righteousness
Which our own hands have done
But we are saved by our Father's grace
Abounding through his Son.

ISAAC WATTS, Neil Robins, and David LaChance,
"The Water and the Blood," © 2011 Sojourn Community Church

God's Grace in Summary

What is the gospel? The gospel is the good news that we enter God's kingdom through God's cross by God's grace (Colossians 1:13 – 14).

What is God's grace? God's wonderful acceptance of us not because we have earned it or deserve it but because he gives it to us freely at Christ's expense (Ephesians 1:6).

What are the enemies of God's grace? The lies that claim we're good enough or that we can work hard enough to earn God's love (Ephesians 2:9).

DANIEL MONTGOMERY AND JARED KENNEDY, *North Star Catechism*,
© 2013 Sojourn Community Church

Grace

The noun translated "grace" suggests gladness or generosity in someone's character;[24] specifically, the word described a person in power granting undeserved favor to someone with less power. In the New Testament, the noun "grace" typically points to God's wonderful acceptance of undeserving sinners not because they have earned it or deserved it but because God has chosen to give it to them freely at Christ's expense. Grace magnifies God's infinite worth by giving sinners the power to delight in God's glory without diminishing God's holiness.[25] This is grace that enables us to stand!

The New Testament term "grace" comes from a verb that meant "to rejoice" or "to be glad." The verb denoted deep inner gladness in response to something delightful. When God gave the Israelites peace in their land, the people spent their days in this sort of gladness (1 Kings 4:20 Septuagint). The prophet Zechariah predicted a future day when God's fulfillment of his promises would produce a celebration so full of gladness that it would seem like a party that extends throughout the cosmos. The hearts of God's people would "be glad as with wine.... In distant lands they will remember [the LORD]" (Zechariah 10:7 – 9).[26] This is grace that staggers our sin-sickened souls!

1. Grace is unearned favor initiated by the stronger and given to the weaker.[27] Grace always flows downhill. In the Old Testament, grace could describe a wealthy landowner showing kindness to the poor, a triumphant army giving compassion to the citizens of a defeated land, or the merciful gaze of God resting on rebellious people (Numbers 6:24 – 26; Deuteronomy 7:2; 28:50; Psalm 31:16; Proverbs 14:31; 28:8; Lamentations 4:16). In the New Testament, it's by grace that the dead are rescued, that the weak find rest, and that outcasts are enfolded into God's glorious plan (Acts 15:11; Romans 4:16; 5:9 – 17; Ephesians 2:1 – 5; 2 Corinthians 12:9 – 10).

2. Grace is an undeserved gift given freely and unconditionally. Grace produces good works, but goodness can never be a condition for receiving or retaining grace. Grace may be "requested, received, and even withdrawn, but never claimed, coerced, or possessed."[28] If grace is anything other than a free and unconditional gift, it isn't really grace (Romans 3:24 – 25; 5:15; 11:6).

3. Grace is unfailing love grounded in God's covenants. God proved his grace in the Old Testament by keeping his promises even when his people failed (Exodus 33:12 – 34:9). The authors of the Old Testament used word-pairs like "compassionate and gracious" and "loving and faithful" to describe God's faithfulness to his covenants (Exodus 34:6; Psalm 25:10; Joel 2:13; Jonah 4:2). In the New Testament, the Holy Spirit inspired the apostle John to use the words "grace and truth" to summarize this unfailing faithfulness and to emphasize the fulfillment of God's covenants in Jesus (John 1:14, 17).[29]

Chapter 2

PLANNED GRACE

*It was God's will that Christ through the blood of the cross ... should
effectively redeem from every people, tribe, nation, and language all
those and only those who were chosen from eternity to salvation and
given to him by the Father.... This plan, arising out of God's eternal love
for the elect, from the beginning of the world to the present time, has
been powerfully carried out and will also be carried out in the future,
the gates of hell seeking vainly to prevail against it (2:8, 9).*

CANONS OF DORT

*This day's been crazy,
But everything's happened on schedule,
From the rain and the cold
To the drink I spilled on my shirt ...
And You know the plans that You have for me,
And You can't plan the end and not plan the means.
And so I suppose I just need some peace,
Just to get me to sleep.*

CAEDMON'S CALL, "Table for Two"

All human plans [are] subject to ruthless revision.

ARTHUR C. CLARKE

MY VACATION PLANS SEEMED SO PERFECT.

In my mind's eye, I envisioned my children skipping arm in arm
along the beach. I saw my wife reclining beside me, shadowed by an

umbrella and surrounded by pristine white sand. I imagined my children constructing a sand castle complete with turrets, moats, and working elevators. After a few days of surf and sand, we might spend a day making memories at a nearby amusement park.

On the final day of our vacation, we would convene in the car for a prayer of thanksgiving, followed by a meandering journey home filled with misty-eyed retellings of each new memory. The sun would be setting as we pull into the driveway. My wife would look deep into my eyes and whisper, "Thank you, honey, this was such a relaxing week for me" — then, with a sly wink and a smile, it would be clear that the joy of this evening isn't over yet.

Vacations rarely turn out the way you imagined.

Instead, after returning home for the third time to retrieve the stuffed unicorn that your youngest child can't sleep without, you find yourself trapped in road construction with children whose bladders have apparently shrunk to the size of peanuts. It's well past midnight when you finally find your hotel. It's a roach-trap that turns out to be nothing like the picture on the website. The room is missing a rollaway bed, and no one on the hotel staff can find the key to unlock the storeroom. You and your spouse wind up sharing a bed with a child who reenacts martial arts films in her sleep.

The next morning is spent purchasing a half dozen items you forgot to pack. You manage to work in two spats with your spouse before arriving at the beach in the hottest part of the afternoon. Your children leap into the surf and immediately exit the water screaming. By the time they reach your umbrella, mysterious welts are swelling around their ankles. An online search reveals that your vacation days have coincided with the shallow-water mating season for a stinging species of jellyfish.[1] Stranded on the beach, your youngest child decides to eat sand while one of the older ones begins screaming because she's gotten suntan lotion in her eyes. Soon, everyone's crying, even your spouse, and your sand-gulper just threw up in the picnic basket.

Except for one miserable morning of endless lines at the amusement park, your family spends the rest of your time together sequestered in a hotel room, dabbing ointment on jellyfish stings while watching television reruns that you could have seen more easily at home. It's two o'clock on Monday morning when you finally pull into your driveway. That's when you discover you've locked yourself out of the house and the stuffed unicorn must have fallen out of the car at your last rest stop. Four hours later, you're headed to work and you can barely keep your eyes open.

You planned for months and emptied your savings for what you hoped would be the perfect holiday. Now you need a vacation to recover from your vacation. You had a plan and you paid the price, but you lacked the power to make it happen.

Welcome to life as a finite creature in a fallen world.

Almost every day, at least a few of our plans fail. Some days — usually when our hopes are highest — everything we've envisioned seems to fall apart at once, and this pattern of human failure runs far deeper than failed vacation plans. Asked to write a story in the fewest possible number of words, one author responded with this snapshot of shattered dreams: "For sale: Baby shoes. Never worn." In only a half dozen words, this miniature story reminds us how even the highest human hopes can fall apart.

You've had hopes fall apart too, haven't you?

For you, perhaps it *was* a baby who never arrived or a lifelong relationship that unraveled in a week, a dream job that turned out to be a nightmare, or a report from your physician that ripped your life apart. Your hopes were riding high, and your plans seemed so perfect. Then everything quickly crumbled — not because you did anything any worse than anyone else but because of circumstances that you never could have predicted or controlled (Luke 13:4).

Not a "Mama Tried" Kind of God

Broken dreams are woven deeply into the fabric of human existence — so deeply that it's easy for us to assume God's plans fail sometimes too. In fact, that's precisely what some theologians have claimed over the past few decades. According to one best-selling book from a Jewish rabbi, God wishes he could make everything right in the world, but he simply doesn't possess the power to make it happen. "Even God," the author claims, "has a hard time keeping chaos in check."[2] This sort of "God" is less like the sovereign Lord of history and more like the well-meaning mother in Merle Haggard's song "Mama Tried." "No one could steer me right but Mama tried," Haggard lamented. "Mama tried to raise me better but her pleading I denied. That leaves only me to blame 'cause Mama tried."[3] Seen from this perspective, God is always doing his best to turn humanity in the right direction. In the end, he just isn't strong enough to do all that he dreams. Still, we really shouldn't blame him because, bless his heart, he tries.

A theological perspective known as "open theism" takes a view of God's sovereignty that's less extreme but no less dangerous. According to open theists, God chose to limit his knowledge when he created the universe. As a result, God may produce a plan that seems perfect, only to discover that the circumstances of his creation have thwarted him again. "God (in a sense) accepts defeat at the hands of creatures not wholly under divine control."[4] Since God doesn't know for certain what people will choose until they make their choice, it's always possible for the first drafts of God's plans to fail.

Why God Has Never Called an Emergency Meeting

The problem with such perspectives is that they contradict everything that the people closest to Jesus had to say about God's plans. God the Father didn't wake up one afternoon in his heavenly hammock and frantically enlist Jesus to be the Savior after noticing that sin was running loose in the world. The apostle John depicted Jesus as a lamb whose sacrifice was already settled when the world was created (Revelation 13:8).[5] Peter proclaimed that Jesus was chosen to die before time began and was betrayed according to "God's deliberate plan" (Acts 2:23; 1 Peter 1:19 – 20). Peter and John testified together that the trial of Jesus was precisely what God's "power and will had decided beforehand should happen" (Acts 4:27 – 28). Long before he created the world, God had already mapped out his people's salvation from beginning to end.

But it wasn't only a plan for salvation that God mapped out in eternity past! According to Paul's letter to the Ephesians, God "works out everything" however he pleases (Ephesians 1:11; see also Psalms 115:3; 135:6). Sovereignty is essential to God's nature. God cannot relinquish his sovereignty over human history any more than God can commit suicide.[6] That's why he's able to promise his people that he will make "everything beautiful" at precisely the right time (Ecclesiastes 3:11; see also Romans 8:28 – 29). His purposes are so secure that they can never be thwarted (Psalm 33:11; Isaiah 14:27). His mapping of history is so meticulous that he can declare "from the beginning ... what is still to come" (Isaiah 46:10).

This doesn't mean that God ordains every event in exactly the same way. Some events God directly causes; others he merely allows — and the distinction between the two is rarely clear to us in this life. But always, God reigns over every quark in every corner of the cosmos. There is no maverick molecule meandering outside God's control anywhere in the universe, and the Trinity has never had to call an emergency meeting to revise heaven's master plan.[7] Everything happens on schedule. "Nothing, not even the smallest virus, escapes his plan and control."[8] Hear the clear declarations of this truth, woven throughout the Scriptures in poetry and songs of praise:

- "I know that you can do all things; no purpose of yours can be thwarted" (Job 42:2).
- The LORD has established his throne in heaven, and his kingdom rules over all (Psalm 103:19).
- Our God is in heaven; he does whatever pleases him (Psalm 115:3).
- All the days ordained for me were written in your book before one of them came to be (Psalm 139:16).

The Beauty of a Plan That Never Fails

It's perfectly possible for you or me to have a plan and pay the price but then lack the power to make it happen. That's why we sometimes need a vacation to recover from our vacations. But that never happens with God. When God makes a plan, he can always pay the price and he never lacks the power to make it happen. God's planning never writes a check that his power can't cash — and that's part of the point that Paul was making when he wrote the opening sentences of his letter to the Ephesians. In this prologue, Paul provided a glimpse into God's sovereign design for our salvation and the restoration of the universe. Paul unpacked planned grace in three parts: the Father's plan to love us, the Son's work to rescue us, and the Spirit's guarantee that we will inherit all that God has planned for us. (Remember, God is a *Trinity*. What this word means is simply that there's one God who lives forever in three Persons — the Father, Son, and Holy Spirit.)

The Father's Plan to Love Us (Ephesians 1:3–6, 11–12)

God the Father loves his children, and his master plan involves choosing them specifically for adoption into his family and then showering them with his blessings and love. Paul couldn't be clearer. The God and Father of our Lord Jesus Christ "has blessed us in the heavenly realms with every spiritual blessing in Christ. For he chose us in him before the creation of the world.... In love he predestined us for adoption to sonship through Jesus Christ, in accordance with his pleasure and will ... which he has freely given us in the One he loves" (Ephesians 1:3–6).

You may be tempted to think this was just Paul slipping his own thoughts into Jesus' message. But Jesus told us this same truth in the simplest of terms! "You did not choose me, but I chose you and appointed you so that you might go and bear fruit" (John 15:16). The apostle Peter called Christians "a chosen people" (1 Peter 2:9). God's grace given to *specific* people is the message of Paul, Peter, Jesus, and the Old and New Testaments—it's the message of God himself! Before time began God *planned* to show his grace to his *chosen* people.

Many people think of "predestination" as a doctrine that pastors like to fight about — theology that divides denominations — and there is no doubt that this doctrine can be contentious. But the authors of the Bible used words like "predestined" and "elected" to bring comfort and hope. One of the reasons that Paul wrote Ephesians was to bring a divided church together. Paul wanted the Christians in Ephesus to see that the sovereign King was also the loving Father of people from every tribe and language and nation. For Paul, this was the key to finding lasting purpose in the midst of conflict and suffering (Ephesians 4:1–16). When our hopes are thwarted and it seems like everything is against us, we can trust that nothing falls into our lives that has not first passed through our Father's hand. He has a plan, and he works all things together for the good of his predestined people (Romans 8:28–29). As pastor Tim Keller has pointed out, we find comfort when we "believe that God has chosen for us exactly what we would have chosen if we knew everything God knows."[9] Even though I never would have chosen

Atonement[10]

The word *atonement* combines the two English words *at* and *one*. This word combination describes how people who were once at odds with each other are brought together or made "at one" again. When we talk about God's atonement for sin, what we're describing is everything that God did through Jesus to bring cosmic traitors like us into fellowship with himself.

	What God accomplished through the work of Christ	Which Scriptures teach this truth
Christ the Substitute *The substitute who takes our penalty*	Atonement by substituting himself in place of particular people, satisfying God's wrath against them and cleansing their sin	Romans 3:25 – 26 Colossians 2:14 Hebrews 2:17 1 John 2:2; 4:10
Christ the Victor *The champion who triumphed over Satan*	Atonement by defeating every power of darkness through death and resurrection	Mark 3:23 – 27 Colossians 2:15 Hebrews 2:14 – 15 1 John 3:8

the hell that I've gone through, I'll also never trade being the person that God has made me by allowing it all to happen in exactly that way. God's eternal plan was to love his children and give us his very best.

The Son's Plan to Rescue Us (Ephesians 1:7 – 10)

Don't you love a good engagement story? You know, one of those stories where the guy just sweeps her off her feet. He knows his girl, and he makes a plan for the whole evening, and then he gets everything just right. What makes some of those stories even more amazing is that everything actually worked out according to plan — the flowers weren't wilted, the car didn't break down, the ring was set and ready right on time. From the guy's perspective, the day of the engagement can be one of the most nerve-racking of his life: "What if she says no?" When her "yes!" finally comes, he wants to shout. When her friends hear her telling about it, they're beaming with joy. He won her heart!

The message of planned grace begins with the truth that God is a loving Father who chose us personally and specifically before time began. It continues with the truth that God is a loving Bridegroom who has accomplished everything necessary to win the heart of his beloved bride. God didn't plan for Christ's work on the cross to extend a certain distance only to discover later that his creatures have somehow thwarted his good intentions. God's grace always goes precisely as far as God planned. God always gets his girl.

When maiden Israel was enslaved, God rescued her from every oppressor—the Egyptian taskmasters who forced her daily labor and the Egyptian gods who emboldened Pharaoh. God rescued her because he loved her. He said, "I will take you as my own people, and I will be your God" (Exodus 6:7). So he carried her off into the wilderness and joined himself with her by exchanging vows (Exodus 20–24). He said, "The LORD your God has chosen you out of all the peoples on the face of the earth to be his people, his treasured possession. The LORD did not set his affection on you and choose you because you were more numerous than other peoples, for you were the fewest of all peoples" (Deuteronomy 7:6–7).

What God did for maiden Israel was a tiny foreshadowing of what he was preparing to do for his bride, the church.

Ages before the forbidden fruit stained our first parents' tongues, God the Father planned for the Bridegroom—God the Son—to do what Adam ought to have done. The Son would go to war against his bride's oppressor and ultimately grind the ancient serpent's skull into the dust (Genesis 3:15; Revelation 12:1–9). Back when humanity first rebelled, God had granted Satan limited dominion on the earth. The serpent from the garden became the ultimate oppressor—"the prince of this world" and "the god of this age" (John 12:31; 2 Corinthians 4:4). Satan meandered the face of the earth, never outside God's power but always seeking to destroy God's chosen people (Job 1:7, 12; 2:6; Revelation 12:13).

But then the long-awaited Bridegroom—the rightful King of the universe—invaded human history amid the amniotic fluids of a Jewish peasant's womb, and nothing would ever be the same again. This child was a warrior-king sent in flesh to set his beloved free — to "break the power of him who holds the power of death — that is, the devil — and free those who all their lives were held in slavery" (Hebrews 2:14 – 15; see Luke 4:18 – 19; 1 John 3:8). That's one reason why Jesus spent so much of his time on earth slinging evil spirits out of people's souls. The Son of God was spoiling Satan's kingdom by seeking the captives and setting them free. The rebel prince of this world was being bound and hurled down "like lightning from heaven" (Luke 10:18). Desperate to preserve his crumbling dominion, Satan conspired to shatter the Son's redemptive plan before the marriage could begin (Luke 22:3; John 13:27; 1 Corinthians 2:6 – 8).[11] And so the Bridegroom from heaven died, his disciples scattered, and all God's good intentions seemed to have failed. But nothing in human history — not even the Son of God spiked and slaughtered on a splintered beam — has ever taken God by surprise. Long before time began, the plot that sent Jesus to the cross had already been a linchpin in God's perfect plan (Luke 22:22; John 19:11; Acts 2:23). Even when Jesus was sentenced to die, no devil or demon, no religious leader or Roman ruler, slipped even a single step outside God's sovereign design. The wedding would go on. In fact, God allowed the crucifixion — the most horrific method of execution known to mankind — knowing that this ghastly crime was simultaneously the event that would win his Bride's heart forever. The cross became the supreme display of God's beauty.

But then, three days after the warrior-king's last breath, his tomb erupted with more life than any earthly power could hold. The victim of the cross was revealed to be the victor over every power in heaven and earth. The death that had seemed like a triumph of darkness turned out to be the dawning of the light. Through the resurrection, God reduced every "rule and authority, power and dominion" into mere footstools for the feet of Christ the King (Ephesians 1:20 – 23).[12]

Through the cross and empty tomb, God destroyed the cosmic powers of darkness who oppressed his young maiden *and* he cleansed the stains that kept her from being presented holy and blameless to her Bridegroom. "Our fundamental problem as human beings is not that outside powers victimize us. The root problem is that we ourselves are radically evil and that we are wrongly related to God himself. Evil powers reign over us because of the evil within us."[13] We are not the devil's victims; we are willing participants in the devil's schemes. Even after the devil's defeat, we remain rebels by nature and sinners by choice — and our sins are not mere misdemeanors that God can brush aside on a day when he happens to be in an indulgent mood. Whenever we sin, we seize a gift that God gave us for our good, and we use that gift in self-indulgence and ingratitude. God's gifts of food and drink are perverted into pathways to gluttony and addiction; sex is twisted into pornography; the natural world is reduced to an economic resource to be exploited; and on and on it goes. The prophet Hosea compared God's people in rebellion to a young wife who received loving gifts from a new husband and then wasted them on other lovers (Hosea 2:5).

Each time we misuse one of God's gifts, we declare that we are the lords of the universe and God is not. This is a form of cosmic treason, a collective thumbing of our noses at the Lord and Ruler of all. The one thing God cannot do in response to our treason is nothing.[14] Shock rocker Alice Cooper clearly described what each sin declares when he sang: "Ain't gonna spend my life being no one's fool. I was born to rock and I was born to rule.... I never learned to bow, bend, or crawl to any known authority. I really want to build my statue tall.... I just wanna be God."[15] Deep inside, this is what we all want — to be our own god.

The penalty for our spiritual unfaithfulness is separation from God and spiritual divorce, in other words, death (Genesis 2:17; Ezekiel 20:21 – 26; Hosea 2:2 – 5; Romans 6:23) — and not just the death of our bodies but the infinite agony of spiritual separation from God for eternity (Revelation 20:13 – 15).

The Bible tells us that the only way to satisfy God's righteousness is if someone who does *not* deserve death dies *our* death in *our* place (Romans 6:4 – 10; 2 Corinthians 5:14; Colossians 2:20; 3:3). This need for a substitute is wired deeply into our souls. It threads its way not only through the story line of Scripture but also through our favorite novels and films and comic books. Before the hideous beast becomes a handsome prince in *Beauty and the Beast,* he must sacrifice his life on his beloved's behalf. At the climax of the Harry Potter series, Harry offers his life to Lord Voldemort in exchange for the lives of his friends. In Christopher Nolan's Dark Knight trilogy, Batman takes the blame for murders he didn't commit and becomes the scapegoat for the sins of Gotham City. At the deepest level of our souls, we know that a substitute is needed to take our sins away, and this knowledge shapes every part of human existence — even the tales we tell.

Our need for a substitute is clearly just that — a deep and desperate *need*. But not one of us deserves the substitute that God's righteousness demands. That's what makes God's "amazing" grace so amazing! On the cross, God did the unimaginable: The Lawmaker took the penalty that lawbreakers deserve. The divine Son became both the sacrifice and the substitute for sinners who did nothing to merit such mercy. "God made him who had no sin to be sin for us, so that in him we might become the righteousness of God" (2 Corinthians 5:21).

Our Bridegroom met that need for us. That's what the apostle Paul was highlighting in the book of Ephesians, when he described how every good gift has been given us "in the One he loves" (Ephesians 1:6). Because the Father chose us in Jesus Christ, we have been united with him in holy union. Through this mystery, a sixteenth-century Reformer named Martin Luther once pointed out, "Christ and the soul become one flesh. And if they are one flesh and there is between them a true marriage — indeed the most perfect of all marriages, since human marriages are but poor examples of this one true marriage" (Ephesians 1:9; 5:31 – 32).[16] When we're joined to Jesus as our Bridegroom, we hold everything in common with him. He goes all the way — mixing up the money and cosigning all of our accounts. He takes what belongs to his bride, and we take what belongs to him. Of course, that's a better deal for us than it is for him. "In him we have redemption through his blood, the forgiveness of sins, in accordance with the riches of God's grace that he lavished on us" (Ephesians 1:7 – 8). As the sacrifice for sins, Jesus satisfied God's wrath against sinners by drinking down the dregs of death and hell in our place (Romans 3:25; Ephesians 2:3; Hebrews 2:17). As the substitute for sinners, Jesus wiped out the penalty that every believing sinner deserves (Acts 3:19; Colossians 2:14; Hebrews 10:14 – 18). This is the way he makes us clean (Hosea 2:19 – 20; Ephesians 5:26 – 27). In the words of Martin Luther:

> Who then can fully understand what this royal marriage means? Who can understand the riches of the glory of this grace? Here this rich and divine bridegroom Christ marries this poor, wicked harlot, redeems her from evil, and adorns her with all his goodness. Her sins cannot now destroy her, since they are laid upon Christ and swallowed up by him. And she has that [right standing] in Christ, her husband, of

Here's a controversial subject that tends to divide
For years it's had Christians lining up on both sides
By God's grace, I'll address this without pride
The question concerns those for whom Christ died
Was he trying to save everybody worldwide?
Was he trying to make the entire world his Bride?
Does man's unbelief keep the Savior's hands tied?
Biblically, each of these must be denied
It's true, Jesus gave up his life for his Bride
But his Bride is the elect, to whom his death is applied.

SHAI LINNE, "Mission Accomplished"

which she may boast as of her own and which she can confidently display alongside her sins in the face of death and hell and say, "If I have sinned, yet my Christ, in whom I believe, has not sinned, and all his is mine and all mine is his," as the bride in Song of Solomon [2:16] says, "My beloved is mine, and I am his."[17]

Christ's death for his bride was personal, but his death was also particular, because Jesus took the place of specific sinners — real people like you and me.

But for whom specifically did Jesus die? That's a central question whenever we talk about God's planned grace. Let's look at three possible answers to that question:

Possibility 1: Jesus Died as a Substitute in Place of Every Person

One of the most popular responses to this question is, "Everyone! Jesus died in place of every person who's ever lived!"[18] But think about it for a moment: If the Father intended his Son's sacrifice to secure everyone's salvation, his eternal plan to redeem humanity has turned out to be a lot like a failed family vacation. God made a plan and he paid the price, but he lacked the power to make it happen. Hip-hop artist Shai Linne makes this point perfectly when he raps, "If saving everybody was why

Christ came in history / With so many in hell, we'd have to say he failed miserably." If God had planned to save every individual throughout all time, "how deplorably" — in the words of Baptist pastor C. H. Spurgeon — "has he been disappointed."[19] But we know that this must not be true. The results of the death of Jesus did not disappoint the Father — far from it! Whatever it was that the death of Jesus accomplished, it "satisfied" God the Father (Isaiah 53:11). If the cross accomplished less than what the Father had hoped, how could the Father possibly have been satisfied? But God the Father *was* satisfied, because Jesus finished every work that his Father had planned for him. He offered himself in place of every individual his Father gave to him (John 17:4 – 10).

Possibility 2: Jesus Died to Make Everyone Savable

Another popular viewpoint is that the purpose of Jesus' death was to make every person's salvation possible.[20] The problem with this perspective is that Jesus didn't die for possibilities — he died in place of actual people. The authors of the New Testament never describe the sacrifice of Jesus as suffering to secure a mere possibility of salvation. According to the angel who first declared the name of Jesus, the Father sent the Son to "save his people" (Matthew 1:21). During his days with his disciples on the dusty roads around Jerusalem, Jesus explained that he would sacrifice his life "for the sheep" (John 10:14 – 15). This flock didn't include everyone (John 10:26 – 27), but it does include those he knows by name (John 10:3). According to a chorus that echoes eternally around the throne of God, the sufferings of Jesus "purchased for God persons from every tribe and language and people and nation" (Revelation 5:9).[21] If the death of Jesus purchased the mere possibility of salvation, why does this song of praise specify his purchase of "persons" — actual human beings from every nation?

Possibility 3: Jesus Died as a Substitute to Secure the Salvation of Particular People

What the song of praise in Revelation suggests is that Jesus gave his life for particular people whose names were known at the throne of God before time began — and this truth does not embarrass God's entourage! The truth of God's planned grace is part of what drives the elders around the throne to fall facedown in worship (Revelation 5:8 – 10).

When did God choose to love and save his people? God planned to love and save his people before the creation of the world. This is planned grace. God maps out our rescue from start to finish (Ephesians 1:4 – 5). The Son didn't just make the world savable — he secured salvation for every individual who repents and believes. The value of his suffering was more than sufficient to atone for every person in the world, but God planned for his death to purchase particular people from every nation. Shai Linne again: "It's true, Jesus gave up his life for his Bride / But his Bride is the elect, to whom his death is applied."[22]

He's won her heart. That's the beauty of planned grace.

The Spirit's Guarantee That God Will Deliver All He Has Promised (Ephesians 1:12 – 14)

Planned grace is worked out by the Triune God. It's a loving plan made by the Father. It's a victorious plan achieved by the Son. It's a guaranteed plan sealed with the power of the Holy Spirit.

As we see in Paul's letter, God the Father predestines *only* those who will believe (1:5). Then the Son redeems (1:7) and the Spirit seals these very same people (1:13). If God the Son had died for the possibility of every person's salvation or as a substitute for everyone who's ever lived, the extent of the Son's redemption would differ from the extent of the work of the Father and the Spirit. You'd have different members of the one Trinity working with different intentions — an absurdity and impossibility.

God is one. Father, Son, and Holy Spirit always work in perfect harmony! Jesus was a perfect high priest who sacrificed his own life for particular persons chosen by his Father and set apart through his Spirit (John 17:9; Hebrews 10:10 – 14).[23] The Son's death purchased — or redeemed — precisely the same people the Father chose and the Spirit seals. This work was *selective*, *effective*, and *definite*. The Father's choice was *selective* because he predestined only those individuals who would believe. The Son's sacrifice was *effective* because he secured the salvation of these same people. The Spirit's sealing is *definite* because his presence in the lives of God's chosen people guarantees that they will remain his forever. The intent of the Father's plan determined the extent of the Son's purchase and the Spirit's pledge.[24]

A Plan That Calls for Praise

Planned grace is a deep and difficult truth — but the deep truths of God should never drive us to despair! Deep truths should be the truths that drive us to worship even on our most difficult days. That's what happened in Scripture whenever the Spirit-inspired writers glimpsed proof of God's planned grace.

The apostle Paul had spent two years chained to a Roman soldier, awaiting his hearing before a pagan emperor. Yet when Paul recalled how God's Spirit was sealing the precise same individuals the Father chose and the Son redeemed, he couldn't stop giving thanks (Ephesians 1:13 – 16). John was sequestered on the island of Patmos because he persisted in proclaiming "the word of God and the testimony of Jesus" (Revelation 1:9). When God pulled back the curtain on human history, the exiled apostle saw perversions of God's truth and persecutions of God's people; the world seemed so broken that no one could ever put it together again (Revelation 5:2 – 4; 6:9 – 11; 13:1 – 17). Yet as soon as John heard how the sacrifice of Jesus had secured the salvation of men and women from every nation, his focus shifted to an endless parade of angels joining the elders around the throne in a glorious chorus of praise (Revelation 5:12 – 14).

When you notice a perfect sunset that swirls a myriad of pink and orange hues across the horizon, you don't need someone to inform you that this is a scene worth seeing. You recognize beauty, and you spontaneously respond. Your response is a bit like what happened when Paul and John and the elders in heaven considered God's planned grace. No one needed to command Paul to thank God for securing his chosen people, and no one had to explain to the elders around the throne why they should bow before the bloodstained Lamb. They saw the beauty of God's unfailing plan, and they surged forward with songs of praise.

So can you.

If you are resting in Jesus alone to be made right with God, that's sure and certain proof that God's planned grace has always included you. Your vacation plans may never turn out right, your loved ones may fade to dust, and your finest dreams may fall apart — but God's plans for your life will never fail. God the Father specifically and particularly loved you before there was time. Jesus Christ purchased your pardon two thousand years ago. Now his Spirit has given you the gift of himself and secured you in God's kingdom forever. This beautiful work of grace frees you to worship with intoxicating joy regardless of your circumstances.

Planned grace is grace that staggers you when you consider the perfections of God's plan, but it's also grace that strengthens you to stand against every force of darkness and fear. Corrie ten Boom — a Dutch woman sent to a concentration camp during the Holocaust because her family sheltered Jewish refugees — made this comment when she considered God's sovereign grace: "You need not fear, even though mountains fall into the sea.... God doesn't have problems, only plans. There is never any panic in heaven. God is faithful, his plans do not fail."[25]

Jesus, Savior, pilot me
Over life's tempestuous sea;
Unknown waves before me roll,
Hiding rock and treacherous shoal.
Chart and compass come from Thee;
Savior, pilot me.

As a mother stills her child,
Thou canst hush the ocean wild;
Boisterous waves obey Thy will,
When Thou sayest to them, "Be still!"
Wondrous Sovereign of the sea,
Savior, pilot me.

EDWARD HOPPER

PROOF FOR LIFE

Meditate on these Scriptures and song lyrics. Work with a friend or family member to memorize the catechism questions and answers.

What Is Planned Grace?

Before time began, God mapped out the plan of salvation from first to last. God planned to adopt particular people as his own children; Christ offered himself as a sacrifice for these people's sins and as their substitute to satisfy God's just requirements (John 10:11 – 18; Ephesians 1:4 – 12).

Planned Grace in the Scriptures

Praise be to the God and Father of our Lord Jesus Christ, who has blessed us in the heavenly realms with every spiritual blessing in Christ. For he chose us in him before the creation of the world to be holy and blameless in his sight. In love he predestined us for adoption to sonship through Jesus Christ, in accordance with his pleasure and will — to the praise of his glorious grace, which he has freely given us in the One he loves. In him we have redemption through his blood, the forgiveness of sins, in accordance with the riches of God's grace.... In him we were also chosen, having been predestined according to the plan of him who works out everything in conformity with the purpose of his will, in order that we, who were the first to put our hope in Christ, might be for the praise of his glory. And you also were included in Christ when you heard the message of truth, the gospel of your salvation. When you believed, you were marked in him with a seal, the promised Holy Spirit, who is a deposit guaranteeing our inheritance until the redemption of those who are God's possession — to the praise of his glory.

EPHESIANS 1:3 – 7, 11 – 14

Planned Grace in Song

Once, we were bound by the chains of darkness,
Locked in sin's embrace.

Once, we were far from the love of Jesus,
Lost in hopelessness.

Darkness fell, on the cross hung Emmanuel.
His blood was spilt, to rescue the guilty ones.

Sing, my soul, adore and wonder,
At my Savior's grace and mercy.

Hushed is the mouth of sin and Satan,
By Jesus' final breath.
Freed from our chains, though the scars remind us,
Of peace that came from death.

BROOKS RITTER, Rebecca Elliott, and T. J. Hester,
"Sing, My Soul," © 2011 Sojourn Community Church

Planned Grace in Summary

When did God choose to love and save his people? God planned to love and save his people before the creation of the world (Ephesians 1:4–5).

How is Jesus our sacrifice? He is the Lamb of God who takes away our sin (Isaiah 53:5). As our propitiation, he satisfies God's wrath; as our expiation, he removes our filth.

What hope does the message of the cross offer to us? We belong to Jesus because he bought us with his blood (1 Corinthians 6:19–20).

DANIEL MONTGOMERY AND JARED KENNEDY, *North Star Catechism*,
© 2013 Sojourn Community Church

Planned Grace for All the World

If Jesus died only for those the Father chose before time began, what does it mean to say that Jesus is "Savior of the world" or that "God so loved the world"? (John 3:16; 4:42). And what about when Jesus declared, "I ... will draw all people to myself"? (John 12:32).

What the biblical writers typically meant by "the world" and "all" was a gathering that included persons from a range of nations.[26] When Jesus declared he would "draw all people" to himself, his point was that he would save not only Jews but also Gentiles, people who weren't Jewish at all (John 12:32).[27] When

43

Paul wrote that the gospel was "growing throughout the whole world," he could not have intended that every individual in the cosmos had embraced — or even heard — the gospel (Colossians 1:6). What Paul meant was that the message of Jesus was multiplying among both Jews and Gentiles. In the same way, to celebrate Jesus as "the Savior of the world" was to declare that no ethnicity — no group of people and no particular culture — can claim a monopoly when it comes to God's planned grace (John 4:42). "For God so loved the world" isn't simply a sweet sentiment to plaster on billboards; it's a cosmic declaration of war against every form of segregation based on status or race (John 3:16).[28]

Keep in mind that this was a difficult truth for many first-century followers of Jesus to embrace. For more than a millennium, the offspring of Abraham, Isaac, and Israel had enjoyed a rather exclusive inside track when it came to knowing God. With the arrival of the Messiah, the loyal love that God had once lavished on the single nation of Israel flowed through one single Israelite — the risen Lord Jesus — into the lives of women and men from *every* nation.[29] That's how law-abiding Jews found themselves being baptized in Jesus' name alongside uncircumcised ex-idolaters with pork on their breath — and that's why both Jews and Gentiles needed reminders that the good news of God's victory in Christ is for everyone (Ephesians 2:12 – 14).

Even today, people employ words like "world" and "all" to describe gatherings that bring together a kaleidoscope of ethnicities. Every couple of years, chosen athletes from around the globe converge in a city to compete in the Olympic Games. Throughout the weeks of competition, sportscasters mention how "all the world" has gathered for this event; they may even talk about the "worldwide reaction" to a particular performance. Yet no viewer takes "the world" to mean that every individual on the entire earth has gathered for the games in London or Sochi or Rio de Janeiro! Nor does any broadcaster presume that a "worldwide reaction" requires every household on the planet to possess a television that's tuned to the Olympic Games. The sports media use the words "world" and "all" in a manner that's similar to how the biblical authors meant the terms. "World" is not an exhaustive description that includes every individual in the universe; it's the declaration of a gathering that draws together a spectrum of people from around the globe.[30] God's grace is *universal* — it includes every class of person in the cosmos (John 3:16) — but it's also *selective*, lavished on particular people that God chose before time began (Romans 9:11 – 13). What this means practically is that God loves every person in some sense and some people in every sense.

A global gospel doesn't mean that everyone in the world will be saved, but it does mean that no one stands beyond the reach of God's grace. God's glorious victory over the powers of darkness is good news that has broken the barriers between "every tribe and language and people and nation" (Revelation 5:9). Jesus alone is the way of salvation, and his grace extends to people in *every* nation.

Chapter 3

RESURRECTING GRACE

Humans were originally created in the image of God and were furnished in mind with a true and sound knowledge of the Creator and things spiritual.... However, rebelling against God at the devil's instigation and by their own free will, they deprived themselves of these outstanding gifts.... Therefore, all people are now conceived in sin and born children of wrath, unfit for any saving good, inclined toward evil, dead in their sins, and slaves to sin; without the grace of the regenerating Holy Spirit, they are neither willing nor able to return to God (3/4:1, 3).

CANONS OF DORT

I was ... stone-cold dead as I stepped out of the womb.[1]

BOB DYLAN AND TIM DRUMMOND, "Saved"

They're dead. They're all messed up.

JOHN RUSSO AND GEORGE ROMERO, *Night of the Living Dead*

ONE EVENING EACH YEAR, SEVERAL THOUSAND BLOODIED BODIES INVADE THE STREETS OF LOUISVILLE, BUT NO ONE SEEMS TO MIND.

The city of Louisville is best known for baseball bats, quality bourbon, and the Kentucky Derby — but there's a lesser-known event in Derby City that's nearly as significant as the annual Run for the Roses.

Each year on Michael Jackson's birthday, the city shuts down Bard-stown Road so that more than fifteen thousand zombies can terrorize unsuspecting passersby.

That's right: *zombies*.

The zombie-costumed participants wander the street for an hour or so and chase down anyone who doesn't happen to be dressed as the living dead. Last year's horde included disemboweled zombies, pirate zombies, pregnant zombies, nurse zombies, but mostly just a lot of very bloody zombies — all of them playing their parts and pursuing any pedestrian who might possess a fresh bit of flesh. It's the Louisville Zombie Attack, and it's the world's oldest and largest annual gathering of people dressed as the living dead.[2] A few photographs might have helped you to understand this event better, but we're trying very hard not to let this book slip too far past a PG rating.

For those of you not acquainted with zombie lore, a zombie is a corpse that's active and moving. Zombies aren't resurrected or even resuscitated bodies. Even though their limbs are lurching and their jaws are snapping, these fictional creatures are dead — but zombies are far more morbid than mere moving corpses. Zombies feed on living flesh. They consume the living, and their appetites control them. You'll never see a zombie slow down to soak in the beauty of a baseball game or stand in awe at the white cliffs of Dover. Zombies are death seeking life, but succeeding only in spreading death. They have neither the capacity nor the desire to trade their death for life. Worst of all, zombies are rotting away even as they are walking around (hence the reference in a recent novel to a zombie family "which, as a result of decay, truly did have 2.5 kids").[3]

Over the past couple of decades, zombie tales have multiplied from a few low-budget films and bits of pulp fiction into a full-fledged cultural phenomenon with slickly produced television programs, blockbuster movies, and even best-selling adaptations of classic novels. ("It is a truth universally acknowledged," begins *Pride and Prejudice and Zombies*, "that a zombie in possession of brains must be in want of more brains."[4]) Zombies have become "a value stock. They are wordless and oozing and brain dead, but they're an ever-expanding market with no glass ceiling."[5]

Why this spurt of interest in the living dead?

According to one recent *New York Times* column, the thought of fighting floods of zombies provides many people with a fitting metaphor for the way they feel about their lives:

> Zombie killing is philosophically similar to reading and deleting four hundred work emails on a Monday morning or filling out paperwork that only generates more paperwork.... The principal downside to any zombie attack is that the zombies will never stop coming; the principal downside to life is that you will never be finished with whatever it is you do.[6]

Put another way, endless waves of the walking dead — never resting but never truly living — echo the unrelenting torrents of tweets, tasks, and to-do lists that seem to deaden our daily lives.

But perhaps there's a reason for this obsession with zombies that runs deeper than our hyperlinked lives, a reason that has to do with humanity's very nature. Zombies are not, after all, the only creatures that are walking dead. Spiritual death is the born predicament of every person on the planet. We may work hard to keep our blood pressure balanced and our cholesterol under control. And yet — apart from God's resurrecting grace — we're walking dead, always on the move but never truly living, always consuming but never satisfied.

We're all zombies.

Perhaps the zombies on our e-readers and cinema screens resonate with the wound of living death that bruises our souls from the moment we're conceived. To understand how humanity ended up this way and why it matters, let's go back to the very beginning.

Zombies in the Garden

Humanity didn't begin as the walking dead. The living God single-handedly created our first parents alive and free. He gave them every gift they could ever need — but the man and the woman became convinced they needed something more. The result was death.

Take a moment to recall the most extravagant gift you've ever received. A computer? A car? An engagement ring? Perhaps even a piece of real estate? Now think about the gifts that God lavished on the first man and woman. God breathed the gift of life into Adam's flesh and handed him an entire planet — and this planet was no secondhand fixer-upper! (Genesis 2:5 – 16). It wasn't like Mercury or Mars where saltwater oceans and a breathable atmosphere still needed to be installed. Every deluxe feature that any human being might need was preinstalled on planet Earth. The Creator included not only water and air but flora and fauna, a thornless garden and abundant fruit (Genesis 1:9 – 31; 3:18). God formed a perfect wife from the man's own body and gave the newlyweds explicit orders to engage in a lifetime of lovemaking and childbearing (Genesis 1:26 – 28; 2:21 – 25). To top it all off, God gave Adam and Eve the gift of his own loyal love, and he called it all "very good" (Genesis 1:31).[7]

The owner's manual for this newly populated planet included only one limitation. It was a single, simple reminder that all these gifts were given for the glory of a greater sovereign than Adam or Eve. "You are free to eat from any tree in the garden," God warned, "but you must not eat from the tree of the knowledge of good and evil, for when you eat from it you will certainly die" (Genesis 2:16 – 17).

All was well with the man and his wife until a serpent slithered into the garden with the soft-pedaled suggestion that God's gifts might not be enough to satisfy their needs (Genesis 3:5). Adam and Eve had been handed an entire planet, furnished and free — but instead of being satisfied with the gifts they received, they traded life in paradise for the fruit of a forbidden tree (Genesis 3:6). And so the man and the woman died.

As it turns out, the most immediate death that Adam and Eve experienced wasn't physical; it was spiritual. This death resulted in separation from God's life and hatred for God's law (Genesis 3:8; Romans 3:10 – 18; 8:7 – 8; Colossians 1:21). The parasite of sin perverted our primeval parents' pleasures and leached away their love for their Creator. But this inward death was far from the most serious result of their sin. What was even worse was the fact that the contagion of death didn't stop with the earth's first sinners.

Zombies from the Womb

"Glinda, why does wickedness happen?" a resident of Oz asks in the opening scene of the musical *Wicked*. "That's a good question. One that many people find confusifying," Glinda the Good replies before proposing two possibilities: "Are people born wicked? Or do they have wickedness thrust upon them?"[8] From the perspective of God's Word, the answer to both possibilities is clearly "yes." People do respond in wicked ways to the circumstances of their lives — but their wicked deeds are rooted in a nature that was inclined toward sin before they were even born.

Ever since that dark moment when mankind first rebelled, every human being has entered the world trapped "inside the future of a shattered past."[9] In Adam's fall, we fell as well, and every part of our lives became death-infected (Romans 5:12 – 21).[10] Now each time the chromosomes align in a mother's womb to form a human embryo, this newly formed person enters the world entangled in a profound and painful paradox: This child is a gift from God whose days will long outlast the rise and fall of all the kingdoms of the earth, but she or he is also wicked from the womb and headed for the grave. This child and all the rest of us are "children of eternity," but we spend our lives "on the run from entropy."[11] We are living likenesses of God, but we are blinded to the life-giving beauty of the gospel (Genesis 1:26 – 28; 2 Corinthians 4:4). We are "fearfully and wonderfully made" (Psalm 139:14), but we are spiritual zombies from the moment we're conceived (Psalm 51:5). "We are all sinners, not only from our birth, but before," medieval theologian John Wycliffe observed, "so that we cannot so much as think a good thought" (see Genesis 6:5; 8:21).[12]

At any moment since the fruit passed our first parents' lips, God would have been perfectly justified if he had simply pulled the sheet over humanity's collective corpse and condemned us all.[13] But God never gave up on his plans for mankind, and he never will. That's because God had already planned a greater gift and a greater promise than anything he lavished on Adam and Eve.[14] In this greater gift, there's good news for the walking dead, but there's a bit of bad news as well.

Good News and Bad News for Spiritual Zombies

God's plan has always been to multiply the fame of his own name by giving new life to the living dead. The price that this plan required was nothing less than the slaughter of a perfect substitute — a gift too great for anyone but God to give, with a price too high for anyone but God to pay. And so God the Son became flesh, and his sinless body was stapled to a wooden beam. There the Son died the death that the living dead deserve, but God refused to let death speak the final word. Three days after the Son released his final breath, "a spike-torn hand twitched. A blood-crusted eyelid opened," and the living Lord checked himself out of his own tomb, alive and well.[15]

Ever since that first resurrection day, all the goodness of Jesus himself has been available as a free gift to anyone who will submit to the reign of the crucified king — and that's good news for us all (Romans 10:5 – 15). Nothing remains for us to do to earn God's favor because Jesus has already delivered everything that God's justice demands. Joined with Jesus in his death, our zombie selves are laid to rest (Romans 6:4 – 7). Through faith in the risen and reigning Christ, we are raised with him to endless life (Colossians 2:12).

But there's bad news in all of this as well — very bad news. The bad news is that, left to ourselves, none of us will ever claim the gift that God has provided. This isn't because human beings are incapable of making choices! Every person possesses, in the words of pastor-theologian Jonathan Edwards, "liberty to act according to his choice, and do what he pleases."[16] We make our choices on the basis of what we most deeply desire — and that's precisely the problem. We are all spiritually dead on arrival, and the reign of the risen Lord Jesus will never be the deepest desire of the spiritually deceased.

Spiritual zombies don't choose the gift of God's grace for the same reason that prison escapees don't show up voluntarily at police stations. It isn't because convicted felons are incapable of locating their local law-enforcement agency. It's because the police represent everything the convict wants to avoid. Ever since our expulsion from Eden, every human being has been a convicted corpse on the run from God's reign. Apart from God's single-handed gift of resurrecting grace, no human being will ever seek God because a death-defeating King who demands that we find our greatest joy in his Father's fame is repulsive to the spiritually dead (John 3:19 – 20; Romans 3:11).

When the living God surveys the inhabitants of the earth, he doesn't discover multitudes of well-intended women and men trying to find their way into his kingdom. What he sees instead are hordes of the walking dead, living with an inward inkling that God is real, but refusing to submit to his sovereign will (Romans 1:18 – 21). Here's how the Scriptures describe humanity's condition:

- "The LORD looks down from heaven on all mankind to see if there are **any who understand, any who seek God. All have turned away**, all have become corrupt; there is no one who does good, not even one" (Psalm 14:2 – 3, emphasis added; see also Psalm 53:2 – 3).
- "Surely I was sinful at birth, sinful from the time my mother conceived me" (Psalm 51:5).
- "We all, like sheep, have gone astray, **each of us has turned to our own way**" (Isaiah 53:6, emphasis added).
- "There is no one who understands; **there is no one who seeks God. All have turned away**" (Romans 3:11 – 12, emphasis added).

Our nature shapes what we choose, and all of us are by nature deadened to God's gospel and destined for God's wrath. That's why God's gift of resurrecting grace is our only hope.

This need for the gift of resurrecting grace is woven throughout every page of Scripture, but it's especially clear in the first few verses of the second chapter of Paul's letter to the Ephesians. There we see clearly why only a single-handed gift from God can raise and save the living dead.

Zombies in Ephesus

"You were dead in your transgressions and sins,
among which you once walked
according to the course of this world,
according to the prince of the authority of the air — the spirit working even
now in the sons of disobedience,
among whom we all once conducted ourselves in the cravings of our flesh,
doing the desires of the flesh and of the mind —
we were by nature children of wrath, even as the rest" (Ephesians 2:1 – 3).[17]

For eighteen months, she talked to him, bathed him, and watched NASCAR races with him; through it all, Charlie never responded once, because he was dead. The sixty-seven-year-old Michigan man had passed away in his recliner, but his housemate never got around to reporting his demise. Instead, she watched television with him, discussed their future together, and even cashed his pension checks. Whenever family members came to check on Charlie, she told them he was "out" or "gone" for the day — both of which were true, from a certain point of view.[18] What she didn't reveal was how far gone Charlie really was. For more than a year, this man's corpse was washed, clothed, and entertained, even though his life was long gone and his flesh was rotting away — much like the men and women in the Ephesian church had been before God's single-handed work of grace disrupted their spiritual decay.

The Ephesians lived in a well-manicured metropolis with abundant parades and athletic competitions, Roman baths and religious rites. Their city seemed alive and full of amusements — but beneath the surface, an unmistakable stench of spiritual death filled the air. Gentiles and Jews alike were caught up in magical practices that were meant to manipulate spiritual powers, and the lives of many citizens revolved around the temple of the goddess Artemis. Despite this dismal backstory, it seems that some Christians in Ephesus may have forgotten how far gone they really were before God's resurrecting grace brought their death to an end.

When Paul recalled these previous patterns of life, he informed the residents of Ephesus that their lives had been dominated by death and the devil (Ephesians 2:1 – 2). Clearly, Paul wasn't interested in writing marketing materials for the Ephesian office of tourism, but his declarations of death didn't stop at the Ephesus city limits. Paul went on to tell his readers that "all of us" share this same deathly starting point (Ephesians 2:3) — not only dabblers in demonic spells like the Ephesians but also self-righteous law-keepers like Paul had been before he encountered Jesus. Before we became believers, this status of spiritual death shaped what we were, what we did, and what we deserved.

What We Were (Ephesians 2:1)

If we're honest, most of us would like to think that our rescue from God's wrath started with something we did. Surely there was some minuscule outpost of goodness deep inside us where God's kingdom first gained a foothold in our lives — perhaps a righteous deed, a willingness to believe, or a flicker of faith that only God could foresee. And so we convince ourselves that salvation is like a divine life preserver that drowning sinners must choose to grasp. Or perhaps we depict our rescue from sin as a poll in which God cast a ballot in favor of our salvation, Satan spoke against it, and the deciding vote was up to us. Either way, we're the ones who make the choice that kick-starts God's rescue effort. God has done his part; now he's waiting for us to do our part, and our salvation depends on us.

But there's a serious snag in this line of thinking: If God waited to give the gift of salvation until one of us made the right response, we would all be damned. That's because, left to ourselves, none of us will ever desire what Jesus requires.

"You were dead," Paul said (Ephesians 2:1).

Not treading water and waiting for a flotation device.

Not agonizing over whether to vote for Jesus in a cosmic popularity contest.

Dead.

When God rescued us, we weren't choking on the waves or waiting our turn at a heavenly polling station. We were deceased in a dung heap of "transgressions and sins" (Ephesians 2:1). And just as the "physically dead cannot communicate with the living, so also those who are spiritually dead cannot communicate with the eternal living God."[19] There are no voting machines in caskets, and corpses have never responded well when asked to grab life preservers.

What We Did (Ephesians 2:2 – 3a)

The primal sin poisoned the roots of every human life — but the carnage didn't stop with a passive status of spiritual death. Death in our roots led to death in our fruits. Humanity didn't simply wallow in sin; from the Garden of Eden forward, every human being has willingly walked in the ways of death. According to Paul's letter to the Ephesians, we have all chosen and chased after

- the patterns of the prevailing culture ("followed the ways of this world," 2:2),

Ephesus

One of the most populous metropolises in the Roman Empire, first-century Ephesus was about the size of Orlando, Florida, and attracted nearly as many tourists. But costumed cartoon characters and amusement parks weren't what brought visitors to Ephesus. Life in Ephesus centered around the temple of Artemis, a structure that one ancient poet described as the most magnificent of the Seven Wonders of the World.[20] The goddess Artemis was "worshiped throughout the province of Asia" (Acts 19:27), and thousands of worshipers planned vacations in Ephesus each spring to gain her good favor. During tourist season, the temple sponsored athletic competitions, musical performances, and parades. There were even souvenirs for sale — terra-cotta images of Artemis and miniature models of her temple, crafted from marble or silver to fit every tourist's budget. For many people, Ephesus was also a magic kingdom. Not only Gentiles but also Jews memorized magical names to manipulate spiritual powers in the space between heaven and earth (Acts 19:17 – 19).[21] That's why Paul's letter highlighted the divine victory that exalted Christ "far above ... every name" and vanquished the rebel ruler "of the kingdom of the air" (Ephesians 1:20 – 21; 2:2).

- the practice of the rebel prince of this world ("followed ... the ruler of the kingdom of the air," 2:2), and
- the passions of our own flesh ("gratifying the cravings of our flesh," 2:3).

These passing pleasures were like painkillers that masked a fatal disease, numbing us to the depth of our spiritual despair.

From time to time, we may have calmed our consciences by pulling the plug on a sinful habit or two. Perhaps we flushed a few pills down the toilet, vowed not to gossip so much about our coworkers, or made a New Year's resolution to stop straying from our spouse or losing our temper with our children. But when it came to quitting sin once and for all, we simply couldn't do it. Sin was as much a part of us as a heart that pumps blood, lungs that breathe air, and skin that produces hair. Even if we succeeded in cutting off one evil habit, a forest of other iniquities soon sprouted in its place. "Inherited sin in a man is like his beard," Martin Luther once commented. "Though shaved off today so the man is very smooth ... it grows back by tomorrow morning."[22]

The theological term for this pervasive presence of sin in every human life is "total depravity" — an unfortunate phrase that sounds at first as if people are completely evil, which isn't true at all.[23] "Depravity" — from the Latin word for "crooked" — simply means that God's design for humanity has been twisted in the wrong direction; "total" reminds us that this twistedness touches everything we are and everything we choose. Every human deed done outside of Christ carries within it a seed of death.

> The stain of sin [has corrupted] us physically, emotionally, psychologically, mentally, morally, and spiritually. That doesn't mean ... we are all brute savages who always carry out every possible evil; it does mean that there is no island of purity from which we might mount a campaign to save ourselves.[24]

"As the salt flavors every drop in the Atlantic, so does sin affect every atom of our nature," Baptist pastor C. H. Spurgeon once pointed out. "It is ... so abundantly there, that if you cannot detect it, you are deceived."[25] Left to ourselves, the death that we inherited from Adam mortifies all that we are, and sin infects all that we do. We cannot cleanse ourselves from this stain, and — as long as we remain dead in our sins — we will never desire the remedy that God has provided.

What We Deserve (Ephesians 2:3b)

Paul hammered the final nail into humanity's coffin with these words: "We were by nature deserving of wrath" (Ephesians 2:3) — or, more literally, we "were by nature children of wrath" (ESV).[26] Sin wasn't merely something we did; sin was by nature who we were. Thus, damnation became our deserved destination before we had even disembarked from our mother's womb.

So what can we do to escape this deathly circumstance?

Nothing.

We are by nature damned and dead, and there is nothing that any of us can do to improve this dismal starting point. Until we receive new life, we will never glimpse the glory of God's kingdom (John 3:3). And yet, as long as we remain spiritually dead, we are "sin-oholics" without the slightest desire to be set free from our addiction to iniquity. That's the dark dilemma of every human life apart from Jesus Christ (Romans 3:9 – 18; Ephesians 2:12) — and that's why the next sentence in Paul's letter is so amazing!

What God Did — and Does (Ephesians 2:4 – 7)

"But God — because of his great love with which he loved us, he being wealthy
    in mercy, we being dead in trespasses —
made us alive with Christ (by grace you have been saved),
raised us with Christ, and
seated us with Christ in the heavenly realms in Christ Jesus
so he might prove,
in the coming courses of time, the surpassing wealth of his grace
in kindness to us
in Christ Jesus" (Ephesians 2:4 – 7).[27]

"But God," Paul declared, "made us alive with Christ."

The Christians in Ephesus had been damned and dead — but God made them alive. He caused them to be born again (John 3:3 – 7). He put their death to death in the death of Jesus and raised them to life through the power of his resurrection! What none of them could do or would do, God did, for the purpose of revealing "the incomparable riches of his grace" (Ephesians 2:7).

And what caused God to display his grace in this way?

It wasn't because certain Ephesians had earned God's favor; they were "by nature deserving of wrath" (Ephesians 2:3). It wasn't because a handful of them had filed requests for resuscitation; they were spiritual corpses, and no corpse has ever requested CPR. It wasn't even because the Christians in Ephesus had made a decision to believe in Jesus. The spiritually dead will never choose God's way or seek God's reign until their death has been traded for God's life (John 3:3, 6 – 7).

How was it, then, that certain sinners in first-century Ephesus moved from death to life in the first place? According to Paul, God delivered their decaying souls because of love and love alone (Ephesians 2:4) — and that's why God enlivens sinners still today.

If you've trusted Jesus Christ, all that you contributed to your own salvation was a sin-bloated spiritual cadaver — blind to God's glory and dead to his grace — that God inexplicably chose to enliven and to love. God lifted your dead soul to a place where you never planned to go and planted life within you that you never could have produced on your own. No human work or will, deed or desire, triggered this miracle (John 3:5 – 8; 6:65; Romans 9:15 – 16). God regenerated you through his Spirit and called you by his grace; your faith and repentance were the fruit of this powerful inward calling. Your salvation was secured from beginning to end through a single-handed work of sovereign love.

New Life for Spiritual Zombies

Some have claimed that God's gift is a response to a human choice — or, at the very least, that God's gift of new life depends on our decision not to resist his grace.[28] But think about it for a moment: When Jesus rescued Lazarus from physical death, what decision did Lazarus make (John 11:38 – 44)? It wasn't as if Lazarus was lying in the tomb, pondering his circumstances, when he suddenly concluded that staying on a stone slab wasn't his most promising career path. Lazarus was *dead*, and the dead can't choose life. But God can, and God did.

The living God has never encountered a corpse that doesn't return to life when he issues the command to live, and he never will. And so the moment Jesus gave the word, the dead man immediately emerged from the tomb alive and well. Lazarus didn't even take the time to change his clothes before leaving the cave behind! He was still "wrapped with strips of linen, and a cloth around his face" when he stepped into the light (John 11:44).

It's a lot like that when God enlivens the spiritually dead. The sovereign king of the cosmos isn't waiting on a permission slip from humanity before he resurrects spiritual zombies — and he certainly isn't pacing the portals of heaven, wringing his hands, hoping someone responds positively to his invitation to the celestial prom.[29] God powerfully sends his church to proclaim the gospel in every nation. As the gospel is shared, God's Spirit pierces the lives of particular people who are spiritually dead and exchanges their death for his life (Acts 2:37; 13:48; Colossians 2:13).

But the miracle doesn't end with new life! God the Father then exalts ex-zombies to heavenly places and joins their lives with the life of his Son (Ephesians 2:6). The gift of spiritual life alone is far greater than anything we deserve. The thought that we are also positioned in the highest places alongside the divine Son should dizzy us with gratitude and joy.

Hope for a Coffee Shop Zombie

Most mornings while writing this book, I [Timothy] consumed my coffee two tables away from a zombie. Bill is pushing eighty years old, and the two of us are daily patrons at the same local coffee shop. Nearly every morning, we spend a few moments talking about everything from local architecture to the merits of farmers' markets and hybrid cars.

Bill's mind is bright and his heart is pumping, but Bill is a zombie. A spiritual zombie.

Despite his probable proximity to the end of life, Bill has no interest whatsoever in the kingdom of God, here or hereafter. The last time I mentioned Jesus in a conversation, Bill changed the subject to a spiritual experience he once had while petting an elk in Montana. (I promise, I am not making this up.)

A couple of days ago, a book entitled *Amazing Grace* was spread on the table while I worked on this chapter. On his way to order his coffee, Bill stopped beside me, glanced at the book title, and snorted.

"Amazing Grace. Hmph. You really think there's grace for someone like me?"

"Bill," I said, "there's grace for anyone who trusts Jesus to be made right with God. God won't turn away anyone who comes to him — not even you." Bill was silent for a moment, but then he shook his thinning shock of snowy hair.

"I've gone too far to think about that," he said. "Too damned far." And he walked away.

Bill is spiritually dead.

And yet, I'm not about to give up on Bill because I believe in resurrecting grace.

Viewed from the vantage of resurrecting grace, Bill is no less likely to trust Jesus than anyone else who's dead in sin and blind to God's kingdom. No one should be written out of God's story, because no one — not Bill, not you, not me, not the self-righteous deacon who's never believed, not the pedophile or the abortionist or the LGBT activist — is too dead to be made alive. Whenever Bill believes, it won't be because of his openness or my eloquence; it will be because of the resurrecting grace of God. Once God breathes new life into Bill, nothing in heaven or on earth will be able to stop him from trusting Jesus. And so, day by day, I seek opportunities to plant the gospel in Bill's life. I plant these seeds with confidence that God can take a foul-mouthed, elk-petting septuagenarian zombie and turn him into a beloved son. Whenever the Holy Spirit regenerates a dead soul in a context where the gospel has been proclaimed and understood, life and faith immediately blossom. And I can't wait for the day when I see it happen in Bill's life! That's the power of resurrecting grace.

But there's an awkward aspect of resurrecting grace as well — one that's tied to the obvious fact that God doesn't regenerate every individual. (If he did, everyone would repent and believe!) God's Spirit enlivens and effectively calls only those men and women the Father chose in Christ before time began (Romans 8:30).

I don't know why God has decided to work in this way. It's a mystery — but it's not a mystery that's exclusive to a particular perspective on God's sovereignty in salvation. No matter where you stand on the doctrine of divine sovereignty, it's clear that a thread of selective grace is woven throughout the Scriptures.

After all, why did God cut a covenant with Abram instead of some other idol-worshiping ancient Near Eastern camel herder (Genesis 12:1)? Why did God prefer Jacob the swindler over Esau his twin (Romans 9:11)? And why did God provide flour and oil for one widow during a deadly drought but not for thousands of others (Luke 4:25 – 26)? For that matter, why did Jesus raise Lazarus from the dead but leave all the other corpses in Bethany to rot in their tombs (John 11:38 – 44)? The primary response that God provides to such questions is, "I will have mercy on whom I have mercy" (Romans 9:15; see Exodus 33:19) — which isn't exactly the logical reply we may think we need when we're wrestling with the question of why God doesn't regenerate everyone.

"There is no group or type of people anywhere in the world that is excluded from salvation, because God desires that the gospel be proclaimed to all without exception.

"Since we don't know who belongs to the number of the predestined and who doesn't,... we work to turn whoever we meet into a sharer of peace."[30]

JOHN CALVIN

In the end, the best answer is simply that "the secret things belong to the LORD" (Deuteronomy 29:29). God has not revealed to us the precise rhythms or reasons that stand behind his resurrecting grace. But for the believer in Jesus Christ, the right response to this mystery isn't frustration, speculation, or selfish pride. It's gratitude, because it wasn't my will or wisdom that caused me to see Jesus in his infinite beauty. I am alive in Jesus because of resurrecting grace and grace alone. I repented and rested in the righteousness of Jesus only because God changed my heart while I was still a rebel.

Whenever God turns dead sinners into living servants, newly reborn rebels freely lay down their weapons at the feet of King Jesus. This new life isn't an achievement that anyone deserved or even desired before God opened their hearts. Our rescue from God's wrath is a work of grace from first to last. It's an unsought and undeserved gift lavished on unresponsive souls who had already enlisted in the rebellion against God's reign before they soiled their first diaper. The only right response to such grace is simply to say, "Thank you," and to share the news of grace with everyone we meet.

PROOF FOR LIFE

Meditate on these Scriptures and song lyrics. Work with a friend or family member to memorize the catechism questions and answers.

What Is Resurrecting Grace?

Everyone is born spiritually dead. Left to ourselves, we will never choose God's way. God enables people to respond freely to his grace by giving them spiritual life through the power of Christ's resurrection (John 5:21; Ephesians 2:1 – 7).

Resurrecting Grace in the Scriptures

"As for you, you were dead in your transgressions and sins, in which you used to live when you followed the ways of this world and of the ruler of the kingdom of the air, the spirit who is now at work in those who are disobedient. All of us also lived among them at one time, gratifying the cravings of our flesh and following its desires and thoughts. Like the rest, we were by nature deserving of wrath. But because of his great love for us, God, who is rich in mercy, made us alive with Christ even when we were dead in transgressions — it is by grace you have been saved. And God raised us up with Christ and seated us with him in the heavenly realms in Christ Jesus, in order that in the coming ages he might show the incomparable riches of his grace, expressed in his kindness to us in Christ Jesus" (Ephesians 2:1 – 7).

Resurrecting Grace in Song

I am ashamed, conceived in sin, I've always been.
Born in a world where Adam's fall corrupts us.
Rooted is the seed of death in life's first breath.
The law demands a perfect heart, but I'm defiled in every part.

All this guilt disturbs my peace; I find no release.
Who will save me from my crime? I'm helpless.
Behold, I fall before your face in need of grace.
So speak to me in a gentle voice, for in your mercies I rejoice.

For only your blood is enough to cover my sin
Only your blood is enough to cover me.

Lord, create my heart anew
Father, come and make us wise
Only you are pure and true
Lead us away from our demise
Lord, you are the remedy
For only your blood can set us free

For only your blood can set us free;
Only your blood can set us free.

No bleeding bird, no bleeding beast
No hyssop branch, no priest,
No running brook, no flood, no sea
Can wash away this stain from me.

For only your blood is enough to cover my sin
For only your blood is enough to cover me.

ISAAC WATTS AND NEIL ROBINS, "Only Your Blood Is Enough,"
© 2009 Sojourn Community Church

Resurrecting Grace in Summary

Who will come to God? We can't reach God, but he reaches us. God calls to his people and they follow him (John 10:27).

Can you come to God in your own power? No. We are dead in sin, and we need the Holy Spirit to make us alive (Ephesians 2:5).

How does the Holy Spirit make us alive? The Holy Spirit helps us to have faith in Jesus (Ephesians 2:1 – 9).

DANIEL MONTGOMERY AND JARED KENNEDY, *North Star Catechism*, ©
2013 Sojourn Community Church

Human Nature: Healthy, Weak, Sickened, or Dead?

The biblical truth that we're born broken has never been particularly popular — and it's especially distasteful in a culture intoxicated by self-esteem. English-speaking adolescents grow up listening to songs that declare, "We are all born superstars ... just love yourself and you're set."[31] According to one of America's most popular religious personalities, everyone is born to be above average (he never answers the obvious question: If everyone exceeds the average, doesn't that simply change the average?).[32] It probably shouldn't surprise us, then, that three-fourths of American adults and more than half of evangelicals are convinced that their children begin life with no natural inclination toward evil.[33] In such a context, informing your pregnant friends that they're giving birth to spiritual zombies isn't likely to land you on anyone's list of most popular godparents.

Even if people admit that their newborns are vipers in diapers, most remain quite convinced that we all possess the power to pull ourselves up by our own bootstraps. "I'm a born sinner," one hip-hop artist recently declared, but then immediately added, "but I'll die better than that."[34]

Our generation is not, however, the first to find the truth of total depravity distasteful! In fact, persons who profess to be Christians have produced no fewer than four different perspectives on humanity's pervasive sinfulness over the past several centuries. Let's look at each one carefully:

1. We are spiritually healthy

Some have claimed that human beings are born spiritually healthy and that people simply need to try harder to do what's right. This perspective is known as "Pelagianism," after a fifth-century proponent named Pelagius.[35]

According to Pelagius, human beings aren't born broken at all; everyone can make the right choices and even take the first steps toward God.[36] So what place remains for grace in this system? For Pelagius, grace wasn't a gift that transforms sinners; grace is strength that God gives in response to human efforts to do what's right. In Pelagianism, the more good works you do, the more grace God gives — sort of like a video game where, the better you play, the more powers and abilities you unlock. Eventually, if people keep putting their quarters in the grace arcade, they can gain enough points to live a perfect life. For Pelagius, grace was a stairway to heaven — it supports you with each step you take, but the first step and the initial effort are yours to make. Grace comes in from time to time to give you a pat on the back and a nudge when you've done something good.[37] Of course, as a pastor named Augustine of Hippo pointed out while arguing against Pelagius, grace that's given in response to human effort isn't grace at all![38] And even though "Stairway to Heaven" happens to be a great fingerpicking exercise for aspiring rock stars, it's a miserable way to live your life. The fifth-century Councils of Carthage and Ephesus condemned Pelagianism as heresy.

2. We are spiritually weak

In the fifth century, a monk named John Cassian came up with a slightly different spin on the issue. He didn't completely agree with Pelagius — but he certainly didn't care for the views of Augustine. So Cassian and some of his fellow monks forged a middle ground — a view that became known much later as "semi-Pelagianism." Trying to have it both ways, Cassian and his followers attributed a tiny but key role to the human will when it comes to overcoming the stranglehold of sin.[39] Grace became, in their schema, a consequence of human obedience. Though weakened by sin, the human will can still take the first step toward salvation. God gives grace in response to this first step.

In Pelagianism, grace had been like a stairway. For semi-Pelagians, grace was more like an escalator. Sometimes sinners step on the escalator of grace in their own power, and sometimes God helps them — but either way, a human choice is the gateway to getting God's grace. If Led Zeppelin's "Stairway to Heaven" is the theme song for Pelagianism, the sound track for semi-Pelagianism is the anthem from the band Rush entitled "Free Will": "I will choose a path that's clear, I will choose free will."[40] Christians rejected the claims of semi-Pelagianism in 529 at the Synod of Orange.

3. We are spiritually sick

Another perspective was that Adam's sin left every human being spiritually ill — and this sickness is no mere sniffle. It's a fatal disease that's already left you nearly dead. In this view, grace is more like an elevator. God finds people and — as long as they don't resist his efforts to save them — places them in the elevator where he lifts them to a place of healing and life. This grace is known as "prevenient grace," and every person possesses the capacity to receive or to resist this grace. If a sinner chooses not to resist God's efforts, prevenient grace produces faith and becomes saving grace. Prevenient grace sees in every person a "faint glimmering ray" that enables them to respond positively to God's work of salvation.[41] Prevenient grace suggests, as Bruce Springsteen once sang, "You can't start a fire without a spark," and every human being possesses at least a slight spark of life.[42] Prevenient grace is irresistible at first — everyone receives it — but once received, it can be resisted. Like unplugging your phone before it's fully charged, humanity has the capacity to disconnect from the current of grace that God initiates. If a sinner resists God's prevenient grace, God leaves the sinner to die.

This was the view of a sixteenth-century pastor and professor named Jacob Arminius and later Arminians such as John Wesley. This view isn't unorthodox because it does recognize that God initiates salvation. The problem with this view is that the sinner's fallen will still has the final say, and that's simply not what Scripture teaches. Arminianism was rejected in 1619 at the Synod of Dort.

4. We are spiritually dead

According to the Scriptures, our status is far more desperate than any of these previous perspectives are willing to admit. We are not — as in Pelagianism and semi-Pelagianism — wandering around the first floor of the shopping mall, looking for a stairway or an escalator to lift us into God's presence. We aren't even — as in Arminianism — lying on the floor, desperately sick but contemplating whether to resist a trip to the top floor on the elevator of grace. We are, as one Puritan prayer put it, dead, "having no eyes to see thee, no ears to hear thee, no taste to relish thy joys, no intelligence to know thee."[43] But we are worse than dead. We are the living dead, running from God's grace and spreading death wherever we go.

If you began life as a spiritual zombie, grace cannot be merely a stairway you climb, an escalator you choose, or an elevator trip that you choose not to resist. Grace is more like a SWAT squad leader who bursts through the glass roof of the shopping mall only to die at the hands of you and a horde of other zombies once he reaches the ground — but not before he mercifully ends the misery of your living death in a hail of gunfire. Then, miraculously and inexplicably, the squad leader and you with him are raised to life. But this new life isn't the living death that you knew before! This is real and joyous life. For the first time, you notice the living death around you. Even though you once loved this life of lurching carcasses and quivering brain tissue, you now find everything about it repulsive. You run to your Savior, who hooks you in a harness, rappels upward with you in his arms, and flies away in a helicopter to a forward position where you are strengthened and trained to do your part to rescue other zombies. God doesn't mess around with sin; he killed sin in the death of Christ, and he single-handedly lifts us to life together with Christ. We cannot claim "a single particle of righteousness" for ourselves without stealing from the "glory of the divine righteousness" of Christ.[44]

Chapter 4

OUTRAGEOUS GRACE

Before the foundation of the world, by sheer grace, according to the free good pleasure of his will, God chose in Christ to salvation a definite number of particular people out of the entire human race.... Election took place, not because of foreseen faith, the obedience of faith, holiness, or any other good quality or attitude.... Election instead took place for the purpose of faith (1:7, 9).

CANONS OF DORT

Amazing grace! (how sweet the sound)
That sav'd a wretch like me!
I once was lost, but now am found,
Was blind, but now I see.[1]

JOHN NEWTON

A crucial eccentricity of the Christian faith is the assertion that people are saved by grace. There's nothing you have to do. There's nothing you have to do. There's nothing you have to do.

FREDERICK BUECHNER

IT'S EASILY ONE OF THE BEST-KNOWN AND BEST-LOVED HYMNS EVER WRITTEN. It's been recorded by everyone from Willie Nelson to the Lemonheads; from Mahalia Jackson to the Dropkick Murphys. The United States Library of Congress has cataloged more than 3,000 varieties of this one song. During U2 concerts, Bono layers the hymn over The Edge's arpeggiated introduction to "Where the Streets Have No Name." Johnny Cash performed the song for thousands of prisoners and said, "For the three minutes that song is going on, everybody is free."[2]

The hymn, of course, is "Amazing Grace."

At some point in your life, you've probably heard the story behind this hymn. It's a touching tale of redemption that's been repeated for decades in Sunday morning sermons and small-group Bible studies. The narrative is typically told something like this: John Newton commanded a slave ship in the eighteenth century. After decades of exploiting Africans, Newton finally glimpsed the wretchedness of his ways during a storm at sea. He immediately renounced the slave trade and became a Christian. After penning the words to the world's best-known hymn, Newton spent the rest of his days working to end slavery.

But there's more to this story than what you've probably been told before.

Much more.

The true story of John Newton's time in the slave trade is far more complicated and quite a bit less heartwarming than the sanitized tale that's been told in too many Sunday sermons. When the future hymnodist became a Christian, he had never yet commanded a slaving vessel. In fact, every slaving voyage that Newton captained happened *after* he embraced God's amazing grace, not before.[3] During Newton's many months in the slave trade, he "never had the least scruple as to its lawfulness." "I was," he later recalled, "satisfied with it, as the appointment Providence had marked out for me."[4] A full decade went by between John Newton's salvation and his first public criticism of the slave trade.

John Newton was simultaneously a son of God and a slave captain, a trafficker in human souls even after his own soul had been saved. That's the truth rarely told or even admitted about the man behind "Amazing Grace."

There's a second truth about God's work in John Newton's life that matters even more than the first one. This truth matters more because it's a biblical truth that has as much to do with you as it does with the author of "Amazing Grace." The second truth is simply this: John Newton was no less a child of God when he was profiting from the purchase of slaves than when he was striving to bring slavery to an end. God's choice to change John Newton into his child had absolutely nothing to do with Newton's future change of heart on the sinfulness of slavery. In fact, if even the slightest sliver of John Newton's sonship ever depended on any deed that God foresaw he might perform, God's grace "would no longer be grace" (Romans 11:6).

The Freedom That Flows from Outrageous Grace

At this point, a few of you may be expecting us to backpedal a bit. Perhaps you think we'll try to whitewash John Newton as a man misled by the customs of his times. Maybe you even suspect we might downplay the savagery of the slave trade by suggesting slavery wasn't all that bad after all.

We have no such plans.

The enslavement of Africans was a horrific crime against humanity. Slave traders traded manufactured goods for human lives, chained human beings in their own waste for weeks at a time, exploited women, and abused men.[5] During the decades of the West African slave trade, more than two million Africans died from torture, disease, and sheer despair.[6] No appeal to misguided customs can justify such atrocities.

At the same time, we stand by this claim that has most likely scandalized every scrap of sensibility and sentimentality in your soul: John Newton the slave captain was no less a son of God than John Newton the campaigner against slavery.

From the instant John Newton first rested in the righteousness of Jesus, God glimpsed his own beloved son every time he looked at this man, even in those many months when he was at the helm of ships crammed with human cargo. The death of Jesus had drowned Newton's entire litany of iniquity, and the resurrection of Jesus crowned him with the very goodness of God. Not one of his sins — past, present, or future — could ever be counted against him again (Romans 4:6 – 8).

God did not choose to lavish this love on John Newton because of any goodness that he foresaw this man might choose. God — fully aware of the whole sordid story of this man's life long before it happened — chose freely and unconditionally to adopt this man as his beloved son. According to the apostle Paul, God's choice to turn particular men and women into his children has never had anything to do with anything they have done or will do, good or bad (Romans 9:11, 16).

Did you catch that?

God's choice to save you had nothing to do with anything that you have done or will do.

You did nothing to gain God's favor, and there's nothing you can do to keep God's favor. All that you can do — which is really no "doing" at all — is to receive what God in Christ has already done. It's only when we realize that nothing we did or might do formed the basis of God's choice to save us that we truly taste the intoxicating joy of God's irresistible grace.

As long as we delude ourselves into thinking that even the tiniest fragment of our righteousness is rooted in our performance, our joy remains shackled to the shifting winds of others' perceptions. When God's grace liberates us from the lie that it was our foreseen faith or personal performance that caused God to save us...

- We can confess our sins freely instead of hiding our failures beneath the feeble fig leaves of our own performance.
- We can rest knowing that we are safe, loved, and accepted by God not just in the future but *today*.
- We can receive correction without feeling devastated because we know that God's choice to make us his children was never based on our performance in the first place.

That's the point Paul was making when he reminded the Christians in Ephesus that God had "predestined" them "for adoption to sonship through Jesus Christ" (Ephesians 1:4 – 5). And what formed the basis of this divine decision to turn dead rebels into living sons? Not their foreseen faith, not their personal performance, not even their choice not to resist God's work. The foundation for God's choice was nothing more or less than God's own "pleasure and will," given without the slightest regard for any deeds that we may do (Ephesians 1:5). "This" — and by "this" Paul meant *everything* that God has done to rescue his people from their sins — "is the gift of God — not by works, so that no one can boast" (Ephesians 2:8 – 9).[7]

Four hundred years ago, a handful of pastors in Holland suggested that God must have — at the very least — foreseen our choice not to resist him and that God chose to adopt us in response to our choice. When pastors throughout Europe gathered to consider the controversy, they rejected this suggestion and reaffirmed their commitment to God's outrageous grace. Here's how they summarized this facet of God's grace:

> Election took place, not because of foreseen faith, the obedience of faith, holiness, or any other good quality or attitude.... Election instead took place for the purpose of faith.... The cause of this undeserved election is exclusively the good pleasure of God. This does not involve his choosing certain human qualities or actions from among all those possible as a condition of salvation, but rather involves his adopting certain particular persons from among the common mass of sinners as his own possession (1:7, 9 – 10).[8]

God's motivation for enlivening rebel corpses and turning them into cherished children was not because he foresaw some faint flutter of faith or hope in a certain segment of humanity. God gives his grace according to his own sovereign design, and his design has never depended on any potential he saw in us. When God chose particular people to become his children, God wasn't looking for highly rated draft picks to take his team deep into the postseason; God — knowing that Jesus would single-handedly defeat every power of darkness — wove the weak into his sovereign design so that he might "shame the strong" (1 Corinthians 1:27). That's how slave captains and swindlers, strumpets and wayward sons can end up as party guests dancing in their Father's front room while the religious professionals spend the night staging a protest on the porch outside (Matthew 21:31; 22:8 – 10; Luke 15:25 – 32).

For by grace you are having been saved, through faith;
this is not from you —
it's God's gift —
this is not from works
so no one should boast.[9]

ΕΡΗΕSIANS 2:8 – 9

Foreknowledge

God's foreknowledge formed the foundation for his predestination. Paul wrote that "those God foreknew he also predestined" (Romans 8:29). But what was Paul's point when he chose to use the word "foreknew"? Some have suggested that God foresaw certain people's faith and that predestination was simply God's response to these people's foreseen faith.[10] Put another way, God saw who would choose him, and God chose them back. This suggestion is highly unlikely for at least two reasons:

1. *The focus of God's foreknowledge is not faith:* What God foreknows isn't faith, it's people. If Paul had meant that God foresaw people's faith, he could have written that "what God foreknew caused him to predestine" — but that's not at all what Paul wrote. What Paul said instead was that "those God foreknew he also predestined" (Romans 8:29).

2. *God's foreknowledge is far more than foresight:* When God "knew" people in the Old Testament, it meant that he loved them with a love that was rooted in his covenants with his chosen people (Genesis 18:19; Exodus 33:17; Jeremiah 1:5).[11] Based on this background, Paul clearly meant far more than "foresaw" when he chose the word that's translated in English Bibles as "foreknew." "Foreknew" pointed to God's eternal and unconditional love for particular people — not to mere foresight of someone's faith.

God Doesn't Need You — and That's Good News

A little more than a decade ago, my wife and I [Timothy] sat at a table in a cramped office that reeked of scorched coffee and mildewed carpet. While social workers shuffled around us, we pored over page after page in a file that never seemed to end.

"Cruelty to animals." "Persistent patterns of theft and destruction of property." "Possible oppositional-defiant disorder." "Acute reactive-attachment disorder."

As the list of disorders and destructive behaviors grew, I whispered to my wife, "Are we sure we want to do this?" We hadn't yet met the seven-year-old girl these files described, but it was clear that — if we chose to go forward with this adoption — nothing in our lives would ever be the same again. From what we could see in those files at that time, this child seemed more likely to be a puppy-flaying arsonist than the delightful daughter we'd dreamed of guiding into adulthood.

And yet we also expected that this child would add something to our lives — and indeed she did. Through her presence, God began to dethrone self-centered patterns that we'd never noticed before and to heal souls scarred by years of infertility and failed adoptions. Our new daughter brought joy that enabled us to laugh again and struggles that drove us to our knees, begging for God's wisdom and strength. Our choice to adopt this child hadn't depended on anything she had to offer us, but her presence in our home brought gifts that both of us desperately needed. (And, as it turned out, only a few of her struggles were the ones described in those files. Sure, she came with some serious challenges, but puppies have fared very well around her, and the only thing she's seriously burned so far was her own forehead while using a hair straightener.)

When it comes to God's choice to turn rebels into sons, each of us has a file as well — and it's filled with far more serious charges than anything my wife and I thumbed through in that social services office. We have been cheaters, liars, gossips, addicts, fornicators, worriers, users of pornography, exploiters of our neighbors, rebels against the King of the universe, and children of the devil himself (John 8:44). We were "without hope and without God in the world" (Ephesians 2:12).

A worse list of iniquities is, however, far from the sole difference between a human adoption of a troubled child and God's adoption of sin-infected zombie rebels. There is another, far deeper distinction as well: no matter how twisted an adoptee's past may have been, there are needs in the lives of the adoptive parents that this new child is likely to fulfill.

That's not the case when it comes to God the Father's choice to predestine particular people to be his children, *because God needs nothing that any of us can provide.* The God described in the Scriptures is the exalted King who owns everything and owes nothing (Job 41:11; Psalms 24:1; 50:10 – 12; Acts 17:24 – 25). This God doesn't even need our love! The Father, Son, and Spirit coexist in a fellowship of perfect love, and they always have. Endless ages before Adam and Eve frolicked among the trees of Eden, the three persons of the Trinity gloried in the infinite

"Adoption is ... costly, exhausting, expensive, and outrageous. Buying back lives costs so much. When God set out to redeem us it killed him."[13]

DEREK LOUX

satisfaction of one another's love, and they needed nothing from us to make their lives complete (John 17:5).

And so, God's choice to adopt us was not based on anything that God needed from us or foresaw in us. The basis of the Father's choice to adopt particular people as his own children was sheer grace, overflowing from the inner life and love of the Trinity. This work of outrageous grace was an act of pure love that cost the Father the life of his Son. This sacrifice gained God nothing that he needed, but through this sacrifice, God purchased for every believer a status higher than anything we could ever deserve. That's why the apostle John exulted in one of his letters, "See what great love the Father has lavished on us, that we should be called children of God!" (1 John 3:1).

"Free grace runs through the whole privilege of adoption," Puritan pastor Thomas Watson pointed out.

> In civil adoption there is some worth and excellence in the person to be adopted; but there was no worth in us, neither beauty, nor parentage, nor virtue; nothing in us to move God to bestow the prerogative of sonship upon us. We have enough in us to move God to correct us, but nothing to move him to adopt us, therefore exalt free grace; ... bless him with your praises who has blessed you in making you his sons and daughters.... Extol and magnify God's mercy, who has adopted you into his family; who, of slaves, has made you sons; of heirs of hell, heirs of the promise.[12]

Meditate on that truth for a moment! Every believer in Jesus Christ began life as an heir of hell, but God turned us into "heirs of the promise." Yet God didn't adopt you or me or John Newton or anyone else on the condition that, after a reasonable period of time, we would turn out to be the type of children who didn't need grace in the first place. God chose us before time and then killed our zombie selves, raised us with Christ, and secured us as his children without the slightest reliance on anything we have done or might do (Ephesians 2:4–6, 16; Colossians

2:12 – 13; 3:1; Titus 3:5). All of this, from beginning to end, God accomplished not due to our deeds but "freely by his grace" (Romans 3:24).

The Scandalous Joy of Outrageous Grace

God's choice to adopt certain sinners as his children solely on the basis of his own good pleasure is sometimes known as "unconditional election." In the simplest possible terms, unconditional election is "God's eternal choice of some persons unto everlasting life — not because of foreseen merit in them, but of his mere mercy in Christ."[14] That's what Paul was getting at when he wrote the opening sentence of his letter to the Ephesians (Ephesians 1:3 – 12). That was also Paul's point in the ninth chapter of his letter to the Christians in Rome. That's where Paul explained to the Romans why God had chosen Jacob as the heir of his promises instead of Jacob's twin brother, Esau.[15]

According to Paul, God didn't make this decision because Jacob's faith or ethics somehow trumped Esau's. Sure, Jacob's twin had a hairy back, strong body odor, and some serious impulse-management issues (Genesis 25:24 – 34; 27:14 – 45) — but Jacob was downright sleazy. Jacob had already managed to convert his mother's birth canal into a wrestling ring by the time he drew his first breath, his livestock deals would have triggered a stroke down at the Better Business Bureau, and we're not even going to mention the man's dealings in the bedroom (Genesis 25:19 – 26; 27 — 34).

Why, then, did God choose Jacob over Esau?

Here's why: "Before the twins were born or had done anything good or bad — in order that God's purpose in election might stand: not by works but by him who calls — [Rebekah] was told, 'The older will serve the younger'" (Romans 9:11 – 12). God made this determination simply so that his own "purpose in election might stand." When God determined in eternity past those he would enliven and call to himself, he didn't make his determination on the basis of any "desire or effort" that he foresaw in any of us (Romans 9:16). God made this decision for his own glory to accomplish his own purpose in his own way. And once again, Paul left the question of why God doesn't save everyone as a mystery (Romans 9:19 – 29; 11:33 – 36). So should we. It is — as a sixteenth-century pastor and theologian named John Calvin once pointed out — "better to limp along the path" clearly revealed in

God's Word "than to rush at full speed outside it" by speculating about perplexities that God has left as mysteries.[16]

So what does all of this have to do with the misconstrued testimony of an eighteenth-century slave trader?

Everything, as it turns out.

Chances are, if we're appalled at the thought of John Newton being chosen as an heir of grace despite the fact that he did nothing to deserve it, we haven't fully embraced the liberating joy of grace in our own lives. We'd rather fudge the chronology of a slave captain's life than face the uncomfortable reality that God's choice to adopt us as his children had nothing to do with anything we might do and everything to do with what God determined to do before time began.

From the perspective of human pride, such grace seems scandalous, outrageous, and unfair—and that's precisely the point. God's grace is a scandal and an outrage that shatters the balance scales where we've meticulously stacked our best deeds for all the world to see.[17] But this same outrageous grace is also the key that opens the door to freedom and joy because it reveals the truth that our standing before God has never depended on how well we perform.

"Weary, working, burdened one, wherefore toil you so?" a Scottish hymnodist once asked before boldly declaring the scandalous implications of such grace: "Cease your doing; all was done long, long ago."

> *Nothing either great or small—*
> *Nothing, sinner, no;*
> *Jesus did it, did it all,*
> *Long, long ago.*
>
> *Till to Jesus' work you cling*
> *By a simple faith,*
> *"Doing" is a deadly thing—*
> *"Doing" ends in death.*
>
> *Cast your deadly "doing" down—*
> *Down at Jesus' feet;*
> *Stand in him, in him alone,*
> *Gloriously complete.*[18]

Seen in this way, the gospel of grace can never be reduced to a doctrine that demands more human doing. The gospel of grace is a divine declaration that Jesus Christ has already secured all that's required to turn zombie corpses into chosen children. The only right response to such a glorious announcement is to discard every concern about what you must do, to cling desperately to what Christ has already done, and to call everyone around you to cling to Christ with you.

> Trust him. And when you have done that, you are living the life of grace. No matter what happens to you in the course of that trusting — no matter how many waverings you may have, no matter how many suspicions that you have bought a poke with no pig in it, no matter how much heaviness and sadness your lapses, vices, indispositions, and bratty whining may cause you — you believe simply that Somebody Else, by his death and resurrection, has made it all right, and you just say thank you and shut up. The whole slop-closet full of mildewed performances (which is all you have to offer) is simply your death; it is Jesus who is your life.... At the very worst, all you can be is dead — and for him who is the Resurrection and the Life, that just makes you his cup of tea.[19]

Every aspect of your salvation — your new life, your faith, your repentance — is a gift from God (Ephesians 2:8 – 9).[20] We were dead, but God made us alive. We were rebels, but God adopted us as his heirs. In all of this, we added nothing because Jesus already accomplished it all. All the performances that you thought might gain God's favor were nothing more than makeup smeared on the rotting face of a cold and bloated corpse.

The cross of Christ marks the end of trying to earn God's favor by keeping the rules and working our way up a stairway to heaven. His empty tomb shouts out the victory that sets us free — free to forgive those who have wronged us because God forgave us when we deserved only hell, free to let go of our possessions because they were never ours in the first place, free to ignore the commercials that correlate our happiness with our buying habits, free to rest in the righteousness of Jesus alone.

That's the scandal and the joy of God's outrageous grace.

The Painful Price of Life under the Law

But outrageous grace doesn't develop in us naturally because grace isn't how our world works. Our world runs by laws that demand performance. You won't receive a paycheck next month unless you do your job now. Dorothy Gale can't receive her wish from the Wizard of Oz until she steals the witch's broom. The prince can't kiss Sleeping Beauty until he slays the fire-breathing dragon and scales the castle wall. Lord Voldemort can't be defeated until Harry Potter dies and the last Horcrux is destroyed. And you're convinced that — if only you try harder and do better — it will all work out and she will finally love you and he will give you a raise and they will tell you for the first time that they're proud of you. "Conditionality is written into the fabric of every society and relationship because it is written into the fabric of every heart and mind."[21]

Every human law — every expectation or condition that demands performance in exchange for blessings — either distorts or derives from the perfect law that God entwined in the tapestry of creation and etched on the stone tablets of Mount Sinai (Psalm 19:7 – 14; Romans 2:15; 7:7 – 12). The world's adaptations of these laws are far from perfect. Yet even the most imperfect human statute hints at humanity's universal awareness that there is a higher and more perfect law, the law of God. What the all-encompassing voice of the law declares is that if you perfectly perform all the right deeds, you can be accepted, blessed, and made right. This is, of course, true. The law of God is "holy, righteous and good" (Romans 7:12). If you were to live in perfect righteousness, keeping all of God's commands from your heart, the result would be nothing less than unending participation in the very life of God (Matthew 10:25 – 28).

The problem is not the law; the problem is us. Not one of us measures up to the standard that the law sets; deep inside, we don't even want to. "The [sinful] mind ... does not submit to God's law, nor can it do so" (Romans 8:7; see also James 2:10). The law — like the birth of a stillborn child — requires painful labor, but this labor leads to despair and death in the very place where we had hoped to find life (Romans 8:1 – 4; Galatians 3:21 – 23). Trying to gain God's favor through your performance is like trying to wring blood from a star; no matter how much effort you put into it, you'll never get what you're looking for, and the effort will ultimately destroy you. No human attempt to do what's right has ever made anyone right (Hebrews 7:18 – 19). That's because the law demands perfection, but the law can never deliver within us what it demands from us.[22]

Some react to this recognition by rebelling against every law, seeking to save themselves through their own pleasure or success. Others try to earn favor from God or their church or their friends by meeting and exceeding every standard. One group rejects the Lawgiver by warring against the law. The other group rejects the Lawgiver by worshiping the law instead of submitting to its Source. Either way, the result is the same: the law kills (2 Corinthians 3:6 – 7).

Why then did God give the law?[23] Let's let the apostle Paul provide the answer: "Through the law we become conscious of our sin" (Romans 3:20). This recognition that sin taints everything we do drives us to cry in desperation, "What a wretched man I am! Who will rescue me from this body that is subject to death?" (Romans 7:24). It's God's gift of the law that drives us to the Savior who fulfilled the law in our place. "We need the Law," Tullian Tchividjian writes,

> to freshly reveal to us that we are worse off than we think we are. We need to be reminded that there is something to be pardoned even in our best works and proudest achievements....
>
> The Law ... leaves us no other option than to cling to the One who has fulfilled the Law in our place. I wish I could say I do everything for God's glory. I can't. Neither can you. What I can say is Jesus' blood covers all my efforts to glorify myself. I wish I could say Jesus fully satisfies me. I can't. Neither can you. What I can say is that Jesus fully satisfied God for me.[24]

The purpose of the law is to point us to the gospel by revealing that there's nothing we can do to earn a place in God's family. Our place in God's family is a gift given to those God chooses in Christ and calls to himself, with no strings attached.

"A rigid master was the law, demanding brick, denying straw," declared one Scottish preacher. "But when with gospel tongue it sings, it bids me fly and gives me wings."[25] And yet, here's the reality that robs our joy: Many of us remain "completely addicted to a legal method of salvation" that tries to barter our best deeds for divine blessings.[26] We trust in the risen Lord Jesus, but we still tie our value to how well we perform — and this pattern doesn't end when we walk through the front doors of our church buildings. Sometimes it even intensifies.

Several years ago, a researcher named William Hendricks interviewed church dropouts to determine what had triggered their drift away from their communities of faith. When it came to the place of grace in their churches, here's what Hendricks discovered:

> "We have to be careful with what we teach about grace because people tend to take advantage of it." The first time I heard one of my interviewees tell me that that, in effect, was what he had been told by a church leader, I felt sad but figured it was just one person's experience. In a way, I could see the leader's point.
>
> The second time I heard it, I thought it coincidental. The third time I heard it, I stopped to consider whether I was being set up. The fourth time I heard it — in the space of three days — and then when I continued to hear it in later interviews, I realized that modern-day American Protestantism has given back a lot of theological ground that Luther, Calvin, and the other Reformers in its heritage paid for in tears, and that Christ paid for in blood.
>
> The retreat is not from whether we are saved by grace.... Almost any evangelical church worth anything will teach that salvation is by grace. But after somebody accepts grace, then grace is virtually forgotten, and the Christian life becomes some combination of faith and works. Most churches preach grace and live works. Story after story bore this out. The results were invariably tragic.[27]

This isn't to say that grace in our churches is like some awkward past event that everyone recalls but no one mentions, like the lampshade incident at your boss's Christmas party. If you spend any time at all in church, chatter about grace surrounds you. The word flits across the video screens in our worship centers almost every Sunday morning. Verses that mention grace echo in our songs, lodge themselves in our memories, and dangle from our walls. Yet whenever we find ourselves face-to-face with a living example of one-way love with no strings attached, our tendency is to change the subject — or to switch the story so that God's grace doesn't land in the lap of an active slave trader or our delusional next-door neighbor or a dancer in some sleazy downtown club. We live by law but call it grace. Such grace isn't amazing because it isn't grace at all; it's law in a cheap mask. And whenever you show up at a party that's hosted by the law, you're the one who's left with the bill.

Outrageous grace does not back away from the truth that the law tells — that God demands obedience and his standard is high. What grace declares is that God's standard is nothing less than perfect holi-

"The life of grace is not an effort on our part to achieve a goal we set for ourselves. It is a continually renewed attempt simply to believe that someone else has done all the achieving that is needed and to live in relationship with that person, whether we achieve or not. If that doesn't seem like much to you, you're right: it isn't. And, as a matter of fact, the life of grace is even less than that. It's not even our life at all, but the life of that Someone Else rising like a tide in the ruins of our death."[28]

ROBERT FARRAR CAPON

ness, that you were born shattered and short of the standard, but that the Son has met the standard once and for all. The God of all grace has invaded human history in the flesh of Jesus Christ, and he has trumped and trampled the treadmill of trying to earn favor by keeping the rules (Hebrews 10:1 – 18). The bill has been paid in advance, and God's disposition toward you no longer hangs on the thread of your performance.

God doesn't simply help you climb the stairway to heaven or provide you with sturdier bootstraps so that you can pull yourself up to his level. God in Christ buries our bootstraps and kicks every stairway out from under our feet so that we fall on the sure and certain mercies of his Son, and he does this completely "apart from the law" (Romans 3:21). God didn't choose to lavish this love on us because of our performance; he gives his grace solely because he has chosen us to be his children, and this choice had nothing to do with anything we have done or will do.

"Because I'm Yours"

I never dreamed that taking a child to Disney World could be so difficult — or that such a trip could teach me so much about God's outrageous grace.

Our middle daughter had been previously adopted by another family. I [Timothy] am sure this couple had the best of intentions, but they never quite integrated the adopted child into their family of biological children. After a couple of rough years, they dissolved the adoption, and we ended up welcoming an eight-year-old girl into our home.

For one reason or another, whenever our daughter's previous family vacationed at Disney World, they took their biological children with them, but they left their adopted daughter with a family friend. Usually — at least in the child's mind — this happened because she did something wrong that precluded her presence on the trip.

And so, by the time we adopted our daughter, she had seen many pictures of Disney World and she had heard about the rides and the characters and the parades. But when it came to passing through the gates of the Magic Kingdom, she had always been the one left on the outside. Once I found out about this history, I made plans to take her to Disney World the next time a speaking engagement took our family to the southeastern United States.

I thought I had mastered the Disney World drill. I knew from previous experiences that the prospect of seeing cast members in freakishly oversized mouse and duck costumes somehow turns children into squirming bundles of emotional instability. What I *didn't* expect was that the prospect of visiting this dreamworld would produce a stream of downright devilish behavior in our newest daughter. In the month leading up to our trip to the Magic Kingdom, she stole food when a simple request would have gained her a snack. She lied when it would have been easier to tell the truth. She whispered insults that were carefully crafted to hurt her older sister as deeply as possible — and, as the days on the calendar moved closer to the trip, her mutinies multiplied.

A couple of days before our family headed to Florida, I pulled our daughter into my lap to talk through her latest escapade. "I know what you're going to do," she stated flatly. "You're not going to take me to Disney World, are you?" The thought hadn't actually crossed my mind, but her downward spiral suddenly started to make some sense. She knew she couldn't earn her way into the Magic Kingdom — she had tried and failed that test several times before — so she was living in a way that placed her as far as possible from the most magical place on earth.

In retrospect, I'm embarrassed to admit that, in that moment, I was tempted to turn her fear to my own advantage. The easiest response would have been, "If you don't start behaving better, you're right, we won't take you" — but, by God's grace, I didn't. Instead, I asked her, "Is this trip something we're doing as a family?"

She nodded, brown eyes wide and tear-rimmed.

"Are you part of this family?"

She nodded again.

"Then you're going with us. Sure, there may be some consequences to help you remember what's right and what's wrong — but you're part of our family, and we're not leaving you behind."

I'd like to say that her behaviors grew better after that moment. They didn't. Her choices pretty much spiraled out of control at every hotel and rest stop all the way to Lake Buena Vista. Still, we headed to Disney World on the day we had promised, and it was a typical Disney day. Overpriced tickets, overpriced meals, and lots of lines, mingled with just enough manufactured magic to consider maybe going again someday.

In our hotel room that evening, a very different child emerged. She was exhausted, pensive, and a little weepy at times, but her month-long facade of rebellion had faded. When bedtime rolled around, I prayed with her, held her, and asked, "So how was your first day at Disney World?"

She closed her eyes and snuggled down into her stuffed unicorn. After a few moments, she opened her eyes ever so slightly. "Daddy," she said, "I finally got to go to Disney World. But it wasn't because I was good; it's because I'm yours."

It wasn't because I was good; it's because I'm yours.

That's the message of outrageous grace.

Outrageous grace isn't a favor you can achieve by being good; it's the gift you receive by being God's. Outrageous grace is God's goodness that comes looking for you when you have nothing but a middle finger flipped in the face of God to offer in return. It's a farmer paying a full day's wages to a crew of deadbeat day laborers with only a single hour punched on their time cards (Matthew 20:1 – 16). It's a man marrying an abandoned woman and then refusing to forsake his covenant with her when she turns out to be a whore (Ezekiel 16:8 – 63; Hosea 1:1 – 3:5). It's the insanity of a shepherd who puts ninety-nine sheep at risk to rescue the single lamb that's too stupid to stay with the flock (Luke 15:1 – 7). It's the love of a father who hands over his finest rings and robes to a young man who has squandered his inheritance on drunken binges with his fair-weather friends (Luke 15:11 – 32). It's God's choice to save a slave trader knowing full well that it would take a decade ɔr this man to recognize the wretchedness of his ways. It's one-way love that calls you into the kingdom not because you've been good but because God has chosen you and made you his own. And now he is chasing you to the ends of the earth to keep you as his child, and nothing in heaven or hell can ever stop him.

When I [Timothy] tuck in my daughters at night, I sometimes ask them something of this sort: "If I could be the daddy of anyone in the world, do you know who I'd choose?" If the girls are in a playful mood, they begin naming other children we know — or, if they're in a particularly zany mood, they might call out random fictional characters, ranging from Frodo Baggins to Bugs Bunny and Luna Lovegood — but each time I reply, "No, that's not who I'd choose." After my girls have exhausted all possibilities, I end our bantering with the same reminder that I've spoken over them hundreds of times before: "If I could choose anyone in the whole world as my baby girls, I would still choose you and you and you. No matter what you say or what you do, I would always still choose you." And I would.

But here's what's amazing about God's outrageous grace: This isn't merely what God the Father *would* do; it's what he *did* do. God could have chosen to save anyone, everyone, or no one from Adam's fallen race. But what God did was to choose a multi-hued multitude of "someones," and — if you are a believer in Jesus Christ — one of those "someones" was you. God in Christ has declared over you, "I could have chosen anyone in the whole world as my child, and I chose you. No matter what you say or do, neither my love nor my choice will ever change." That's grace that's truly amazing.

PROOF FOR LIFE

Meditate on these Scriptures and song lyrics. Work with a friend or family member to memorize the catechism questions and answers.

What Is Outrageous Grace?

God chose people to be saved on the basis of his own sovereign will. He didn't base this choice on anything that anyone did or might do (John 15:16; Ephesians 2:8 – 9).

Outrageous Grace in the Scriptures

"For those who are led by the Spirit of God are the children of God. The Spirit you received does not make you slaves, so that you live in fear again; rather, the Spirit you received brought about your adoption to sonship. And by him we cry, '*Abba*, Father'" (Romans 8:14–15).

"Rebekah's children were conceived at the same time by our father Isaac. Yet, before the twins were born or had done anything good or bad — in order that God's purpose in election might stand: not by works but by him who calls — she was told, 'The older will serve the younger.' Just as it is written: 'Jacob I loved, but Esau I hated.' What then shall we say? Is God unjust? Not at all! For he says to Moses, 'I will have mercy on whom I have mercy, and I will have compassion on whom I have compassion.' It does not, therefore, depend on human desire or effort, but on God's mercy. For Scripture says to Pharaoh: 'I raised you up for this very purpose, that I might display my power in you and that my name might be proclaimed in all the earth.' Therefore God has mercy on whom he wants to have mercy, and he hardens whom he wants to harden. One of you will say to me: 'Then why does God still blame us? For who is able to resist his will?' But who are you, a human being, to talk back to God? 'Shall what is formed say to the one who formed it, "Why did you make me like this?"' Does not the potter have the right to make out of the same lump of clay some pottery for special purposes and some for common use?" (Romans 9:10–21).

"In love he predestined us for adoption to sonship through Jesus Christ, in accordance with his pleasure and will.... It is by grace you have been saved, through faith — and this is not from yourselves, it is the gift of God — not by works, so that no one can boast" (Ephesians 1:4–5; 2:8–9).

Outrageous Grace in Song

Oh Lord, our Father God and Friend,
Your Majesty knows no end,
When we were helpless, wrecked with sin,
You spoke to life the hearts of men.

All you saints! Adopted ones!
Sing to him enthroned on high,

Who calls us sons and heirs of light,
He sent his son, the ransom for our crimes.
Should thieves or death or demons try,
To cheat us of this new birth-right,
We're safe within the First-Born's sacrifice.

Creation wearied, waits in death,
For life again with God's elect,
By faith, Christ's blood in us perfects,
Eternal hope we now possess.

Though scenes of hell appear today,
Our Savior stands in victory
None shall be taken from his hand,
Our Sovereign God, the Great I AM!

"ALL YOU SAINTS, ADOPTED ONES,"
adapted by Brooks Ritter from Gadsby Hymn 624,
© 2013 Sojourn Community Church

Outrageous Grace in Summary

Who can obey God's law? No one but Jesus can obey God's law perfectly (Romans 3:23; Hebrews 4:15).

If no one can obey God's law, why did God give it? God gave the law to show us his goodness, to show us our sin, and to show us we need Jesus (John 5:39; Romans 3:20).

How is Jesus our righteousness? His perfect life counts for us (Romans 4:4 – 8, 25).

DANIEL MONTGOMERY AND JARED KENNEDY,
North Star Catechism, © 2013 Sojourn Community Church

Justification

"If this one doctrine stands in purity, Christianity will remain pure and good," Martin Luther once noted. "But if this one doctrine stumbles, it is impossible not to fall into error."[29] So what is "this one doctrine" by which the church stands or falls? It's justification by faith alone. And what does it mean to say we are justified by faith alone?

1. **Justification is a legal verdict that declares believers righteous.** Justification makes us right with God — but not by making us perfectly righteous in this life! Justification is a divine decision that declares us righteous even though we aren't righteous yet. "Justification is God's verdict that in Christ and on the basis of Christ's life, death, and resurrection our sins are forgiven and we are counted as those who are perfectly obedient in his sight."[30]

2. **Justification is a verdict from the end of time that God declares here and now.** This divine verdict is, however, no mere fiction in which God acts like we're righteous even though we aren't and never will be! God will make every believer righteous at the end of time. Our future justification is so certain that God declares his end-time verdict of justification now, in the very moment that we first rest in the finished work of Jesus. "When we come to faith in Christ, our justification in the present is the same justification that will be declared publicly in the future at the resurrection and judgment."[31] Our justification is already our possession and, at the same time, not yet fulfilled.

3. **Justification is found in Jesus alone.** Faith is the means that God uses to incorporate us into Jesus Christ. Joined with Jesus through faith, we are forgiven because Jesus suffered our death in our place, and we are declared righteous because God credits all the goodness of Jesus to our account.[32] Sometimes "justified" has been defined as "just as if I'd never sinned" — a definition that, while true, represents only one small slice of the truth. To be justified is to be declared not only "just as if I'd never sinned in the past" but also "just as if I'm already living the perfect life that Jesus lived right now."

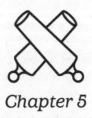

Chapter 5

OVERCOMING GRACE

Just as from eternity God chose his own in Christ, so within time God effectively calls them, grants them faith and repentance, and, having rescued them from the dominion of darkness, brings them into the kingdom of his Son.... Where before the rebellion and resistance of the flesh had dominated their hearts, now eager and sincere obedience from the Spirit begins to overcome (3/4:10, 16).

CANONS OF DORT

The whole point of irresistible grace is that rebirth quickens someone to spiritual life in such a way that Jesus is now seen in his irresistible sweetness.

R. C. SPROUL, *Chosen by God*

Methods are inscrutable.
The proof is irrefutable...
Simply irresistible.

ROBERT PALMER, "Simply Irresistible"

NEAR THE END OF THE TWENTIETH CENTURY, a frightening mutation of the influenza virus developed. If this "bird flu" virus had metamorphosed into a form that could spread person to person, scientists estimate that one-third of humanity would have died.[1] A few years later, fragments of viruses from humans, birds, and pigs fused into a single "swine flu" virus. The result was a pandemic that took the lives of more than a quarter-million people, mostly in Africa and southeast Asia.[2]

About the time the first waves of swine flu subsided, a movie studio responded in the most American of ways: They assembled an all-star cast to convert people's pandemic fears into a box-office blockbuster. The movie was entitled *Contagion*, and it pretty much turns you into an obsessive hand washer for several days after leaving the theater. It also causes your spouse to become reluctant to share the soda straw with you in the theater, which can cause your evening to end less pleasantly than it began. Trust me on this one. In any case, once the pandemic in *Contagion* is identified, the search begins not only for a vaccine to overcome the virus but also for "patient zero" — for the victim who first infected everyone else. As millions die and people manipulate one another for profit and survival, it becomes clear that nothing spreads like fear.

Except maybe sin.

There is, after all, another contagion far deadlier than any pandemic that's been splashed across the silver screen. In the beginning, God created the human will healthy and free.[3] When the first man and woman rejected God's way, Adam and Eve became patient zero. They not only died spiritually, but their wills — their inner dispositions and desires — became sin infected, and a deadly contagion raced through all creation (Romans 8:19–22). But unlike the virus movies where some people are clean and others aren't, this disease *affects* us all because it *infects* us all (Romans 5:12–14). We sense the sting of the infection in every choice we make, and yet we cannot seem to keep ourselves from sinning (Romans 7:18).[4] And so we experiment with all sorts of home-brewed remedies to deal with our infected wills. Some of us numb the pain with the pleasures of substances and sex while others try to appease God through religion, but God alone has created the only vaccine that works.

God's remedy is grace that overcomes. Through this overcoming grace,[5] God changes his chosen people one by one so that they abandon their rebellion, long for holiness, and freely surrender to Jesus. He overcomes their idolatrous self-reliance and gathers them into communities that share in the multiplication of God's kingdom around the world (Matthew 16:18; Luke 10:19; John 16:33; Romans 16:20; 1 John 5:4–5). This grace begins with a calling that heals our contagion. It's the call that Paul hinted at in his letter to the Ephesians when he mentioned "the hope to which [God] has called you" (Ephesians 1:18).

Over the years, theologians have sometimes dubbed this calling "irresistible grace" — a term that, while true, can be a bit confusing since people can and do resist many expressions of God's grace! In fact, left to ourselves, we will always refuse to respond positively to God's outward call to submit to the reign of the risen King (Acts 7:51; Romans 3:11).

But there is another call of grace, a powerful and effective call that overcomes the contagion within us and gives birth to repentance and faith. This inward call is the starting point for what we've called "overcoming grace." Overcoming grace reaches only into the lives of those God has chosen and enlivened, and it's a call that never fails. This is the call that caused the Christians in Ephesus to find their hope in Jesus Christ alone (Ephesians 1:18). It's the same inward call that the apostle Paul was describing when he declared that "those [God] predestined, he also called; those he called, he also justified; those he justified, he also glorified" (Romans 8:30). God's effective inward call isn't like an initial inoculation that includes everyone at first, but then requires people to request the right booster shots to maintain their immunity! The precise people God predestined before time are the same ones he calls, justifies, and guarantees he will glorify at the end. And God doesn't wait for our response before he floods our lives with his grace! God's call overcomes our resistance completely apart from any contribution from us. "Our nature is so corrupt ... that unless God does a supernatural work in our souls, we will never choose Christ. We do not believe in order to be born again; we are born in order that we may believe."[6]

"There may be several things which may help to make the life fair in the eyes of men; but nothing will make it amiable in the eyes of God, unless the heart be changed and renewed. All the medicines which can be applied, without the sanctifying work of the Spirit, though they may cover, they can never cure the corruption and diseases of the soul."

GEORGE SWINNOCK

God Is Not a Gentleman

But this perspective on how God saves us isn't popular in most churches today.

One of the most common contemporary depictions of our salvation portrays a chasm of sin between God and humanity that's bridged by the cross of Jesus. And, up to a point, this is a helpful and appropriate image. The problem with this picture is that it sometimes leaves humanity on one side of the chasm and God on the other. There, on his end of the bridge, God waits for sinners to find their own way across. He beckons us and begs us, but he never crosses the bridge himself. Well-meaning Christian teachers make this same point in different words when they claim that "God is a gentleman, and he waits for people to come to him."[7]

But that's not even close to how the Scriptures describe God's saving work.

The God of the Scriptures is no debonair gentleman who waves to us from the opposite side of a chasm, hoping we will find it in our hearts to respond. In Jesus Christ, God himself crossed the chasm between himself and humanity (John 1:14; 12:27). He came as a righteous shepherd who sacrifices his life to snatch his sheep from the jaws of the beast (Ezekiel 34:10; Matthew 18:12–14; John 10:11–15). He entered space and time as a sovereign lord in humble disguise, seeking to transform a broken woman into his pure and perfect bride (Ezekiel 16:1–14; Hosea 3:1; Ephesians 5:25–27). He came as a medic on an emergency mission to breathe life into sin-infected souls (Mark 2:17). Now, through the power of his Spirit and the proclamation of his gospel, this same Jesus is shattering every resistance to his reign in the lives of those he has chosen. He is planting outposts of his kingdom where love and justice grow, and he is beginning the healing of his people's sin-infected souls. Jesus Christ came to seek and to save his people who were lost, and he isn't asking anyone's permission to finish this mission (Matthew 1:21; Luke 19:10). That's the power and the beauty of overcoming grace.

Through overcoming grace, God unshackles us from the enslaving contagion of sin so that we glimpse the overwhelming beauty of Jesus and his kingdom. Our immediate response to this work of grace is "repentance toward God and faith in the Lord Jesus Christ."[8] This response doesn't happen forcibly, with God running roughshod over our wills. Instead, God changes our desires so that we love holiness and long to see God's justice flow all around us. With wills healed and hearts transformed, we run to Jesus "freely, being made willing by his grace."[9]

Now, how exactly does God accomplish this inward calling that cures our contagion by joining us with Jesus?

We have no idea.

Scripture doesn't provide us with the specifics of how God accomplishes this work. But it happens only as the gospel of Jesus Christ is proclaimed to every nation. And, to paraphrase a few lines from pop vocalist Robert Palmer — who most likely wasn't thinking a lot about theology when he wrote these words — whenever God calls us, though his "methods are inscrutable, the proof is irrefutable," and Jesus becomes "simply irresistible."[10] God's overcoming grace transforms us into "God's handiwork" or "his making" — a phrase from Paul's letter to the Ephesians that identifies God's people as a new creation no less miraculous than God's initial creation of the cosmos (Ephesians 2:10)). Just as God once effectively called a world into being, so he now calls sinners to himself and creates new life in them that overcomes the contagion of sin.[11]

Inward Call and Outward Call

Whenever the gospel is proclaimed, God *outwardly calls* everyone who hears the good news; unbelievers can and do resist this call (Acts 7:51). But when God gives new life to one of his chosen children, God *inwardly calls* this newly regenerated sinner; God's inward calling never fails. Jesus clearly distinguished between these two callings when he said, "Many are invited, but few are chosen" — in other words, all who hear the gospel are called outwardly but God's chosen children are also called inwardly (Matthew 22:14).

Jesus described the impact of this irresistible inward calling in John's gospel: "All that the Father gives to me will come to me.... No one can come to me unless the Father who sent me draws him" (John 6:37, 44 NASB).[12] Some biblical scholars claim that this drawing is "nothing more than a way of saying *convincement* or *persuasion*."[13] But such a reading simply doesn't fit the biblical text. When the Father "draws" a sinner in the sense that Jesus declared here, his work of grace isn't a gentle tug that tests whether we might choose Jesus on our own. Look carefully at how the verb translated "draws" (John 6:44) functions throughout the rest of the New Testament:

- "Simon Peter, who had a sword, *drew* it and struck the high priest's servant" (John 18:10).

- "He said unto them, 'Cast the net on the right side of the boat.' ... Now they were not able to *draw* it for the multitude of fishes.... Simon Peter ... *drew* the net to land, full of great fishes" (John 21:6, 11 ASV).

- "When her masters saw that the hope of their gains was gone, they caught Paul and Silas, and *drew* them into the marketplace" (Acts 16:19 KJV).

- "Do not rich men oppress you, and *draw* you before the judgment seats?" (James 2:6 KJV).

In each of these instances, the word translated "draw" pointed to a powerful and particular pull that did not fail. So it is when the Father raises and calls his chosen children.[14]

The Intoxicating Joy of a Life That's Overcome

In that moment when we freely flee to Jesus in faith, God the Father accomplishes the most amazing miracle of all: He joins our life with the life of Jesus, his Son. United with Christ, we have a new identity. Our new identity *includes* the perfections of Jesus credited to our account — but it doesn't end there! United with Christ, we begin to become what we already are in Christ.

In Christ, we are not cursed but blessed with new life (Ephesians 1:3). We are not rejected whores but a chosen bride (1:4). We are not judged and condemned but redeemed and forgiven (1:7). We are not forgotten. We were remembered before the foundation of the world (1:10 – 11).

You are not lost but marked and sealed by the Spirit (1:13). You are no longer a zombie but alive with new life in Christ (2:4 – 5). Before we were second-class citizens, but now we are "seated ... with [God] in the heavenly realms" (2:6). You are not left over and ugly. You are part of God's new creation (2:10).

You may feel like your past defines you. But Paul tells us that even though you were once far away from God, he has brought you near (2:13). You were a prodigal with respect to God's promised inheritance, but now you're family — you've been written into the will (3:6). You were once an illegal alien — barred from God's presence — but now you have free access to the very throne of God. You can approach him with confidence (3:12).

Think of how much energy we put into making ourselves something in this world. From Facebook profiles to fashion, from what we eat and don't eat to where we get an education. There's this crazy cycle of "I've got to get into a good school and get a good job and find a good spouse and make a lot of money so that my children can find a good school and get a good spouse" and around and around we go. It's a merry-go-round of meaninglessness ... of trying to make our miserable lives mean something. We're desperately reaching out for a sense of self. Let's listen to the words of a prophet — not a biblical prophet, but a pagan prophet — on our situation. This is from Madonna, twenty years ago in *Vanity Fair* (April 1991):

> All of my will has always been to conquer some horrible feeling of inadequacy. I'm always struggling with that fear. I push past one spell of it and discover myself as a special human being and then I get to another stage and think I'm mediocre and uninteresting. And I find a way to get myself out of that. Again and again. My drive in life is from this horrible fear of being mediocre. And that's always pushing me, pushing me. Because even though I've become Somebody, I still have to prove that Somebody. My struggle has never ended and it probably never will.

And I wish I could say that this is just a problem outside the church, but the cycle can be just as pathetic within the church. The only difference is that we hide behind our religion and superficial spirituality. We need to hear God's shout: *"You are my workmanship, you are my masterpiece, created anew in Christ Jesus."* Our culture bombards us with calls to "Be extraordinary, be different, be special!" And God's shouting, *"By grace through faith — you are extraordinary, you are different, you are special. You are my workmanship!"* There's nothing greater than being made new by the living God.

"For we are his making, having been created in Christ Jesus for good works, which God prepared before the foundation of the world so we would walk in them" (Ephesians 2:10).[15]

From Deadly Contagion to New Creation

Your Predicament Outside Christ	God's Provision in Christ	God's Precept for Our Lives in Christ	God's Promise in Christ
You were alienated (Ephesians 2:12)	Jesus was alienated	Predestination	You are chosen (Ephesians 1:4)
You were an object of God's wrath (Ephesians 2:3)	Jesus was condemned	Propitiation	You are forgiven (Ephesians 1:7)
You were dead (Ephesians 2:1)	Jesus endured death	Regeneration	You are alive (Ephesians 2:4–5)
You were guilty (Ephesians 2:13)	Jesus was rejected	Justification	You are accepted (Ephesians 2:13)
You were abandoned (Ephesians 2:12)	Jesus was forsaken by his Father	Adoption	You are adopted (Ephesians 1:5–11)
You were enslaved (Ephesians 2:3)	Jesus was set free from death	Redemption	You have been set free from sin (Ephesians 2:6)
You were defiled (Ephesians 2:2)	Jesus ascended to his Father	Sanctification	You are being set free from sin (Ephesians 2:7, 21)
You were hopeless (Ephesians 2:12)	Jesus will come again	Glorification	You will be set free from sin. All things — including you — will be made new (Ephesians 2:22)

ADAPTED FROM STEVEN L. CHILDERS, *True Spirituality: The Transforming Power of the Gospel*, © copyright 2003, version 4.0.

Behold one of the most mysterious and beautiful facets of God's dealings with humanity: From the moment that you first rest in Jesus Christ as your only hope, you are forever joined with Jesus in such a way that God the Father sees you always and only in Jesus. Through faith, the deeds of Jesus become your deeds,[16] his life becomes your life, and all his goodness is credited to your account (John 17:20–23; Romans 4:22–25; 5:17–19; 6:11; Colossians 3:3).[17] Jesus Christ on the cross joined himself with sins that were not his own. United with him by faith, you receive righteousness that you never could have earned.

Here's what this means for your life: In that moment when the baptized body of Jesus burst through the surface of the Jordan River, the heavens thundered with the words that your heart hungers to hear: "You are my Son, whom I love; with you I am well pleased" (Mark 1:11). These words from God the Father were meant first and foremost for Jesus, of course. Of all the billions of men and women who have lived and died from the dawn of time to the end of the age, Jesus alone deserves such praise. And yet, through the work that Jesus accomplished through his perfect life and sacrifice, these words have reached far beyond the Son of God to include every human being who is "in Christ."

Deep inside, you are starving for someone whose opinion really matters to declare once and for all that you belong, that you're loved, and that he is pleased with you. The good news of grace is that someone already has, and not even the slightest measure of his pleasure is based on anything that you will ever do. It's based solely on what Jesus has already done.

In Christ, whatever Jesus inherits, you inherit with him (Romans 8:17). You don't deserve this inheritance, and you never will—but Jesus does, and the Father sees you in him.

In Christ, whatever love God the Father has for Jesus, he has for you as well. Nothing you do could ever merit this love—but Jesus could and did, and the Father sees you in him.

In Christ, you are joined to Jesus in such a way that God the Father can never think anything less of you than he thinks of Jesus. Your failures are wiped away, your short-fallings no longer fall short, and your future is secure.

In Christ, the deepest reality in your life isn't the rapidly wrinkling flesh that stared back at you from the mirror this morning. Your deepest reality is the fist-battered face of the one who looked down at men whose spit had clotted with his blood and who pleaded with his Father for their forgiveness (Luke 23:34). Your truest identity isn't the failure-prone fool who never seems to lose enough weight or gain enough ground to impress the people around you. Your life is "hidden with Christ in God" (Colossians 3:3; see also Galatians 3:26; Philippians 3:9; Colossians 1:2 – 4; Hebrews 3:14).

In Christ, you have already been convicted and executed, raised from death and vindicated once and for all (Romans 6:11; Ephesians 2:5 – 6; Hebrews 10:10 – 18). You have no failures to hide and no triumphs to hide behind. The risen King has become your righteousness, and your standing before God no longer depends on you (Romans 4:24; 1 Corinthians 1:30; Philippians 3:9).

This single truth of being "in Christ" changes everything, and it has all been given to you in the free gift of faith (Ephesians 2:8 – 9).

Union with Christ

Union with Christ may be the most important doctrine you never knew you needed to know. It's a doctrine that's woven throughout almost every page of the New Testament, yet it's rarely discussed in many churches. Virtually every occurrence of phrases such as "in Christ," "into Christ," "with Christ," and "through Christ" — hundreds of instances in all — hints somehow at union with Christ. Jesus specifically mentioned his people's union with himself when he prayed on the night before his crucifixion: "I have given them the glory that you gave me, that they may be one as we are one — I in them and you in me" (John 17:22 – 23). Then there are the repeated promises from Jesus to his first followers: "You are in me, and I am in you," and "If you remain in me and I in you, you will bear much fruit" (John 14:20; 15:5). Union with Christ is the golden strand that ties together every aspect of God's gracious plan to save sinners.[18]

So what is union with Christ?

Union with Christ is nothing less than identification with God's Son that leads to participation in God's life and to incorporation into God's people through faith in Jesus Christ (Romans 5:17; 6:11; Colossians 3:3). Part of what this means for your daily life is that, from the moment you place your faith in Christ,[19] you are "in Christ" in such a way that God the Father regards you in the same way that he regards Jesus.

- Jesus was the righteous Son of God; "in Christ," God adopts you, and you gain the privilege of calling God your Father (Romans 8:9 – 17).
- Jesus suffered for the sake of his people; "in Christ," your pain has a purpose because your sufferings are joined with his sufferings (Colossians 1:24).
- Jesus was raised from the dead and exalted to the highest place in the heavens; "in Christ," you share this glory now, and you will share this glory more fully in the future (Ephesians 2:6).[20]

1. Union with Christ determined before time

"Union with Christ is not something 'tacked on' to our salvation; it is there from the outset, even in the plan of God."[21] Before time began, God the Father planned for Christ to be crucified, and he chose in Christ every person who would ever trust in Christ (Acts 2:23; 4:27 – 28; Ephesians 1:4 – 5).[22] Even in eternity past, those who would be saved were never contemplated by the Father apart from union with his Son.[23] "As in the womb, head and members are not conceived apart, but together,... so were we and Christ ... formed together in that eternal womb of election,... us with him, and yet us in him."[24]

2. Union with Christ accomplished within time[25]

- *Christ united with humanity by becoming flesh:* In the womb of the Virgin Mary, God the Son was united with human flesh for the sake of his people. Because he became one with humanity through the incarnation, he was able also to become the substitute for human beings through his sufferings and sacrificial death (Hebrews 2:17; 1 John 2:2).[26] In the words of an ancient pastor named Augustine of Hippo, "The Son of God became the Son of Man so that sons of men could become sons of God."[27] Through the resurrection, God the Father vindicated Jesus Christ and proved that he was the Righteous One predicted by the ancient prophets (Acts 2:22 – 33; 3:13 – 15).
- *Christ united with believers through faith:* Whenever a sinner trusts Jesus as the sole and certain source of righteousness, that sinner receives the very righteousness of Christ and becomes united with Christ (Romans 6:4 – 6; Galatians 2:20; 2 Corinthians 5:21; 2 Timothy 2:11).[28] This union is made possible by the life-giving work of God's Spirit (Ephesians 2:4 – 5, 10), actualized through faith in Jesus Christ (Ephesians 1:13; 3:17), and guaranteed to persist past the rise and fall of all the kingdoms of the earth (Romans 8:38 – 39). It is through union with Christ that believers experience the twofold gift of being declared righteous (justification)

and growing in righteousness (sanctification).[29] But the importance of union with Christ doesn't end with justification and sanctification! Union with Christ also provides the vital basis for unity in the church (John 15:4 – 5; Romans 6:4, 11; 1 Corinthians 6:17 – 20; Galatians 3:28; Ephesians 2:13; Colossians 3:11).

3. Union with Christ guaranteed beyond time

When Christ returns to earth in triumph and time draws to an end, every believer will be transformed to participate fully in Christ's glory (1 Corinthians 15:22 – 23; 1 Thessalonians 4:16 – 17). In a renewed heaven and earth, the glorious union that God planned before time will grow throughout eternity.

Faith That Overcomes the World (Ephesians 2:10)

But God's gift doesn't stop with the inward call that unites us with Christ and results in repentance and faith. In fact, this initial transformation is only the beginning. God doesn't simply cure our sin-infected souls by forgiving us and declaring us righteous in Christ ("justification" is the theological term for this part of God's work). God also begins to heal the lingering contagion of sin in our souls by cultivating his own righteousness within us (this part of God's work is known as "sanctification"). The gift of faith keeps on giving! Immediately after Paul reminded the Ephesians that God had saved them "by grace ... through faith," the apostle went on to say, "We are God's handiwork, created in Christ Jesus to do good works, which God prepared in advance for us to do" (Ephesians 2:8, 10).

God's grace changes us, and then he sends us. First, he makes us new — giving us new birth as his children. Then, as the apostle John makes clear, "Everyone born of God overcomes the world" (1 John 5:4). Why? "[Because] this is the victory that has overcome the world, even our faith" (1 John 5:4). God overcomes our legal sentence of death by making Christ's obedience count for us, and then God overcomes the world by transforming us and sending us on a mission. God's grace is not merely his pardon for your sin — it is his power at work in your powerless life.

Some people experience God's saving grace like a flower that buds slowly, over time. For others, like Paul — the persecutor of Christians turned missionary — grace is a volcanic eruption that hurls them to the ground without warning and rearranges their lives.

I [Daniel] happen to belong to this second group.

When my family moved from Southern California to a conservative southeastern city nestled in a comfortable notch of the Bible Belt, I thought I would be able to change my life. I even told my parents that I wouldn't be drinking as much as I had before. (Can you imagine? A teenager informing his parents that he wasn't going to drink *as much*? But that's what I did.)

Still, my drug use, drug dealing, and drunkenness kept spiraling further out of control. I hated my addictions — but I also craved the substances and the thrills, and I couldn't escape their clutch. There were moments when I wanted out of this downhill spiral of death, but I was powerless to change. Many of my father figures were already in prison. I knew I was headed in the same direction, and I sensed that the contagion of sin had a stranglehold on my will.

I finally struck rock bottom when I was sixteen. Kicked out of my house and suspended from school, I ended up standing on a corner in Winslow, Arizona, where I was arrested for possession of a stolen vehicle. It was not a fine sight to see.

I logged three days in a detention center before someone from Young Life offered me a chance to go to one of their camps. I went, mostly because it seemed preferable to anywhere else I was going at the moment. By the third day of that weeklong retreat, I found myself whispering, "I can't do this anymore. I can't keep fighting. I want life, but I can't do it." On the outside I looked like a rebel, but on the inside I knew I was a slave — a slave to my own desires.

At that moment, something happened that I never expected. Though I didn't hear an audible voice, I clearly sensed the voice of God speaking to me.

"I know you can't," the voice said. "But I can. And I *will*."

Immediately, I stood up and said out loud, "I believe."

I had heard the gospel before, many times in fact. But this time, God chose to flip the switch on my dead, sin-addicted heart. God conquered my rebellion and changed my will. I found that something had been changed in me, and I could no longer keep myself from surrendering my will to the reign of Jesus the King.

For the first time in my life, I found that I wanted nothing to do with drugs or sleeping around. And no one needed to tell me that it was a good idea to tell other people about Jesus! Wherever I went, I wanted people to know the freedom I had experienced, I wanted them to hear about God's glorious grace. So I started sharing my story with everyone I knew. There was no training, no complicated apologetics, nothing but the true story of one life changed. As I told my story, God began working in the lives of my friends as well, and many of them turned to Jesus. Nothing in this transformation was the result of my own efforts — I had tried and failed to change my life many times before. This new life I was experiencing was the result of God overruling my rebellion.

The same miracle that God accomplished in me, God carries out in the life of every believer in Jesus Christ. This miracle may look different in each person's life, "but to each one of us grace has been given as Christ apportioned it" (Ephesians 4:7). Through grace, God soothes the contagion of sin that has scarred our souls — but he doesn't stop at dealing with us as individuals. God's desire from the beginning was that, "through the church, the manifold wisdom of God should be made known to the rulers and authorities in the heavenly realms" (Ephesians 3:10).

A Community of Overcomers (Ephesians 3:10 – 13)

God designed his overcoming grace to flow through the church — through the people of God clustered in communities all around the globe. Someone had to share the gospel of grace with us in the first place, and — once we've embraced the gospel — it's through the community of faith that God's Spirit works to kill the residue of sin that remains within us. We cannot experience this grace alone any more than we can get married alone.

> There may be religions that come to you through quiet walks in the woods, or by sitting quietly in the library with a book, or rummaging around in the recesses of your psyche. Christianity is not one of them. Christianity is inherently communal, a matter of life in the Body.... Jesus did not call isolated individuals to follow him. He called a group of disciples. He gathered a crowd.... Privacy is not a Christian category. We are saved from our privacy by being made part of a people who can tell us what we should do with our money, with our genitals, with our lives. We have been made part of a good company, a wonderful adventure, so that we no longer need "mine."[30]

It's through the craziness of this "good company" that God reveals the wonders of his overcoming grace. But this is no social club where resistance is negligible and risks are few! The church has been called together to overcome (Revelation 2:7; 3:5, 12, 21; 12:11).

Because we are people called to overcome, opposition is inevitable. Jesus himself made clear that people will "insult you, persecute you and falsely say all kinds of evil against you because of me" (Matthew 5:11). For comfortable American Christians who live in a land of religious liberty, it may seem like this kind of oppression can be avoided, but this is not the case for the majority of Christians throughout the world. But even in our relative comfort, Christians are constantly at war with Satan, sin, and death. "For our struggle is not against flesh and blood, but against the rulers, against the authorities, against the powers of this dark world and against the spiritual forces of evil in the heavenly realms" (Ephesians 6:12).

Think about the ways that you are defeated on a daily basis. Maybe you're battling depression. Maybe you're fighting a losing battle with habitual lust and pornography. Maybe you're just losing a battle to the snooze button on Sunday morning. You have no problem admitting that when you try to live for Jesus, there is very real opposition. So how can we say that the church will overcome?

The answer is that God has saved you by grace alone, but he hasn't saved you to be alone. The grace that transforms us places us in a community that together overcomes. And Paul tells us that God's grace equips the church for the fight. He has gifted the people of the church to spur one another on:

> But to each one of us grace has been given as Christ apportioned it.... So Christ himself gave the apostles, the prophets, the evangelists, the pastors and teachers, to equip his people for works of service, so that the body of Christ may be built up until we all reach unity in the faith and in the knowledge of the Son of God and become mature, attaining to the whole measure of the fullness of Christ (Ephesians 4:7, 11–13).

And he has called the church to fight together with his mighty power:

> Finally, be strong in the Lord and in his mighty power. Put on the full armor of God, so that you can take your stand against the devil's schemes (Ephesians 6:10–11).

Earlier in the chapter, I [Daniel] told you the story of how God's grace transformed me. But it didn't take long for me to slip into the delusion that my rescue had happened, at least in part, because of me. A couple of years later, a friend reminded me that even my faith had been the fruit of God's work in my life. My first response was to make fun of her, and that's when she began reading aloud the ninth chapter of Paul's letter to the Romans. Despite my derision, she refused to stop, and God's Word pierced my stubborn heart. As she read, I began to see more clearly than ever before that I had been saved by grace alone. Grace *alone*! My transformation hadn't been a two-handed work, with God reaching down and waiting for me to do my part. God had seized me, loved me, and lifted me when I couldn't raise an arm in surrender or even so much as clasp my hand around his little finger. God alone deserved the credit for saving me, because nothing good that I did or desired to do had originated with me.

In that instance, God used his church — another Christian — to point me back to the truth. She took the sword of the Spirit — God's Word (Ephesians 6:17) — and my own wrestling with the Spirit through prayer (Ephesians 6:18) to open my mind to God's sovereign grace. That's an example of the overcoming work of God through his church. Apart from the Word of God being preached, no one will ever hear of this glorious grace that saves us, sanctifies us, and sends us into the world. And apart from the work of God's Spirit giving us new life, strengthening us through the sacraments, and empowering us to live this new life, the contagion of sin would overwhelm us all.

Let's look at three clear examples of God's overcoming grace at work in the world.

In the fourth century, a young man named Aurelius grew up in the region of Africa known today as Algeria. He and his friends stole for the thrill of the theft and slept with as many women as possible without the slightest thought of love or marriage. "I was not in love," Aurelius later wrote, "I was in love with love" — and this love of love revolved around his own pleasure and prestige. While still a teenager, the young man contracted a concubine, but not for love — at least not at first. "I chose her," he said, "only because my restless lusts happened to land on her." At one point, he prayed, "God, grant me purity, but not yet" — not until he had his full fill of sexual thrills.[31]

It was in Rome that the news of a famous philosopher's conversion intersected with the ongoing emptiness in the soul of Aurelius. He was seated beneath a tree in a park, wondering if he would ever turn to Jesus, when he heard a child singing, "*Tolle lege, tolle lege.* Take up and read, take up and read." Aurelius opened a New Testament and began reading the first text he saw. What he read were these words from Paul's letter to the Romans (13:13 – 14):

> Let us walk properly as in the daytime, not in orgies and drunkenness, not in sexual immorality and sensuality, not in quarreling and jealousy. But put on the Lord Jesus Christ, and make no provision for the flesh, to gratify its desires.

This was game over for Aurelius Augustine's old life. God's grace overcame the contagion of sex addiction in this man's life and turned this whore of a man into one of the greatest pastors and theologians in church history: St. Augustine of Hippo.

Fast-forward fourteen centuries. It is just before four o'clock in the morning in London, England, on February 24, 1807. There is great excitement in the House of Commons. British parliament members are on their feet applauding because the slave trade has just officially ended. One man sat with his head bowed, weeping. This man, who was once known as a lazy socialite, who fought off the call of Christ because he thought it would cost him his upper-class lifestyle and career, was William Wilberforce. This man who was once only concerned with his own comfort and enjoyment was overcome by the grace of God and, just a few short years after his conversion, God used him to overcome the tyranny of slavery in the British Empire. God's grace moved through a broken sinner and overcame an entire nation's oppression of Africans.

Fast-forward another two hundred years...

Sojourn Community Church is now a few years old, and one of the elders says he and his wife are feeling called to the horn of Africa. He had been raised there as the son of a missionary and desired to return. We have to keep their names and location secret because of the intense, violent persecution Christians are experiencing in their country. They labored for several years when God suddenly began stirring in the hearts of the indigenous people — they were working in an area that had literally never heard the name of Jesus or of his gospel. A few men were saved and they immediately began sharing the gospel with their friends and family. The Sojourn missionary also develops a relationship with the head of the state church to the north and is able to place a Bible in literally every church in the northern part of the country. Each church has one single Bible now and it's checked out like a library book for weeks at a time by grateful families. Today, there are literally thousands of Christians in dozens of new churches worshiping Jesus in the horn of Africa. God's grace overcame the fear of leaving home, the hostility of violent God-haters, the ignorance of the gospel, the lack of Bibles, and is this very day reaping a harvest of souls. Sojourn Community Church deserves none of the glory for any of this. Sojourn is nothing more than a single drop in the vast and overwhelming tidal wave of God's overcoming grace. What the stories of Augustine and Wilberforce and Sojourn and you and me reveal is the grandeur of a God whose healing grace is not only personal but also global and missional. The plan and the power belong to God, and so does the glory.

"By grace you have been saved, through faith," Paul reminded the Ephesians, "and this is not from yourselves, it is the gift of God.... We are God's handiwork" (Ephesians 2:8 – 10). God's salvation is a gift. We were nothing but corpses on the run from God's reign. But God, in his grace, chased us down, overcame our resistance, and began to heal our sin-infected will. His grace gives us hearts of compassion, love for neighbors and friends, and it empowers us with boldness to share the message of redemption. God's grace is an overcoming grace.

PROOF FOR LIFE

Meditate on these Scriptures and song lyrics. Work with a friend or family member to memorize the catechism questions and answers.

What Is Overcoming Grace?

God works in the lives of his chosen people to transform their rebellion into surrender so that they freely repent and recognize Christ as the risen King (John 6:44, 65; Ephesians 2:4 – 10).

Overcoming Grace in the Scriptures

"'Stop grumbling among yourselves,' Jesus answered. 'No one can come to me unless the Father who sent me draws them, and I will raise them up at the last day.' … He went on to say, 'This is why I told you that no one can come to me unless the Father has enabled them'" (John 6:43–44, 65).

"For we are God's handiwork, created in Christ Jesus to do good works, which God prepared in advance for us to do" (Ephesians 2:10).

"His intent was that now, through the church, the manifold wisdom of God should be made known to the rulers and authorities in the heavenly realms, according to his eternal purpose that he accomplished in Christ Jesus our Lord.… But to each one of us grace has been given as Christ apportioned it" (Ephesians 3:10–11; 4:7).

Overcoming Grace in Song

Not any government on earth, no law that God has given,
No will of man, no blood, no birth can raise a soul to heaven
The sovereign will of God alone prepares the heirs of grace
Born in the image of his Son, a chosen holy race.

It's through your Spirit,
Through your sacrificial Son.

We are changed, no longer in chains
Once were enslaved but the Son has come
And conquered the grave, so we are changed.
We are changed not by the things we've arranged
Not by the work our hands have done
It's through your Son that we are changed.

Our quickened souls awake and rise from sin and shame and death.
On heavenly things we fix our eyes; his praise employs our breath.

DAVE MOISAN, Bobby Gilles, and Neil Robins,
"We Are Changed," © 2008 Sojourn Community Church

Overcoming Grace in Summary

How does the Holy Spirit make us alive? The Holy Spirit helps us to have faith in Jesus (Ephesians 2:8).

What is growth? Growth is a lifelong partnership with the Holy Spirit to change and become like Jesus (Colossians 1:28 – 29).

What is the evidence of a changed life? The fruit of the Spirit is the evidence of a changed life (Galatians 5:22 – 23).

DANIEL MONTGOMERY AND JARED KENNEDY,
North Star Catechism, © 2013 Sojourn Community Church

Chapter 6

FOREVER GRACE

Those who have been converted could not remain standing in this grace if left to their own resources. But God is faithful, mercifully strengthening them in the grace once conferred on them and powerfully preserving them in it to the end.... As it has pleased God, by the preaching of the gospel, to begin this work of grace in us, so he preserves, continues, and perfects it by the hearing and reading of his Word, by meditation on it, and by the exhortations, threats, and promises contained in it, as well as by the use of the sacraments (5:3, 14).

Canons of Dort

His words hold true, he's the covenant keeper,
 We can't be separated, he's loving me deeper....
 We persevere 'cause of his preservation,
 My eyes tear 'cause he made reservations.[1]

Believin' Stephen, "Perseverance of the Saints"

Though Christians be not kept altogether from falling, yet they are kept from falling altogether.[2]

William Secker

Jesus put the down payment on your salvation at the cross — but you have to keep up the payments!"

That's the message that my [Timothy's] father heard from a preacher as a young man. The message was probably well-intended, but it certainly wasn't true — and the lie nearly destroyed my father's life. My father knew he could never keep up the payments on his salvation. By the time he became a teenager, he was already drinking heavily. Long before he turned sixteen, he was careening at high speeds along the gravel roads that crisscross the Ozark foothills. All three of the friends with whom he had shared his first drink of alcohol died before they turned twenty-one, and there was no reason to believe that his life would turn out any different. Eventually, he ended up in Kansas City, where he found the love of his life. But marriage did little to change his love for the bottle. The pattern of heavy drinking and parties spiraled further and further out of control.

After watching two men leave one party dragging a drunken woman behind them, my mother informed my father that, if the drinking didn't stop, she wouldn't be there the next time he came home. A few weeks later, the two of them piled two children and a handful of possessions into a Chevrolet sedan that was so rusted out that dust rolled through the floorboards on gravel roads. They left the city behind and, in a two-room house in rural Missouri, my father began working to reform his ways. Yet, even after leaving the bottle behind, he knew that he lacked the power to straighten out his life on his own. He regularly and violently lost his temper, and his drinking had nearly cost him his marriage. How could he possibly keep up the payments on any changes that he made in his life?

But then he found himself in a tiny Southern Baptist church where the preacher claimed that we don't keep ourselves saved. God in Christ has already made every payment necessary to save everyone who would ever trust in him. And so, no payments remain for us to keep up; Jesus has paid it all, and there is nothing for us to do or to contribute to keep God's good favor. You don't keep up your salvation; God does.

Not long after learning this truth, my father made his way down a creaky wooden aisle at Mount Pisgah Baptist Church during an invitation to respond to the message. "Are you wanting to join the church?" the pastor asked him. "No," he replied, "I've got something more important that I need to take care of first." There and then, he knelt at the altar and received God's payment for his sins.

Forever grace saved my father's life.

All Is Grace from Beginning to End

Not every preacher would say it as bluntly as that preacher from my father's younger years, but the idea that we have to keep up our salvation is alive and well still today. Seen in this way, our salvation begins with God's grace — but then it's up to us to stay saved. Whether or not we remain in God's good graces depends on our choices. Perhaps there are certain unpardonable sins that must be avoided or certain levels of growth that must be maintained or even religious rites that must be performed. Jesus starts it, but we finish it. But God, according to the Scriptures, doesn't only start our salvation; he plans it and guarantees it from beginning to end. When we looked at planned grace, we pointed out that one of the best reasons to believe in planned grace is the threefold harmony of the Trinity. It's the same when it comes to forever grace! It's clear throughout the Scriptures that the Father, Son, and Holy Spirit are working together at all times to sustain our salvation to the very end of time.

- The Father plans our salvation to the end: "He who began a good work in you will carry it on to completion until the day of Christ Jesus" (Philippians 1:6).
- The Son promises to carry out our salvation to the end: Jesus is both "the pioneer and perfecter" of our faith (Hebrews 12:2). In other words, Jesus doesn't start our faith as the pioneer, but then leave us to finish the project. Jesus is the one who brings it to completion as "the perfecter" of our faith as well.
- The Spirit guarantees our salvation to the end: God "put his Spirit in our hearts as a deposit, guaranteeing what is to come" (2 Corinthians 1:22).

That's good news for believers in Jesus Christ because it means you don't have to keep up the payments on your salvation! If you've trusted Jesus, it's not because you planned that faith in your fleeting and faulty wisdom. It's because God set his heart on you from eternity past; God made this choice knowing everything about you — past, present, and future! As a result, nothing can change his choice to pour out his grace on you.

Not your sin.

Not your fears.

Not the darkness that gnaws at your heart that no one else knows about.

Nothing in your future.

Nothing in your past.

Nothing in all creation.

Nothing at all can separate you from God's love.

God proved his love for you once and for all through the cross of Jesus and the empty tomb — and nothing can change his determination to save you by his grace.

That's the promise of forever grace.

Forever grace means that God *preserves* us in his grace and that we *persevere* by this same grace. Both of these realities are rooted in God's gracious work. Neither one is a work that originates in us, and both truths are essential. We can glimpse both of these truths at the same time in the same verse in Paul's letter to the Ephesians: "And do not grieve the Holy Spirit" (that's a command to persevere) "with whom you were sealed for the day of redemption" (4:30) — that's an assurance that you will be preserved. Let's look carefully at each of these twin truths of forever grace in Paul's letter to the Ephesians.

God Preserves Us in His Grace

One of the ways that the apostle Paul pictured the truth of God's preservation was with the image of a seal, the imprint on a clump of clay that kept ancient scrolls secure. "When you believed," Paul wrote to the Ephesians, "you were marked in him with a seal, the promised Holy Spirit" (Ephesians 1:13). A seal in the ancient world implied at least three distinct realities: *possession, protection,* and *proof.*[3]

So when Paul wrote that God seals us through his Holy Spirit, he was declaring, first, that we are God's *possession* — and no one steals God's stuff because no one can overcome God's power or slip undetected past God's defenses![4] That's what Jesus was getting at when he said, "This is the will of him who sent me, that I shall lose none of all those he has given me, but raise them up at the last day.... My sheep listen to my voice; I know them, and they follow me.... My Father, who has given them to me, is greater than all; no one can snatch them out of my Father's hand" (John 6:39; 10:27 – 29). If you are God's property —

someone who has been transformed by God's power — no one, not even you, can remove you from God's hand.

A seal also suggests *protection*. When Jesus said, "They shall never perish" (John 10:28), he reminded us that we can never leave God's fold. Death comes from sin, and since the power of sin has been removed from us, so has every form of death that lasts past this life. "Jesus, as emphatically as possible, states that those to whom he gives eternal life will never be lost, will never be cast into hell.... This is one of the strongest statements of God's preservation of his people in the whole Bible, and it comes from the lips of Jesus, the Savior of the world."[5] God's grace is based on who he is, not on who we are. His plan is fixed and his hand is steady. He does not change his mind, he does not get nervous, and he does not hesitate. When God chose us, he declared, "These people belong to me." There is nothing in the universe strong enough to remove God's chosen ones from his hands. Believers don't merely enter eternal life when they die; eternal life enters us when we believe and it can never leave — if it did leave us, it wouldn't have been eternal!

This seal of possession and protection provides, according to Paul, an unbreakable promise. When we trusted Jesus in response to the Spirit's work of resurrecting grace, the Holy Spirit became in our lives "a deposit guaranteeing our inheritance until the redemption of those who are God's possession" (Ephesians 1:14). God chose us as his portion and possession (Ephesians 1:11) and then placed his Spirit within us as "a deposit" — a down payment or first installment — promising that he will redeem us at the end.[6] Think about what this means for us: If anyone who trusts Jesus ("when you believed," Ephesians 1:13) is lost, that would mean God made a down payment and claimed a property as his own, but then defaulted on his payments. That means we would no longer be able to sing, "Jesus paid it all, all to him I owe," but "Jesus paid it partly, and it depends on me whether he pays the rest" — which would drop a bit of a damper not only on our theology but also on our music.

Remember: God's planning never writes a check his power can't cash! Paul made that point clear when he described the faith of Abraham: "He did not waver through unbelief regarding the promise of God." And what was the assurance that undergirded Abraham's belief? He was "fully persuaded that God had power to do what he had promised" (Romans 4:20 – 21). Whatever God promises, he possesses the power to do, and his down payment through the Spirit is his promise that he will finish all that he started.[7] The same God who "began a good work in you will carry it on to completion" until his kingdom comes (Philippians 1:6).

We Persevere by God's Grace

But God's preservation isn't the only truth about forever grace! Wherever God's saving grace is present, not only preservation but also perseverance are present too. Let's be clear about what perseverance *isn't*, though, before we look at what perseverance *is*: Perseverance is *not* you contributing your part to your salvation so that you and God are partnering together to keep you saved.

Your salvation depends solely on what Jesus has already done, not on anything you have done or might do! The certainty of your justification forms the foundation for your perseverance, and your perseverance is no less a work of God's grace than your justification and preservation. In preservation, God places his Spirit within you and guarantees your salvation. In perseverance, God transforms you and works through you so that you grow in holiness and never let go. "Preservation is God's work of keeping us, and perseverance is our work of keeping on."[8] But even our keeping on is ultimately a work of God's grace. One preacher put it this way: "You take the first step, God will take the second step, and by the time you get to the third step, you will know that it was God who took the first step."[9]

Here's how the apostle Paul described the process of perseverance in his letter to the Ephesians: "I urge you to live a life worthy of the calling you have received" (4:1). Living a worthy life doesn't gain God's calling or keep God's calling. If you're a believer in Jesus Christ, you have already experienced God's effective calling. (Remember, your regeneration and calling were the cause of your faith and repentance, so — if you're trusting Jesus right now — that's positive proof that God has called you!) What Paul told the Ephesians was to live a life "worthy" of the calling they had already received.

So what happens when someone fails to persevere in faith? Here's the difficult truth that we sometimes don't want to hear: If someone rejects "a life worthy of the calling," there is no reason to believe that God has called that person to himself, and there is every reason to fear for their soul. It doesn't matter how many times they've walked the aisle at church or raised their hand or prayed a prayer.

Years ago I [Daniel] worked with a man who had once said he was a Christian. Now he claimed to be an agnostic, and he was proud of it. Whenever he mentioned his "Christian phase," he described it with a condescending sneer.

At one point I simply quoted a couple of verses from Paul's letter to Timothy: "Turn away from godless chatter and the opposing ideas of what is falsely called knowledge, which some have professed and in so doing have departed from the faith" (1 Timothy 6:20–21).

He didn't like it.

In fact, he was incredulous and blurted out, "Are you saying I was never saved?"

Imagine that.

In his new way of thinking, he never could have been saved because what he himself had declared wasn't sufficient evidence to believe in anyone who might save him! And yet, when I pointed to Paul's words to suggest that he had "departed from the faith," he was shocked.

"What I'm saying," I replied, "is that you have no assurance of salvation and you have every reason to fear for your soul."

This individual had been taught that God preserves anyone who believes — but he hadn't been taught that saving faith perseveres. And so his thinking ran something like this: "I don't believe in God and I'm not going to live as a Christian, but, hey … *once saved, always saved!* If I happen to be wrong about God, I am still safe because, once upon a time, I prayed a prayer and said I believed that Jesus saves."

So did this individual lose his salvation?

Not at all.

Unless he repents and returns to faith, what this young man's rejection of Jesus revealed was that his faith in Jesus had never been real. Years ago, I heard a revival preacher put it this way: "Faith that fizzles before the finish was flawed from the first." It's a little corny, but it's totally true. If we don't persevere to the end, our faith never really existed in the first place. That's why the apostle John wrote these words about some who had abandoned the faith: "They went out from us, but they did not really belong to us" (1 John 2:19).

Grace is free and it is forever, but when God lavishes his grace on you, it changes you. It enables and inspires you to live your faith openly, in a way that produces far more goodness than when we try to earn our salvation by good works, apart from grace. One writer put it this way: "Works is a barren mother; she will never have any children, much less gracious children. Grace is fruitful; her children are many, and they all work hard."[10] God's grace isn't just his pardon for your sin; it's his power at work in your powerless life. And that's why grace isn't opposed to working *out* our salvation; grace is opposed to working *for* our salvation.

Perseverance isn't about performance that earns God's favor; it's about putting in effort to bring to fulfillment what God has already accomplished and guaranteed.

But if God has already guaranteed our salvation, why do the work of persevering? Why not sit around and watch movies all day? Or, worse yet, why not spend the rest of your life in total debauchery? After all, God has already paid the price and guaranteed the outcome, hasn't he?

Perseverance Is a Proof of Grace

A call to trust Jesus is a call to holiness. This holiness is both a *position* and a *pursuit*. God sets us apart as his own children and positions us in Jesus so that he sees us always and only in his Son. But God also works within us so that we love and long for holiness. If there is no pursuit of holiness in someone's life, there is no reason to believe that God has authentically saved that person. And what about when a Christian falls into sin? The question isn't whether people who profess Christ can or will fall into sin — we do! — it's how we respond when the Spirit convicts us and the congregation confronts us. Our response to the conviction of the Holy Spirit and the discipline of the church reveals whether our faith is real. That's what happened in the church at Corinth when a man was having an affair with his stepmother. Sleeping with your father's wife is not only perverted — as in after-hour cable television show perverted — it broke at least two of the top ten laws that God had engraved in stone on Mount Sinai. Not surprisingly, Paul declared that the man must be handed "over to Satan for the destruction of the flesh" — but when this same man turned from his sin, Paul wrote "to forgive and comfort him" (1 Corinthians 5:5; 2 Corinthians 2:7). The man's repentance and return to a pursuit of holiness provided practical evidence that his profession of faith was real. If the man had not turned from his sin, the Christians at Corinth would have had to assume — though they couldn't know everything about his heart in that moment — that his profession of faith was something other than authentic.

This perseverance in holiness isn't our work of proving we're worthy to receive God's grace. If God watched and waited to save us until we prove ourselves worthy, that would be like a new mother waiting to admit that her newborn belongs to her until the child proves he can care for her in her old age! Perseverance requires effort from us but earns nothing for us. That's because perseverance isn't something we're doing in our own power. Perseverance is God working through us to reveal the authenticity of our faith for the good of God's people and the fame of God's name — and this is no less a gift of grace than our initial rescue from God's wrath. Jesus himself is the proof of grace. What our perseverance provides is evidence that Jesus is present in our faith, working his works through us.

Warnings! A Means of God's Grace

But perseverance isn't only a proof of grace — the warnings that call us to persevere are also a means of grace. God works his very works in us through our perseverance to save us in the end. Where there are no works, there will be no salvation — but not because our works contribute to our salvation! Our works are necessary for our salvation without being the ground of our salvation. We grow and keep ourselves in God's holiness, but we know that when we grow, it's ultimately because God is keeping us and working in us. That's what Jude was getting at when he commanded his readers to "keep yourselves in God's love," but then he added almost immediately that it's God who keeps "you from stumbling" (Jude 1:21, 24). Perseverance is not perfection; it is a new direction.[11] Maintaining this new direction is both evidence that God has saved us and a means by which God will save us.

> The path of spiritual growth in the riches of Christ is not a passive one. Grace is not opposed to effort. It is opposed to earning.... You have never seen people more active than those who have been set on fire by the grace of God. Paul, who perhaps understood grace better than any other mere human being, looked back at what had happened to him and said: "By the grace of God I am what I am, and his grace toward me did not prove vain; but I labored even more than all of them, yet not I, but the grace of God with me" (1 Corinthians 15:10).[12]

Sometimes the doctrine of forever grace is termed "once saved, always saved." This clause is certainly true — once you're saved, your salvation is certain and secure. But "once saved, always saved" limits salvation to a past event, whereas — in the New Testament — "salvation" primarily points to our future and final rescue from God's wrath.[13] The result of this unfortunate phrasing is that people might miss the deeply biblical truth that salvation includes perseverance to the end. If we disown our Savior and never return, Jesus "will also disown us" (2 Timothy 2:12). This isn't because we forfeited our salvation. When Jesus himself described this disowning that would happen at the end of time, his words to the disowned were not "I once knew you but now I don't"; they were, "I never knew you" (Matthew 7:23).[14] Where there is no perseverance in faithfulness, there was no faith in the first place.

Living in the Covenant

Most of the rest of Paul's letter to the Ephesians spells out what this life of perseverance looks like. Central to this life is "speaking the truth in love" (Ephesians 4:15) — which doesn't merely mean saying kind words when we correct one another! "Speaking the truth in love" hints at all-important Old Testament phrases such as "steadfast love" and "faithfulness" that summarized God's faithfulness to his covenant despite humanity's unfaithfulness. Paul's point was to urge the Ephesians to reflect God's faithful love in their relationships with one another — but this also clearly roots our salvation in God's covenants with humanity.

Most agreements we make — agreements to work a particular job or to purchase a certain house — are sealed by contracts. A contract lasts for a limited time and focuses on an object or an obligation. If either party fails to provide an expected benefit, the contract may be renegotiated or reneged.[15] But God doesn't work primarily in contracts. God has chosen to structure his work with humanity around a series of covenants. In covenants, the persons do not merely agree regarding a set of abstract obligations; they give themselves to one another in relationships of loyal love. Covenants persist far past the capacity for reciprocity. Covenants bind people together in lasting communions of spirit and flesh, tears and blood.

Perseverance

Can Christians forfeit God's saving grace in their lives? Scripture seems to say that a Christian's salvation can never be shipwrecked (John 10:27 – 30; Philippians 1:6). And yet, if Christians *can't* lose their salvation, what's the point of biblical texts that warn against "falling away" and "shrinking back" (see, for example, Hebrews 2:1 – 4; 3:7 — 4:13; 5:11 — 6:12; 10:19 – 39; 12:1 – 29)? The perspective of PROOF is that every authentic believer perseveres to the end and produces fruit along the way. The biblical warnings and believers' responses are both a *means of grace* and a *proof of grace* (the two middle columns in the chart below). Believers' repentant responses to biblical warnings reveal and refine their faith.

	Loss-of-Salvation View	Means-of-Grace View	Proof-of-Grace View	Loss-of-Rewards View
What is the point of the believer's perseverance?	By repenting in response to warnings, believers safeguard their salvation for the end of time.	By repenting in response to warnings, believers demonstrate the authenticity of their faith.	By producing godly fruit, believers demonstrate the authenticity of their faith.	By producing godly fruit, believers secure rewards for themselves for the end of time.
What is the point of the warning passages?	Warnings urge obedience by calling into question whether a Christian will receive salvation.	Warnings urge obedience by calling Christians to repent, recognizing that saving faith perseveres to the end.	Warnings urge obedience by calling Christians to test themselves, looking for evidence that exemplifies saving faith.	Warnings urge obedience by calling into question whether a Christian will receive rewards.
What happens if a professed believer disowns Jesus or persists in unrepentant sin?	The believer was once saved but forfeits his or her salvation and becomes lost.	The professed believer was likely never an authentic believer; the individual's refusal to respond to warnings as a means of grace casts doubt on the authenticity of the individual's profession of faith.	The professed believer was likely never an authentic believer; the absence of evidence and the presence of persistent sin cast doubt on the authenticity of the individual's profession of faith.	The believer loses future rewards but remains saved even if he or she no longer believes or lives his or her profession of faith.
What assurance does this perspective provide?	Present assurance of salvation is only as good as one's proof and perseverance.	Present assurance of salvation is provided, but not apart from perseverance.	Present assurance of salvation is provided, but not apart from proof.	Present assurance of salvation is unrelated to proof or perseverance.

How should we respond to this view?	The loss-of-salvation view should be rejected because it fails to account adequately for scriptural affirmations that God preserves his children to the end. This view represents a defective view of how saving grace secures believers.	The means-of-grace view is helpful because it rightly recognizes that the warning passages are to be taken as authentic warnings of condemnation and that, if a professed believer fails to persevere, this person is eternally condemned because his or her faith was never authentic.	The proof-of-grace view is helpful because it rightly recognizes that authentic faith results in faithfulness and that, if the life of a professed believer fails to produce evidence of faith, this person is eternally condemned because his or her faith was never authentic.	The loss-of-rewards view should be rejected because it fails to account adequately for scriptural affirmations that saving faith perseveres and produces fruit. This view represents a defective view of how saving faith transforms believers.

Developed in part from Thomas Schreiner and Ardel Caneday,
The Race Set Before Us (Downers Grove: InterVarsity, 2001), 21 – 45,
with the hypothetical loss-of-salvation view excluded.

So when God chose to cut a covenant with Abraham, he commanded the patriarch to hew five creatures in two, and God bound himself to Abraham by passing between these halved haunches and heads (Genesis 15:7 – 21). Although the patriarch's descendants failed to fulfill their part of this covenant (Jeremiah 11:10), God's faithfulness never faltered. Before it was all over, God went so far as to fulfill both sides of the covenant himself in Jesus Christ and to make a new covenant through the broken body of his beloved Son (Luke 22:20). This new covenant stretches far beyond Abraham's descendants to embrace all who will find their rest in Abraham's crucified offspring (Galatians 3:15 – 18; Ephesians 2:11 – 14). God in Christ fulfilled both halves of his covenant with humanity so that anyone "in Christ" is seen by God as one who has fully fulfilled every requirement of the covenant.

So what does this have to do with forever grace?

God's covenant with us is no longer conditioned on our obedience. It's conditioned solely on the obedience of Jesus Christ. Once we are in Christ, the Father cannot reject his covenant with us without rejecting his beloved Son. And can someone who is in this covenant ever be removed? Here's what Jesus himself had to say about such a possibility:

"No one will snatch them out of my hand. My Father, who has given them to me, is greater than all; no one can snatch them out of my Father's hand" (John 10:28 – 29). What this means is — in the words of Michael Horton — that

> you can gauge your life by God's decision for you and not the other way around. You can keep going when you know that this is God's program, God's project, and that God's interest in you creates within you an interest in him.

> I remember how as a child I used to ask Jesus into my heart over and over again. Each time I intended to make absolutely certain that I was saved. Why do we do that? Why is it that in some churches we see the same people walking down the aisle week after week? Perhaps it is because we are looking to something we can do, or have done, to secure the kind of assurance we need. But we can't trust our feelings or our abilities of either will or effort, so we're left with having to trust in the ability of God, "who is able to keep you from falling" (Jude 24).

> We have the responsibility to "go on to maturity" (Heb. 6:1). So we are responsible to persevere, but not for our perseverance. We are responsible to be saved, but not for our salvation.

> To lose our salvation, we would have to return to a condition of spiritual death. What sort of regeneration would the Holy Spirit be the author of if those whom he resurrected and [had] given eternal life are capable of dying spiritually again?

> "Well, can't we commit spiritual suicide?" one might ask. Not if we take seriously the claim of 1 Peter 1:23: "For you have been born again, not of perishable seed, but of imperishable."[16]

Jesus Never Forgets

Forever grace is no abstract theological discussion. I [Timothy] discovered a couple years ago it's a truth that provides Christians with encouragement to live well and assurance to die well. In the five decades after my father walked down that aisle in a tiny church in southern Missouri, he served as a deacon, a teacher, and eventually a pastor. He faltered at times in his pursuit of God's plan, but he always returned to the Savior who had rescued him in the first place. And then one day, I stood beside a physician's assistant as she clicked through a half-dozen scans of my father's cranial cavity.

An undetected tumor in his left lung had sown four, perhaps five, cancerous lesions in his skull. Viewed from that inadequate perspective in which the body is a machine to be repaired if possible and discarded if necessary, no hope remained for him. Seen from the standpoint of the resurrection of Jesus Christ, these results signaled that a time was approaching when the "last enemy to be destroyed" would rend my father's spirit from his flesh (1 Corinthians 15:26) until that future moment when the risen Christ returns for his own. And so we watched and waited as a country pastor who had previously devoured multiple books every week became incapable of assessing whether his newspaper was right side up. Calloused fingers that had turned raw lumber into furniture and shaped simple chords on the neck of a guitar now clenched into gristly knots. Sentences once spoken with an inescapable Ozarks twang disintegrated into unaccented grunts and finally into silent, liquid stares. Walking gave way to a wheelchair, and wheeling a chair gave way to lifting and turning, feeding and diapering.

On one of my family's many long trips to care for my father, a small voice from the backseat broke an extended silence.

"Daddy?"

"Yes, Skylar?"

Our nine-year-old stretched her head upward, and I saw two worried eyes in the rearview mirror.

"What if Grandpa forgets about Jesus before he dies? Where will he go?"

It was an understandable question. A month or two earlier, Skylar and I had discussed why no one could be saved apart from explicit faith in Jesus. Over the past week, she had watched my father lose the names of children, grandchildren, and longtime acquaintances. What if the same lesions that were leaching his awareness of family and friends and basic bodily functions misplaced his memories of Jesus as well?

Several seconds slipped by before I could speak past the lump that had lodged in my throat.

"Skylar," I finally said, "what matters most is not whether Grandpa remembers Jesus, but whether Jesus remembers him. God turned

Grandpa's heart to trust him many years ago, and Jesus will never forget him. No matter what, Jesus never forgets."

That simple assurance was possible solely because we serve a God who operates not in terms of contractual reciprocity but on the basis of covenantal fidelity. Christ's commitment to his people does not depend on our capacity to remember, but on God's capacity to sustain us and preserve us. It depends on a covenant that has been engraved in flesh and confirmed in blood.

One Sunday evening, about the time my father would typically have finished preaching his Sunday evening message, he opened his eyes and began to breathe in deep, ragged heaves. We sang his favorite hymn, "Amazing Grace," and he passed from this life at "bright shining as the sun." On the first day of fall that year, we planted my father's flesh in the stony red soil of southern Missouri. There his body awaits the spring of resurrection, the consummation of the new covenant, the death of death itself. "For the trumpet will sound, the dead will be raised imperishable, and we will be changed.... Thanks be to God! He gives us the victory through our Lord Jesus Christ" (1 Corinthians 15:52, 57). That's the certainty and assurance of forever grace.

PROOF FOR LIFE

Meditate on these Scriptures and song lyrics. Work with a friend or family member to memorize the catechism questions and answers.

What Is Forever Grace?

God seals his people with his Holy Spirit so that they are preserved and persevere in faith until the final restoration of God's kingdom on the earth (John 10:27 – 29; Ephesians 1:13 – 14; 4:30).

Forever Grace in the Scriptures

"My sheep listen to my voice; I know them, and they follow me. I give them eternal life, and they shall never perish; no one will snatch them out of my hand. My Father, who has given them to me, is greater than all; no one can snatch them out of my Father's hand. I and the Father are one" (John 10:27 – 30).

"And you also were included in Christ when you heard the message of truth, the gospel of your salvation. When you believed, you were marked in him with a seal, the promised Holy Spirit, who is a deposit guaranteeing our inheritance until the redemption of those who are God's possession — to the praise of his glory" (Ephesians 1:13 – 14).

"In all my prayers for all of you, I always pray with joy because of your partnership in the gospel from the first day until now, being confident of this, that he who began a good work in you will carry it on to completion until the day of Christ Jesus" (Philippians 1:4 – 6).

Forever Grace in Song

Mistaken souls, they dream of heaven
And make their empty boast
Of inwards joys and sins forgiven
While slaves to greed and lust.

Vain is the will of mortal men
If faith is cold and dead
None but a living power unites
To Christ the living head.

Pray for a living faith
That leads us to trust this grace
We cannot come to God on our own.
A faith that truly sees
That drives us to bended knee
Looking for hope in the cross of Christ alone.

True faith will purify the soul
And faith will work by love
It forces sinful thoughts to go
And lifts our minds above.

This faith will conquer earth and hell
By God's celestial power
This is the grace that will prevail
In the decisive hour.

BROOKS RITTER AND BOBBY GILLES,
"Living Faith," © 2008 Sojourn Community Church

Forever Grace in Summary

How do I know that I belong to God? The Holy Spirit marks us as God's children forever (Ephesians 1:13 – 14).

What does the Holy Spirit use to change Christians? God's Word, prayer, and trials (Acts 2:42; James 1:2 – 3).

Will the church ever be free from sin? Yes. When Jesus returns, we will appear with him — changed into his image and totally free from sin (1 John 3:2).

DANIEL MONTGOMERY AND JARED KENNEDY,
North Star Catechism, © 2013 Sojourn Community Church

	Our Position in Christ	**Our Practice on Earth**
	Planned Grace: What God has done for us, focus is on God's sovereignty (Ephesians 1:1 – 23) Resurrecting Grace and Outrageous Grace: What Christ has done in us, focus is on God's grace (Ephesians 2:1 – 10)	Overcoming Grace: What Christ has done between us, focus is on our reconciliation in Christ (Ephesians 2:11 — 3:21) Forever Grace: What God will continue to do for us, focus is on: Our new unity (Ephesians 4:1 – 16) Our new walk (Ephesians 4:17 — 6:9) Our new strength (Ephesians 6:10 – 20)
Emphasis	Doctrinal Vertical relationship with God	Practical Horizontal relationship with others
Key Phrase	"He chose us in him." (Ephesians 1:4)	"Live a life worthy of the calling." (Ephesians 4:1)
Subjects	Declaration of heavenly truth God's accomplishment	Exhortations for earthly living The church's assignment

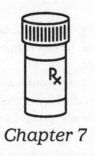

Chapter 7

LIVING PROOF

From the Scriptures ... we gather proof that God's grace is not given according to works.... God doesn't simply give grace where there are no good works; he gives grace where there have been only evil works.

AUGUSTINE, bishop of Hippo, "On Grace and Free Will"

The all-embracing slogan of the Reformed faith is this: the work of grace in the sinner is a mirror for the glory of God.

GEERHARDUS VOS, "The Doctrine of the Covenant"

Reformed theology is not an end in itself. It is simply a window to the awe-inspiring universe of God's truth, filled with glory, beauty, and grace.

GREG DUTCHER, *Killing Calvinism*

AS MANY AS SIX HOURS AT A TIME.

Nearly every day.

For years.

That's how much time a certain sixteenth-century monk spent confessing his sins — only to feel crushed a few seconds after his confession ended because he recalled a sin he'd forgotten to mention. After months of listening to these constant confessions, the monk's mentor muttered to him, "If you expect Christ to forgive you, come in here with something to forgive—murder of a family member, blasphemy, adultery—instead of all these small offenses!" Still, he kept at it, confessing every sin he could remember almost every day.

The problem wasn't that the monk was a slacker. "I kept the rule of my order so strictly," he recalled later, "that if ever a monk could have gotten to heaven by his monkery it was I." And his sins weren't the sort that get you on *The Jerry Springer Show*—or even on the church prayer list, for that matter. His own superiors saw his sins as a constant stream of minor offenses. The monk's problem was that he saw how far even his best deeds fell short of God's perfect standard.

The most popular plan of salvation during these decades could be summarized in a single sentence: "Do what is in you."[1] According to this religious teaching, God's grace prepared people to do good deeds. If people chose to perform these deeds, they could receive perfect credit for less-than-perfect works. It was sort of like a cosmic version of doing below-average work in a class but still getting top marks because the professor noticed how hard you tried and plugged in a lot of extra credit. Just do your best, and God will grade on a curve. According to the top theologians of the day, this works-for-merit system was how sinners became righteous—not perfectly righteous, mind you, but righteous enough to merit forgiveness sometime after their earthly lives ended. Even on the other side of the grave, people might have to spend a few centuries in purgatory before a spot opened up for them in the presence of God.[2]

This system was meant to provide comfort for less-than-perfect people. But for this particular monk, the system triggered only terror. "Do what is in you" couldn't help him because he saw how sin festered even in his finest works. If every work he did was tainted by sin, how could his efforts merit anything other than God's wrath? And if sin-tainted works earned God's wrath instead of God's favor, how could anyone be saved? "Love God?" he cried out at one point. "I hate him!"[3]

Still, the monk longed to be made right with God. Day after day, he kept confessing every sin, no matter how slight. He slept without a robe or blankets. He fasted for days at a time, trying to barter his own discomfort for divine favor. Yet all these deeds of penance only drove the monk to deeper despair.[4]

Grace on the Toilet

At one point, the monk found himself meditating on a passage from
Paul's letter to the Romans. It was through this text that God transformed
Martin Luther's despair into freedom and joy. Luther the monk had read
the letters of Paul many times — but this time, he glimpsed a truth that
he'd never noticed before. Martin Luther later claimed that this epiph-
any occurred while he was "on the toilet."[5] (Toilet humor was common
for Martin. His Christmas sermon once included the story of a monk
who said his prayers on the commode. Satan accused the monk of being
sacrilegious; the monk simply replied, "I am purging my bowels while
worshiping.... You can have what goes down, while God gets what goes
up."[6]) In this instance, Luther most likely meant the phrase to be taken
metaphorically. "On the toilet" was sixteenth-century slang that meant
"down in the dumps" — feeling vulnerable, helpless, and in despair.

Regardless of whether he was reading on the john or at a desk, Martin Luther was broken by these words from the apostle Paul: "For in
the gospel the righteousness of God is revealed — a righteousness that
is by faith from first to last, just as it is written: 'The righteous will
live by faith' " (Romans 1:17). When Luther read this text, he saw for
the first time that God's righteousness includes not only his righteous
anger and hatred of sin but also his gracious willingness to give the very
righteousness of Jesus to undeserving sinners.[7] What Luther realized
was that God's verdict of righteousness isn't given on the basis of any
human deed or desire. It is a one-way work of God that comes by grace
through faith "from first to last" (Romans 1:17; Ephesians 2:8 – 9). This
message of undeserved mercy was the good news that Martin Luther
had missed during his many years in the monasteries.

After decades of groping in the darkness, light finally flooded Martin Luther's soul. "This passage of Paul became to me a gate of heaven,"
he later wrote. "I felt myself to be reborn and to have gone through
open doors into paradise." The way to God — Luther now saw — was
not a winding stairway of human merit; it was an open gateway of
divine grace. Nothing remained for him to do to gain God's righteousness. God in Christ had already delivered everything that God's justice
demanded.

"You, Lord Jesus, are my righteousness and I am your sin," Luther
prayed when he recalled all that God had done for him. "You have taken

"We are so weak and uncertain that if [our salvation] depended on us, not even a single person would be saved; the devil would surely overpower us all. But since God is dependable ... we still have hope in the face of sin."[9]

MARTIN LUTHER

on yourself what you were not, and you have given me what I am not."[8] It was this renewed recognition of the gospel of grace that blossomed into a movement of revival and reform that became known as the Protestant Reformation.

Grace in the Cellar

Within a few decades, the leadership of the Reformation had multiplied far beyond a solitary monk in Germany to include Ulrich Zwingli in Zurich, Martin Bucer in Strasbourg, and John Calvin in Geneva. These "Reformers" rejected the most popular religious systems of their day—systems that tried to barter human works for divine merit. They "ranted and raved endlessly ... about the falseness of the notion that the gasoline of grace could be made to give better mileage if you put into it the additive of some more perfect performance."[10] What started as a moment of relief "on the toilet" became

a time when men went blind, staggering drunk because they had discovered, in the dusty basement of late medievalism, a whole cellar full of fifteen-hundred-year-old, two-hundred proof Grace—of bottle after bottle of pure distillate of Scripture, one sip of which would convince anyone that God saves us single-handedly. The word of the Gospel—after all those centuries of trying to lift yourself into heaven by worrying about the perfection of your bootstraps—suddenly turned out to be a flat announcement that the saved were home before they started.[11]

After centuries of wandering in the merciless deserts of works-for-merit, men and women throughout Europe were thirsty for this message of unmerited favor. And yet it wasn't long before some grew nervous—uncomfortable with the thought that God saves us single-handedly. The response was to tilt the scales back, ever so slightly, in the direction of human decisions. That's what happened in the land of Holland near the end of the sixteenth century.

Grace in the Land of Windmills and Wooden Shoes

Less than a century after Martin Luther's renewed recognition of the gospel, a new debate over grace developed in the land of tulips, windmills, and wooden shoes. In the city of Leiden, a professor named Jakob Hermanszoon reacted against certain teachings in the Reformed churches.[12] Hermanszoon began to call for a reworking of the statements about salvation in the Reformed confessions of faith. By the time the controversy reached its height, Hermanszoon had rejected the belief that God saves people single-handedly. Instead, he and his followers insisted that God gives every person just enough grace to choose whether to resist God's saving work and that remaining a Christian may depend on what a person does *after* choosing not to resist the Spirit's work.[13] According to Hermanszoon and his followers, "The death of Christ ... satisfied the justice of God in such a way that it rendered all people savable without actually making anyone's salvation certain."[14]

After Hermanszoon died, his followers issued a series of five articles called "the Remonstrance" — writings that repudiated certain teachings from the earlier Reformers, particularly those that had to do with God's sovereignty in salvation. These articles of Remonstrance earned Hermanszoon's followers the title "Remonstrants." You may have never heard of the Remonstrants, but we're sure you'll agree that it was better than the "Hermanszoonians." In fact, if you've heard of these folks at all, you most likely know them neither as Hermanszoonians nor as Remonstrants but as "Arminians," from Jakob Hermanszoon's Latin surname "Arminius."

To be fair, the Arminians weren't suggesting a return to the works-for-merit system of the past. But they had reworked the earlier Reformers' claim that salvation is God's sovereign and single-handed work, and other heirs of the Reformation saw this as a serious problem. In 1618, Reformed pastors throughout Europe — not only from the Netherlands but also from England, Germany, and Switzerland—journeyed to the Dutch village of Dort to decide how to respond to this challenge to the message of grace.

Six months after gathering, these pastors published a five-point response to the Arminian Remonstrance.[15] Their response represented a careful exposition of the biblical truths that the sixteenth-century Reformers had rediscovered when they returned to the Scriptures.[16] The focus of these five points was the grace-filled wonder of God's single-handed work of salvation. The five points from Dort were:

1. God chose in Christ a definite number of particular people for salvation.
2. Christ effectively redeemed these people.
3. No one is naturally willing or able to turn to God in their own power.
4. Everyone to whom God's Spirit gives new life turns to Christ and trusts in him.
5. God preserves, continues, and finishes the work of salvation in the life of everyone who trusts Christ.

These weren't new truths, of course. These were teachings that had been widely known among the earliest Christians and highlighted in the writings of a fifth-century pastor named Augustine of Hippo. These truths had been neglected in the Middle Ages, but they were never quite lost even then. The Reformation had been a time of retrieval, a time of rediscovering old truths from the Scriptures and from faithful leaders in the early church. Now these rediscovered truths were highlighted anew in the dispute at Dort. In the centuries that followed this dispute, a broad assortment of Christians—Baptists, Puritans, and even, briefly, an Eastern Orthodox patriarch—embraced the biblical truths about salvation that were summarized at Dort.[17]

Grace and Its Labels

Up to this point, we've made only a handful of references to the Protestant Reformer John Calvin, but the view of grace that we're advocating here is sometimes known as "Calvinism"—a term that has caused far more confusion than clarity and that neither of us much likes. In

Five Points from the Synod of Dort

1. **Christ effectively redeems:** "This death of God's Son is … more than sufficient to atone for the sins of the whole world.… It was God's will that Christ through the blood of the cross … should effectively redeem from every people, tribe, nation, and language all those and only those who were chosen from eternity to salvation and given to him by the Father.… It was the entirely free plan and very gracious will and intention of God the Father that the enlivening and saving effectiveness of his Son's costly death should work itself out in all the elect" (Isaiah 53:10; John 10:15; Galatians 2:20).

2. **No one is naturally willing to turn to God:** "All people are conceived in sin and born children of wrath,… neither willing nor able to return to God.… Regeneration … is a completely supernatural work. This work is simultaneously most powerful and most pleasing; it is a marvelous, mysterious, and inexpressible work, not less than or inferior in power to that of creation or of the resurrection of the dead" (Genesis 6:5; Psalm 51:5; Jeremiah 17:9; Ephesians 2:1 – 5).

3. **God chose in Christ:** "Before the foundation of the world, by sheer grace,… God chose in Christ to salvation a definite number of particular people.… This election took place, not on the basis of foreseen faith … but rather for the purpose of faith.… Holy Scripture most especially highlights this eternal and undeserved grace" (Acts 13:48; Romans 8:30; Ephesians 1:4 – 6, 11).

4. **Everyone to whom God's Spirit gives new life turns to Christ:** "All those in whose hearts God works in this marvelous way are certainly, unfailingly, and effectively reborn, and they do actually believe.… Where before the rebellion and resistance of the flesh had dominated their hearts, now eager and sincere obedience from the Spirit begins to overcome" (1 Corinthians 4:7; Ephesians 1:19; Philippians 2:13).

5. **God will finish the work that he begins:** "God … does not take the Holy Spirit from his own completely, even when they fall grievously.… God preserves, continues, and finishes this work by the hearing and reading of the gospel; by meditation on it; by its exhortations, threats, and promises; and, by the use of the sacraments.… The bride of Christ … has always tenderly cherished this teaching and defended it steadfastly as a priceless treasure. God, against whom no plan can avail and no strength can prevail, will ensure that the church will continue to do so. To this God alone — Father, Son, and Holy Spirit — be honor and glory forever. Amen" (John 10:28 – 29; Romans 8:32 – 39; 1 Corinthians 1:8).[18]

Calvin's own lifetime, the willing acceptance of such a title would have been seen as ridiculous at best, offensive at worst. John Calvin was far from the sole architect of Reformed theology, and he would have deplored the thought that any movement might bear his name. Calvin didn't even want his name to appear on his own gravestone! His request was to be buried in an unmarked pit alongside the common citizens of Geneva.[19]

The term "Calvinism" emerged in the sixteenth century as a derogatory title to disparage Calvin's view of the Lord's Supper.[20] In the centuries that followed the fellowship at Dort, the five points from Dort became less and less linked with God's singlehanded works of grace and more connected with the name of John Calvin. Before long, the word "Calvinism" ended up tied to five points that didn't emerge until more than a half century after John Calvin died! By the nineteenth century, if people knew the five points at all, they filed them under the unfortunate title "the five points of Calvinism."[21]

If you've heard of these five points before — and it's fine with us if you haven't — you've most likely heard them tied to a flower — a tulip, to be exact. But no one in the Reformation or at the Synod of Dort would have dreamed of such a mnemonic device. It was in the early twentieth century that the five points of Calvinism went floral and were transformed into a tulip. Around 1905, a Presbyterian pastor in Brooklyn developed an acrostic to help people remember the five points. He selected a single phrase to describe each point and rearranged the points to fit the name of a flower.[22] The flower that he picked was a tulip, and his acrostic went like this:

1. T: Total depravity
2. U: Universal sovereignty[23]
3. L: Limited atonement
4. I: Irresistible grace
5. P: Perseverance of the saints

In some ways, picking a tulip for this task made perfect sense. After all, even in the seventeenth century, the lands around Dort were known for their tulips (as well as windmills, wooden shoes, and water canals — all of which would have made even worse acrostics than TULIP).[24] And yet, several petals of the TULIP have created far more confusion than clarity when it comes to God's work in salvation.

The trouble with the TULIP is that some of the changes required to turn the five points into the acrostic "TULIP" have little to do with the decisions made at Dort — or with the theology of the Reformation.[25] Total depravity? That sounds more like a cable-television series that Christians ought to avoid than a biblical description of human nature. What's more, it almost gives the impression that people are as evil as they can be, which no Reformed theologian has ever claimed. And how about limited atonement? There's no mention of "limited atonement" in the decisions from Dort! What the pastors at Dort declared was that the death of Jesus was "more than sufficient to atone for the sins of the whole world" and that this sacrifice was effective for everyone whom God had chosen.

Despite these limitations, the TULIP took off. By the midpoint of the twentieth century, the Scripture-saturated decisions from Dort had been recast as "the five points of Calvinism," and this barebones framework had been further reworked to fit the name of a flower. TULIP became the most common tool for explaining the Reformed doctrine of salvation among English-speaking people.[26]

Even though we find the title "Calvinist" distasteful and we would prefer to lose the TULIP completely, we agree wholeheartedly with central points from the pastors at Dort. These five points are, in fact, the foundation for the five aspects of grace that we've highlighted in *PROOF.* But the point of *PROOF* is not to convince you that Calvinism is true. In fact, part of our purpose is to point you *away* from Calvinism — or, perhaps more precisely, to push your focus away from Calvinism as a system and toward the gospel of God's grace. You may be a Calvinist, an Arminian, neither one, or someone who's about to Google both terms because you have no clue what we're talking about — but no matter where you stand or where you land, we long for you to drink deeply from the well of God's grace and to share this grace with others.

The Trouble with Calvinists

If you were to use Google to look for data about Calvinism, part of what you would discover are some brutally honest stereotypes about Calvinists. Google relies on an algorithm to suggest the most popular queries, so when users type questions about churches or denomina-

PROOF in Scripture and at the Synod of Dort

	Key Truths from Scripture	Key Points from the Pastors at Dort
Planned Grace	God's plan from eternity past: "The good shepherd **lays down his life for the sheep....** I am the good shepherd" (John 10:11 – 18). "In him **we were also chosen, having been predestined according to the plan** of him who works out everything in conformity with the purpose of his will" (Ephesians 1:11).	"It was the entirely free **PLAN** and very gracious will and intention of God the Father that the enlivening and saving effectiveness of his Son's costly death should work itself out in all the elect." (2:8)
Resurrecting Grace	Humanity's condition after the fall: "Surely I was sinful at birth, **sinful from the time my mother conceived me**" (Psalm 51:5). "**You were dead** in your transgressions and sins ... by nature deserving of wrath.... **God ... made us alive** with Christ even when we were dead in transgressions — it is by grace you have been saved" (Ephesians 2:1 – 5).	"All people are conceived in sin and born children of wrath.... Regeneration ... is a marvelous, mysterious, and inexpressible work, not less than or inferior in power to that of creation or of the **RESURRECTION** of the dead." (3/4:12)
Outrageous Grace	God's choice and God's work: "It does not, therefore, depend on human desire or effort, but **on God's mercy**" (Romans 9:16). "He predestined us ... in accordance with his pleasure and will" (Ephesians 1:5).	"Holy Scripture most especially highlights this eternal and **UNDESERVED GRACE.**" (1:15)
Overcoming Grace	Humanity's transformation in response to God's work: "No one can come to me unless the Father who sent me draws them.... No one can come to me unless the Father has enabled them" (John 6:44, 65). "He saved us **through the washing of rebirth and renewal** by the Holy Spirit" (Titus 3:5).	"Where before the rebellion and resistance of the flesh had dominated their hearts, now eager and sincere obedience from the Spirit begins to **OVERCOME.**" (3/4:16)

Forever Grace	God's guarantee for the future: "My sheep listen to my voice.... I give them eternal life, and they shall never perish; **no one will snatch them out of my hand**. My Father, who has given them to me, is greater than all; **no one can snatch them out of my Father's hand**" (John 10:27 – 29). "He who began a good work in you **will carry it on to completion** until the day of Christ Jesus" (Philippians 1:6).	"God **PRESERVES, CONTINUES, AND FINISHES** this work.... To this God alone — Father, Son, and Holy Spirit — be honor and glory **FOREVER.**" (5:14 – 15)

tions, Google's auto-complete feature fills in the rest. Kate Shellnut of *Christianity Today* typed in "Why are Calvinists ..." and this is what came up:[27]

Why are Calvinists *so mean*?
Why are Calvinists *so arrogant*?
Why are Calvinists *so smug*?
Why are Calvinists *so negative*?

The trouble with Calvinists is that these perceptions are often true. John Piper unpacks one of the reasons why:

There is an attractiveness about [the doctrines of grace] to some people, in large matter, because of their intellectual rigor. They are powerfully coherent doctrines, and certain kinds of minds are drawn to that. And those kinds of minds tend to be argumentative.

So the intellectual appeal of the system of Calvinism draws a certain kind of intellectual person, and that type of person doesn't tend to be the most warm, fuzzy, and tender. Therefore this type of person has a greater danger of being hostile, gruff, abrupt, insensitive, or intellectualistic.

I'll just confess that. It's a sad and terrible thing that that's the case. Some of this type aren't even Christians, I think. You can embrace a system of theology and not even be born again.[28]

On top of all this, Calvinism has turned trendy in certain circles. *Time* magazine has called Calvinism an evangelical "success story" and even identified Calvinism as one of the top ten ideas currently changing the world. Conferences aimed at Calvinist church leaders attract thousands. Church-planting networks with Calvinistic confessions of faith are sending pastors to start new congregations around the world. Hip-hop artists like Flame and Shai Linne crank out tunes with clearly Calvinist lyrics ("Everybody's not elect, the Father decides / And it's only the elect in whom the Spirit resides," says Shai Linne). T-shirts and infant pullovers mingle slogans from the Reformation with such quirky anachronisms as, "Jonathan Edwards is my homeboy" and "TULIP girl."

Two decades ago, when the two of us embraced the doctrines that popular imagination has linked with the name of John Calvin, Calvinism was far from cool. Daniel had recently turned to Christ after being busted for possession of a stolen vehicle; Timothy was attending a tiny non-Calvinist Bible college in Kansas and playing guitar in a heavy-metal band. Back then, a teenager with "TULIP girl" on her shirt would have been assumed to be aiming for a career in floriculture, DC Talk's "I Luv Rap Music" represented the theological high-water mark for most Christian hip-hop, and Jonathan Edwards was far removed from the lofty status of homeboy. In these contexts, Calvinism didn't capture our minds because the system was popular — it wasn't. What drove us to Calvinism was a Scripture-saturated vision of a vast and glorious God who reigns over human history and who saves his people singlehandedly. We glimpsed this vision in books by John Piper, in sermons from a nineteenth-century pastor named Charles Haddon Spurgeon, and in VHS videotapes that we scrimped and saved to purchase from Ligonier Ministries — tools that challenged our presuppositions and drove us deeper into the Scriptures.

But now Calvinism has turned into a trend. And, whenever a theological system turns trendy, it's easy for the system to end up overshadowing its own original purpose. Instead of the system functioning as a tool that fuels devotion and drives us deeper into the Scriptures, the defense of the system itself becomes our focus. Greg Dutcher describes the dilemma this way:

> I am concerned that many Calvinists today do little more than celebrate how wonderfully clear their theological windshield is. But like a windshield, Reformed theology is not an end in itself. It is simply a window to the awe-inspiring universe of God's truth, filled with glory, beauty, and grace. Do we need something like a metaphorical wind-

shield of clear, biblical truth to look through as we hope to marvel at God's glory? Absolutely. But we must make sure that we know the difference between staring at a windshield and staring through one.[29]

When pristine windshields become the focus, what attracts people to our theological system isn't a God-centered passion for God's glory to be glimpsed around the globe, but a human-centered fixation on intellectual rigor and logical consistency. (If you're a Calvinist who keeps your ribbon marker in Romans 9 and who's spent more time in the last month arguing about Calvinism than sharing the gospel with the lost, that last sentence was for you.)

At times Calvinists — the two of us included — have defended these five points about grace in ways that showed little grace toward fellow believers. And, for that, it's time to repent. Calvinism for the sake of Calvinism is not worth fighting for — but grace is always worth fighting for.

Grace Worth Fighting For

The battle over God's grace has been ongoing since Jesus' day. Good religious people have always resisted the notion that only God's grace is strong enough to save us. When Jesus arrived on planet Earth, the Pharisees were working to maintain God's favor by keeping God's commands and human traditions (Mark 7:1 – 16).

Then a group of popular teachers in the days of the apostle Paul proclaimed that the sacrifice of Jesus was the right place to start, *but* if folks were really serious and wanted to finish the race with Jesus, there was a bit of flesh beneath the men's loincloths that needed to be sacrificed too (Acts 15:1; Galatians 5:1 – 12). And what happened in the early church? Paul and Barnabas actually left the mission field and returned to Jerusalem to address the issue. One pastor describes the scene like this:

> Can you imagine Paul and Barnabas listening to all of this? They've been out on the front lines witnessing the most incredible revival in history and have stopped everything to enter into this debate. Paul might have jumped in at some point and said, "Okay, let me get this straight. You want us to go back to all the cities where people have

become Christians and say, 'How's your faith going? Great. Oh, yeah … um, there's just one thing we forgot to tell you …'"

Thankfully, there are a couple of moments in which smart leaders take a stand on what really matters. Peter says, God "made no distinction between us and them, for he purified their hearts by faith.… We believe it is through the grace of our Lord Jesus that we are saved, just as they are." Finally, James drives home the right answer in one sentence. I wish every leader in every church would write this one down and post it where it can be seen every day: "It is my judgment … that we should not make it difficult for the Gentiles who are turning to God."[30]

But the battle for grace didn't end there. In the fifth century, a British-born monk named Pelagius claimed that human beings were capable of taking the first step toward God. Throughout the Middle Ages, salvation through the church's sacraments coupled with human contributions overshadowed the message of grace until a monk named Tetzel was meandering around Saxony singing, "Whenever a coin in the coffer does ring, a soul from purgatory does spring." That triggered Martin Luther's demand to debate the issue of grace and works. Then a century later came Jacob Arminius and the Synod of Dort — but not even the five points from Dort could settle the issue. Scottish common-sense philosophy mingled with American democracy to produce revivalists like Charles Finney, who identified conversion as a rational human decision instead of as a work of divine grace. In the twentieth century, well-intended fundamentalists worked to guard the authority of God's Word but, in the process, ended up so focused on separation from the world that the Christian life became defined by disengagement from the culture; a little book by Carl F. H. Henry entitled *The Uneasy Conscience of Modern Fundamentalism* called for a renewal of gospel-centered cultural engagement that continues to reshape evangelicalism today. These were not battles over intellectual minutiae. They were fights to keep grace central in the church's mission.

The Responsibility of Our Generation: Recover and Rally

In the centuries that followed the Reformation, five phrases emerged to describe the central emphases of the Reformers:[31]

- *Sola Scriptura* — By this we mean that Scripture *alone* is the word of God spoken to us. The Bible is completely true and without any mistakes. It is our authority — our rule for life. The Bible is clear — it is not always understood, but it *can* be understood. The Bible is sufficient — it is enough, that is, everything we need for life with God. Second Timothy 3:16 – 17 says, "All Scripture is God-breathed and is useful for teaching, rebuking, correcting and training in righteousness, so that the servant of God may be thoroughly equipped for every good work."[32]

- *Sola Fide* — By this we mean that salvation is only for those who trust and believe in who Jesus is, what he has done, and all he has promised to do. Hebrews 11:6 says, "And without faith it is impossible to please God, because anyone who comes to him must believe that he exists and that he rewards those who earnestly seek him."

- *Sola Gratia* — By this we mean that you are wonderfully accepted by God not because you have earned it or deserved it but because God has freely given it to you at Christ's expense. You are saved by grace *alone*. Ephesians 2:8 – 9 says, "For it is by grace you have been saved, through faith — and this is not from yourselves, it is the gift of God — not by works, so that no one can boast."

- *Solo Christo* — By this we mean that Jesus himself is the only mediator between God and mankind and the only one who provides salvation. First Peter 3:18 says, "For Christ also suffered once for sins, the righteous for the unrighteous, to bring you to God. He was put to death in the body but made alive in the Spirit." Because Christ is our sacrifice and mediator, we find salvation in belonging to him. Romans 14:8 says, "If we live, we live for the Lord; and if we die, we die for the Lord. So, whether we live or die, we belong to the Lord."

- *Soli Deo Gloria* — By this we mean that the purpose and goal of everything is to reveal and declare God's glory — the great fame of his goodness and greatness shining out to the world. Habakkuk 2:14 says, "For the earth will be filled with the knowledge of the glory of the LORD as the waters cover the sea." To God *alone* be the glory!

We still need these rally cries today. Why?

Because some things never change.

Today's most popular perspectives on God treat him like a butler in the background or a therapist whose purpose is to make our lives more comfortable. We need the glorious God of the Bible! The doctrines of grace recovered in the sixteenth and seventeenth centuries turn the spotlight toward a sovereign God against whom — in the words of the gathering at Dort — "no plan can avail and no strength can prevail" (5:4).

Television preachers tell us that it's up to us to take the first step in God's direction. But the Reformation taught us that salvation comes by *grace alone* through *faith alone* in *Christ alone*. The knowledge that we are by nature "neither willing nor able to return to God"[33] reminds us that anytime we make a move toward God, it's only because God already made the first move toward us. Human religion claims that we gain God's favor based on how well we perform. But a gospel of "sheer grace" celebrates the truth that God gives his favor freely at Christ's expense, releasing us from the burden of pleasing and performing.

For God's glory alone! The Bible alone! Grace alone! Faith alone! Christ alone!

Another rallying cry rooted in the Reformation is *ecclesia semper reformans, semper reformanda*. In plain English, this means "the church is always reformed, always reforming." The battle cry is a reminder that, even as we stand on the shoulders of great pastors and theologians from the past, our present context needs a fresh vision of grace. We believe that our generation needs to recover these rally cries, but we would also like to suggest five new rally cries for our generation — cries that we have woven throughout this book.

- *Mystery* — Our first new rally cry is "Mystery!" "Because God is infinite and we are limited, we can never fully understand God … God is incomprehensible in the sense that he is 'unable to be *fully* understood.'"[34] This is not mystery in the Sherlock Holmes sense (or even in the sense that Paul used the term). It is not something that's been held back or hidden. It is an acknowledgment that God's paths are unsearchable, his judgments inscrutable. After logically unpacking the doctrine of election (Romans 9 – 11), Paul ended with a poetic exultation, celebrating the wonders of God's mystery:

Oh, the depth of the riches of the wisdom and knowledge of God!
How unsearchable his judgments,
and his paths beyond tracing out!
"Who has known the mind of the Lord?
Or who has been his counselor?"
"Who has ever given to God,
that God should repay them?"
For from him and through him and for him are all things.
To him be the glory forever! Amen.

ROMANS 11:33 – 36

We must approach God with awareness that he is beyond us and that we will never *fully* understand him (Job 37:5; Psalm 147:5; Jeremiah 33:3; Romans 11:33 – 36; 1 Corinthians 2:7).

- *Paradox* — The second of our new rally cries is "Paradox!" Paradox seems like a strange rally cry, but, as Søren Kierkegaard has said, "One should not think slightingly of the paradoxical; for the paradox is the source of the thinker's passion, and the thinker without a paradox is like a lover without feeling: a paltry mediocrity."[35] Like children, we are called to accept things that perhaps don't make logical sense to us when we first encounter them. Maybe they won't make logical sense to us on this side of heaven. But our own lack of understanding shouldn't frustrate us or shake our faith. After all, if the doctrines of grace are true, our ability to get them right — our performance — had nothing to do with God's choice to love us. God remains true to his saving purposes and, at the same time, remains beyond us. He is God and we are not. "'For my thoughts are not your thoughts, neither are your ways my ways,' declares the LORD. 'As the heavens are higher than the earth, so are my ways higher than your ways and my thoughts than your thoughts'" (Isaiah 55:8 – 9).

- *Beauty* — God's beauty is that attribute of God whereby he is the sum of all desirable qualities.[36] "Beauty exists and emanates from God himself. Beauty does not define God; God defines beauty. In all his qualities, God is perfect unity, harmony, and splendor."[37] When a man is first smitten by a woman's beauty, he wants to have her on his arm as they walk in restaurants or shopping malls or parks. He is not ashamed of her; he is pleased to be seen with her and to show her off. There is nothing wrong with that! The closet Calvinist may grudgingly see the truth of the doctrines of grace, but he does not find them beautiful. At the heart of the Reformed tradition is a response of awe before a grand and powerful God, seen in the majesty of sky and sea, and in the transformed lives of those whose stories are recounted in Scripture.[38] One of the goals of this book is to encourage closet Calvinists to come out by helping them to see the joy and delight of knowing the sovereign God who single-handedly saves helpless sinners. After all, learning to delight in a God of wild, abundant, shocking beauty is one of the chief aims of the Christian life. "One thing I ask from the LORD, this only do I seek: that I may dwell in the house of the LORD all the days of my life, to gaze on the beauty of the LORD and to seek him in his temple" (Psalm 27:4). "Whom have I in heaven but you? And earth has nothing I desire besides you" (Psalm 73:25).

- *Community* — Delving into the depths of who God is can be overwhelming. The sheer complexity of our God points us to the reality that we neither can nor were ever intended to figure this out all alone. We need both historical and communal reflection to plumb these truths. You aren't the first to wrestle through these questions, and you won't be the last. In order to experience these truths to their fullest, we need to understand, reflect, and grow in them within the context of community.

- *Mission* — The doctrines of God's sovereign grace can become divorced from God's mission in the world. But, historically, the truth that God can overcome any barrier to his grace has been a force that drives missions! Many of the early missionaries in the modern missions movement — people like William and Dorothy Carey, Hudson and Maria Taylor, Ann and Adoniram Judson — embraced the truth of God's sovereign grace. Mission has always stood at the heart of true Calvinism. It still does today, and that's why *PROOF* isn't merely about updating old truths — it's about gathering God's people for God's mission in the world.

That's what we've seen happen in the congregation where we're privileged to serve, and that's what we long to see in your life as well.

At the church where we both teach and serve, we have seen over and over again how God uses this timeless message of grace to set people free. One young woman we know attended church as a child, then turned to a life of alcoholism, had an abortion, and later an affair. She tried to straighten out her life and attended a church that focused on "social justice," but she couldn't shake the feeling that "something was missing." Some friends invited her to attend a service where she heard the gospel of grace for the first time. After becoming a believer, she said, "The message here was vastly different from what we were used to! Learning that there is no way to earn God's forgiveness was so *freeing*."

Grace sets people free.

"I thought that working hard and quitting drugs would be enough to cover my shame and depression, but nothing worked," a young man told us. After hearing how God single-handedly changes people through the gospel, he found his righteousness and rest in Jesus Christ alone. "Peace didn't fill my heart as a result of quitting drugs," he said afterward. "Peace filled my heart when I realized that the perfect life of Jesus has replaced my life of shame." Now this former drug addict serves in children's ministry.

Grace gives rest and peace.

A pastor's kid, now in his thirties, heard the message of God's sovereign grace for the first time and realized that he had never truly embraced the gospel. When we baptized him, he said, "I no longer feel I need to prove things to people because Christ has proven himself to God on my behalf. I am valuable because I am made in God's image, he chose me, and his Son suffered on the cross for me."

Grace leaves us with nothing to prove because, in Christ, everything that needs to be proven has already been provided.

Maybe you think that you have it all together. Or maybe you know that your life is on the toilet. Wherever you are, the joy you are thirsting for (the satisfaction that you hunger for) is found in the beautiful mystery — the wonderful paradox — of God's sovereign grace. God is calling to every sinner who sees their need:

> *"Come, all you who are thirsty,*
> *come to the waters;*
> *and you who have no money,*
> *come, buy and eat!*

Come, buy wine and milk
*   without money and without cost.*
Why spend money on what is not bread,
*   and your labor on what does not satisfy?*
Listen, listen to me, and eat what is good,
*   and you will delight in the richest of fare.*
Give ear and come to me;
*   listen, that you may live."*

ISAIAH 55:1 – 3

His offer is free.
You can't earn it or deserve it.
Come thirsty and empty-handed.
Drink deeply and dance for joy.
It's on the house.

PROOF FOR LIFE

Meditate on these Scriptures and song lyrics. Work with a friend or family member to memorize the catechism questions and answers.

The Source of Joy in the Scriptures

"For in the gospel the righteousness of God is revealed — a righteousness that is by faith from first to last, just as it is written: 'The righteous will live by faith'" (Romans 1:17).

"Oh, the depth of the riches of the wisdom and knowledge of God! How unsearchable his judgments, and his paths beyond tracing out! 'Who has known the mind of the Lord? Or who has been his counselor?' 'Who has ever given to God, that God should repay them?' For from him and through him and for him are all things. To him be the glory forever! Amen" (Romans 11:33 – 36).

"May the God of hope fill you with all joy and peace as you trust in him, so that you may overflow with hope by the power of the Holy Spirit" (Romans 15:13).

The Source of Joy in Song

Come, ye sinners, poor and needy,
Weak and wounded, sick and sore;
Jesus ready stands to save you,
Full of pity, love and pow'r.

Come, ye thirsty, come, and welcome,
God's free bounty glorify;
True belief and true repentance,
Every grace that brings you nigh.

Come, ye weary, heavy-laden,
Lost and ruined by the fall;
If you tarry till you're better,
You will never come at all.

Let not conscience make you linger,
Not of fitness fondly dream;
All the fitness He requireth
Is to feel your need of Him.

JOSEPH HURT AND BROOKS RITTER, "Come Ye Sinners"

The Source of Joy in Summary

How do people enter God's kingdom? We must turn from sin and have faith in Jesus (Acts 16:30 – 31).

What does it mean to have faith in Jesus? To trust only Jesus to save us (Romans 1:17).

What gift do we receive when we repent and believe? Forgiveness of sins and life with Jesus forever (1 John 5:11).

DANIEL MONTGOMERY AND JARED KENNEDY,
North Star Catechism, © 2013 Sojourn Community Church

Appendix 1

PROOF TEXTS

Planned Grace

Job 42:2 "I know that you can do all things; no purpose of yours can be thwarted."

Isaiah 46:9 – 11 "I am God, and there is no other; I am God, and there is none like me. I make known the end from the beginning, from ancient times, what is still to come. I say, 'My purpose will stand, and I will do all that I please.' From the east I summon a bird of prey; from a far-off land, a man to fulfill my purpose. What I have said, that I will bring about; what I have planned, that I will do."

Psalm 139:16 Your eyes saw my unformed body; all the days ordained for me were written in your book before one of them came to be.

John 10:11, 14 – 16 "I am the good shepherd. The good shepherd lays down his life for the sheep.... I know my sheep and my sheep know me — just as the Father knows me and I know the Father — and I lay down my life for the sheep. I have other sheep that are not of this sheep pen. I must bring them also. They too will listen to my voice, and there shall be one flock and one shepherd."

Acts 13:48 When the Gentiles heard this, they were glad and honored the word of the Lord; and all who were appointed for eternal life believed.

Romans 8:29 – 30 For those God foreknew he also predestined to be conformed to the image of his Son, that he might be the firstborn among many brothers and sisters. And those he predestined, he also called; those he called, he also justified; those he justified, he also glorified.

Ephesians 1:11 In him we were also chosen, having been predestined according to the plan of him who works out everything in conformity with the purpose of his will.

Titus 2:14 [Jesus Christ] gave himself for us to redeem us from all wickedness and to purify for himself a people that are his very own.

Revelation 5:9 And they sang a new song, saying: "You are worthy to take the scroll and to open its seals, because you were slain, and with your blood you purchased for God persons from every tribe and language and people and nation."

Resurrecting Grace

Deuteronomy 32:39 "See now that I myself am he! There is no god besides me. I put to death and I bring to life, I have wounded and I will heal, and no one can deliver out of my hand."

Psalm 51:5 Surely I was sinful at birth, sinful from the time my mother conceived me.

Isaiah 26:19 Your dead shall live, LORD; their bodies shall rise — let those who dwell in the dust wake up and shout for joy — your dew is like the dew of the morning; the earth will give birth to her dead.

Ezekiel 37:11 – 14 Then he said to me: "Son of man, these bones are the people of Israel. They say, 'Our bones are dried up and our hope is gone; we are cut off.' Therefore prophesy and say to them: 'This is what the Sovereign LORD says: My people, I am going to open your graves and bring you up from them; I will bring you back to the land of Israel. Then you, my people, will know that I am the LORD, when I open your graves and bring you up from them. I will put my Spirit in you and you will live, and I will settle you in your own land. Then you will know that I the LORD have spoken, and I have done it, declares the LORD.'"

John 11:25 – 26 Jesus said to her, "I am the resurrection and the life. The one who believes in me will live, even though they die; and whoever lives by believing in me will never die. Do you believe this?"

Romans 4:17 God … gives life to the dead and calls into being things that were not.

Romans 3:9 – 12 What shall we conclude then? Do we have any advantage? Not at all! For we have already made the charge that Jews and Gentiles alike are all under the power of sin. As it is written: "There is no one righteous, not even one; there is no one who understands; there is no one who seeks God. All have turned away, they have together become worthless; there is no one who does good, not even one."

Ephesians 2:1 – 5 As for you, you were dead in your transgressions and sins, in which you used to live when you followed the ways of this world and of the ruler of the kingdom of the air, the spirit who is now at work in those who are disobedient. All of us also lived among them at one time, gratifying the cravings of our flesh and following its desires and thoughts. Like the rest, we were by nature deserving of wrath. But because of his great love for us, God, who is rich in mercy, made us alive with Christ even when we were dead in transgressions — it is by grace you have been saved.

Outrageous Grace

Deuteronomy 9:6 Understand, then, that it is not because of your righteousness that the LORD your God is giving you this good land to possess, for you are a stiff-necked people.

Luke 15:20 – 24 "So he got up and went to his father. But while he was still a long way off, his father saw him and was filled with compassion for him; he ran to his son, threw his arms around him and kissed him. The son said to him, 'Father, I have sinned against heaven and against you. I am no longer worthy to be called your son.' But the father said to his servants, 'Quick! Bring the best robe and put it on him. Put a ring on his finger and sandals on his feet. Bring the fattened calf and kill it. Let's have a feast and celebrate. For this son of mine was dead and is alive again; he was lost and is found.' So they began to celebrate."

John 6:44 "No one can come to me unless the Father who sent me draws them, and I will raise them up at the last day."

Romans 9:11 – 16 Yet, before the twins were born or had done anything good or bad — in order that God's purpose in election might stand: not by works but by him who calls — she was told, "The older will serve the younger." Just as it is written: "Jacob I loved, but Esau I hated." What then shall we say? Is God unjust? Not at all! For he says to Moses, "I will have mercy on whom I have mercy, and I will have compassion on whom I have compassion." It does not, therefore, depend on human desire or effort, but on God's mercy.

Romans 9:19 – 21 One of you will say to me: "Then why does God still blame us? For who is able to resist his will?" But who are you, a human being, to talk back to God? "Shall what is formed say to the one who formed it, 'Why did you make me like this?'" Does not the potter have the right to make out of the same lump of clay some pottery for special purposes and some for common use?

Ephesians 2:8 – 9 For it is by grace you have been saved, through faith — and this is not from yourselves, it is the gift of God — not by works, so that no one may boast.

2 Timothy 1:9 [God] has saved us and called us to a holy life — not because of anything we have done but because of his own purpose and grace. This grace was given us in Christ Jesus before the beginning of time.

Titus 3:4 – 7 But when the kindness and love of God our Savior appeared, he saved us, not because of righteous things we had done, but because of his mercy. He saved us through the washing of rebirth and renewal of the Holy Spirit, whom he poured out on us generously through Jesus Christ our Savior, so that, having been justified by his grace, we might become heirs having the hope of eternal life.

Overcoming Grace

Ezekiel 36:26 – 27 "I will give you a new heart and put a new spirit in you; I will remove from you your heart of stone and give you a heart of flesh. And I will put my Spirit in you and move you to follow my decrees and be careful to keep my laws."

Matthew 16:18 "And I tell you that you are Peter, and on this rock I will build my church, and the gates of Hades will not overcome it."

Luke 10:19 "I have given you authority to trample on snakes and scorpions and to overcome all the power of the enemy; nothing will harm you."

John 6:37 "All those the Father gives me will come to me, and whoever comes to me I will never drive away."

John 16:33 "I have told you these things, so that in me you may have peace. In this world you will have trouble. But take heart! I have overcome the world."

Acts 16:14 The Lord opened her heart to respond to Paul's message.

Romans 5:18 – 21 Consequently, just as one trespass resulted in condemnation for all people, so also one righteous act resulted in justification and life for all people. For just as through the disobedience of the one man the many were made sinners, so also through the obedience of the one man the many will be made righteous. The law was brought in so that the trespass might increase. But where sin increased, grace increased all the more, so that, just as sin reigned in death, so also grace might reign through righteousness to bring eternal life through Jesus Christ our Lord.

Romans 16:20 The God of peace will soon crush Satan under your feet. The grace of our Lord Jesus Christ be with you.

2 Corinthians 2:14 But thanks be to God, who always leads us as captives in Christ's triumphal procession and uses us to spread the aroma of the knowledge of him everywhere. For we are to God the pleasing aroma of Christ among those who are being saved and those who are perishing. To the one we are an aroma that brings death; to the other, an aroma that brings life. And who is equal to such a task?

Ephesians 2:10 For we are God's handiwork, created in Christ Jesus to do good works, which God prepared in advance for us to do.

1 John 5:4 – 5 For everyone born of God overcomes the world. This is the victory that has overcome the world, even our faith. Who is it that overcomes the world? Only the one who believes that Jesus is the Son of God.

Revelation 17:14 "They will wage war against the Lamb, but the Lamb will triumph over them because he is Lord of lords and King of kings — and with him will be his called, chosen and faithful followers."

Forever Grace

Psalm 23:6 Surely your goodness and love will follow me all the days of my life, and I will dwell in the house of the LORD forever.

Jeremiah 32:40 I will make an everlasting covenant with them: I will never stop doing good to them, and I will inspire them to fear me, so that they will never turn away from me.

John 10:27 – 30 "My sheep listen to my voice; I know them, and they follow me. I give them eternal life, and they shall never perish; no one will snatch them out of my hand. My Father, who has given them to me, is greater than all; no one can snatch them out of my Father's hand. I and the Father are one."

Romans 8:32 – 35, 38 – 39 He who did not spare his own Son, but gave him up for us all — how will he not also, along with him, graciously give us all things? Who will bring any charge against those whom God has chosen? It is God who justifies. Who then is the one who condemns? No one. Christ Jesus who died — more than that, who was raised to life — is at the right hand of God and is also interceding for us. Who shall separate us from the love of Christ? Shall trouble or hardship or persecution or famine or nakedness or danger or sword? . . . For I am convinced that neither death nor life, neither angels nor demons, neither the present nor the future, nor any powers, neither height nor depth, nor anything else in all creation, will be able to separate us from the love of God that is in Christ Jesus our Lord.

Romans 11:29 God's gifts and his call are irrevocable.

2 Corinthians 1:21 – 22 Now it is God who makes both us and you stand firm in Christ. He anointed us, set his seal of ownership on us, and put his Spirit in our hearts as a deposit, guaranteeing what is to come.

Ephesians 1:13 And you also were included in Christ when you heard the message of truth, the gospel of your salvation. When you believed, you were marked in him with a seal, the promised Holy Spirit.

Ephesians 4:30 And do not grieve the Holy Spirit of God, with whom you were sealed for the day of redemption.

Philippians 1:6 He who began a good work in you will carry it on to completion until the day of Christ Jesus.

1 Thessalonians 5:23 – 24 May God himself, the God of peace, sanctify you through and through. May your whole spirit, soul and body be kept blameless at the coming of our Lord Jesus Christ. The one who calls you is faithful and he will do it.

Jude 1:24 To [God] who is able to keep you from stumbling and to present you before his glorious presence without fault and with great joy.

Appendix 2

PROOF DISTILLED

PROOF Distilled in Doctrinal Statements[1]

P — Planned Grace	**Canons of Dort:** It was the entirely free plan and very gracious will and intention of God the Father that the enlivening and saving effectiveness of his Son's costly death should work itself out in all his chosen ones, in order that he might grant justifying faith to them only and thereby lead them without fail to salvation. In other words, it was God's will that Christ through the blood of the cross (by which he confirmed the new covenant) should effectively redeem from every people, tribe, nation, and language all those and only those who were chosen from eternity to salvation and given to him by the Father. (2:8)
	Westminster Confession: God did, from all eternity, decree to justify all the elect, and Christ did, in the fullness of time, die for their sins, and rise again for their justification: nevertheless, they are not justified, until the Holy Spirit does, in due time, actually apply Christ unto them. (chapter 11, paragraph 4)
	The First London Baptist Confession: Christ Jesus by His death did bring forth salvation and reconciliation only for the elect, which were those which God the Father gave Him.... The gospel which is to be preached to all men [is] the ground of faith. (chapter 21)
	The New Hampshire Baptist Confession: The salvation of sinners is wholly of grace, through the mediatorial offices of the Son of God; who ... by his death made a full atonement for our sins. ("Of the Way of Salvation," chapter 4)

	Abstract of Principles: He perfectly fulfilled the Law, suffered and died upon the cross for the salvation of sinners.... He ever liveth to make intercession for His people. He is the only Mediator; the Prophet, Priest, and King of the Church; and, Sovereign of the Universe. ("The Mediator," article 7)
	The Baptist Faith and Message: In His substitutionary death on the cross He made provision for the redemption of men from sin.... Jesus Christ ... by His own blood obtained eternal redemption for the believer. (chapters 2, 4)
R — Resurrecting Grace	**Canons of Dort:** Therefore, all people are conceived in sin and are born children of wrath, unfit for any saving good, inclined to evil, dead in their sins, and slaves to sin; without the grace of the regenerating Holy Spirit they are neither willing nor able to return to God, to reform their distorted nature, or even to dispose themselves to such reform. (3/4:3)
	Westminster Confession: Man, by his fall into a state of sin, has wholly lost all ability of will to any spiritual good accompanying salvation: so as, a natural man, being altogether averse from that good, and dead in sin, is not able, by his own strength, to convert himself, or to prepare himself thereunto. (chapter 9, paragraph 3)
	The First London Baptist Confession: All since the Fall are conceived in sin, and brought forth in iniquity, and so by nature children of wrath, and servants of sin, subjects of death, and all other calamities due to sin in this world and for ever, being considered in the state of nature, without relation to Christ. (chapter 4)
	The New Hampshire Baptist Confession: All mankind are now sinners, not by constraint but by choice; being by nature utterly void of that holiness required by the law of God, positively inclined to evil; and therefore under just condemnation to eternal ruin, without defense or excuse. ("Of the Fall of Man," chapter 3)
	Abstract of Principles: Through the temptation of Satan, [the man] transgressed the command of God, and fell from his original holiness and righteousness; whereby his posterity inherit a nature corrupt and wholly opposed to God and His law, are under condemnation, and as soon as they are capable of moral action, become actual transgressors. ("The Fall of Man," article 6)
	The Baptist Faith and Message: Through the temptation of Satan man transgressed the command of God, and fell from his original innocence whereby his posterity inherit a nature and an environment inclined toward sin. Therefore, as soon as they are capable of moral action, they become transgressors and are under condemnation. (chapter 3)

O — Outrageous Grace	**Canons of Dort:** The fact that some receive from God the gift of faith within time, and that others do not, stems from his eternal decision. For "all his works are known to God from eternity." (1:6; see Acts 15:18; Ephesians 1:11)
	Westminster Confession: By the decree of God, for the manifestation of His glory, some men and angels are predestinated unto everlasting life; and others foreordained to everlasting death. (chapter 3, paragraph 3)
	The First London Baptist Confession: Touching his creature man, God had in Christ before the foundation of the world, according to the good pleasure of His will, foreordained some men to eternal life through Jesus Christ, to the praise and glory of His grace. (chapter 3)
	The New Hampshire Baptist Confession: Election is the eternal purpose of God, according to which he graciously regenerates, sanctifies, and saves sinners; ... being perfectly consistent with the free agency of man, it comprehends all the means in connection with the end; ... it is a most glorious display of God's sovereign goodness, being infinitely free, wise, holy and unchangeable; ... it encourages the use of means in the highest degree. ("Of God's Purpose of Grace," chapter 9)
	Abstract of Principles: Election is God's eternal choice of some persons unto everlasting life — not because of foreseen merit in them, but of his mere mercy in Christ — in consequence of which choice they are called, justified and glorified. (article 5)
	The Baptist Faith and Message: Election is the gracious purpose of God, according to which He regenerates, justifies, sanctifies, and glorifies sinners. It is consistent with the free agency of man, and comprehends all the means in connection with the end. It is the glorious display of God's sovereign goodness, and is infinitely wise, holy, and unchangeable. It excludes boasting and promotes humility. (chapter 5)

O — Overcoming Grace	**Canons of Dort:** Just as from eternity he chose his own in Christ, so within time he effectively calls them, grants them faith and repentance. (3/4:10)
	Westminster Confession: All those whom God hath predestinated unto life, and those only, He is pleased, in His appointed time, effectually to call, by His Word and Spirit, out of that state of sin and death, in which they are by nature, to grace and salvation, by Jesus Christ; enlightening their minds spiritually and savingly to understand the things of God, taking away their heart of stone, and giving unto them an heart of flesh; renewing their wills, and, by His almighty power, determining them to that which is good, and effectually drawing them to Jesus Christ: yet so, as they come most freely, being made willing by His grace. (chapter 10, paragraph 1)
	The First London Baptist Confession: The elect, which God has loved with an everlasting love, are redeemed, quickened, and saved, not by themselves, neither by their own works, lest any man should boast himself, but wholly and only by God of His free grace and mercy through Jesus Christ. (chapter 5)
	The New Hampshire Baptist Confession: Regeneration ... is effected in a manner above our comprehension by the power of the Holy Spirit, in connection with divine truth, so as to secure our voluntary obedience to the gospel. ("Of Grace in Regeneration," chapter 7)
	Abstract of Principles: Regeneration is a change of heart, wrought by the Holy Spirit, who quickeneth the dead in trespasses and sins, enlightening their minds spiritually and savingly to understand the Word of God, and renewing their whole nature, so that they love and practice holiness. It is a work of God's free and special grace alone. ("Regeneration," article 8)
	The Baptist Faith and Message: Regeneration ... is a change of heart wrought by the Holy Spirit through conviction of sin, to which the sinner responds in repentance toward God and faith in the Lord Jesus Christ. (chapter 4)

F — Forever Grace	**Canons of Dort:** God is faithful, mercifully strengthening them in the grace once conferred on them and powerfully preserving them in it to the end. (5:3)
	Westminster Confession: They, whom God has accepted in His Beloved, effectually called, and sanctified by His Spirit, can neither totally nor finally fall away from the state of grace, but shall certainly persevere therein to the end, and be eternally saved. (chapter 17, paragraph 1)
	The First London Baptist Confession: Those that have this precious faith wrought in them by the Spirit, can never finally nor totally fall away; and though many storms and floods do arise and beat against them, yet they shall never be able to take them off that foundation and rock which by faith they are fastened upon, but shall be kept by the power of God to salvation. (chapter 23)
	The New Hampshire Baptist Confession: Such only are real believers as endure unto the end: ... their persevering attachment to Christ is the grand mark which distinguishes them from superficial professors; ... a special providence watches over their welfare, and ... they are kept by the power of God through faith unto salvation. ("Of Perseverance of the Saints," chapter 11)
	Abstract of Principles: Those whom God hath accepted in the Beloved, and sanctified by His Spirit, will never totally nor finally fall away from the state of grace, but shall certainly persevere to the end; and though they may fall, through neglect and temptation, into sin, whereby they grieve the Spirit, impair their graces and comforts, bring reproach on the Church, and temporal judgments on themselves, yet they shall be renewed again unto repentance, and be kept by the power of God through faith unto salvation. ("Perseverance of the Saints," article 13)
	The Baptist Faith and Message: All true believers endure to the end. Those whom God has accepted in Christ, and sanctified by His Spirit, will never fall away from the state of grace, but shall persevere to the end. Believers may fall into sin through neglect and temptation, whereby they grieve the Spirit, impair their graces and comforts, and bring reproach on the cause of Christ and temporal judgments on themselves; yet they shall be kept by the power of God through faith unto salvation. (chapter 5)

PROOF Distilled for Proclamation and Teaching

PROOF in Ephesians

Planned Grace: Ephesians 1:3 – 14

Resurrecting Grace: Ephesians 2:1 – 7

Outrageous Grace: Ephesians 2:8 – 9

Overcoming Grace: Ephesians 2:10 — 4:16; 4:17 — 6:9

Forever Grace: Ephesians 1:13 – 14; 6:10 – 20

PROOF in John

Planned Grace: John 1:1 – 14; 10:7 – 18

Resurrecting Grace: John 3:1 – 8; 11:1 – 44

Outrageous Grace: John 6:35 – 40; 15:16

Overcoming Grace: John 6:41 – 51; 10:22 – 30

Forever Grace: John 17:1 – 12; 20:30 – 31

PROOF in the Story Line of Scripture

Planned Grace: Isaiah 46:9 – 10; Ephesians 1:4

Resurrecting Grace: Genesis 3:1 – 24; Romans 5:12

Outrageous Grace: Deuteronomy 7:7 – 8; John 15:16

Overcoming Grace: John 19:28 — 20:17; Ephesians 2:1 – 10

Forever Grace: John 10:27 – 30; 1 Thessalonians 5:1 – 24

PROOF Distilled through Redemptive History

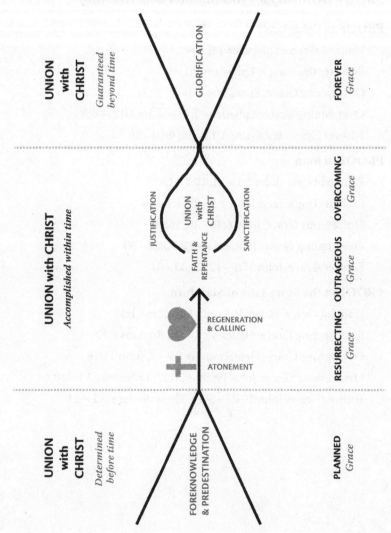

UNION with CHRIST
Guaranteed beyond time

GLORIFICATION

FOREVER
Grace

UNION with CHRIST
Accomplished within time

JUSTIFICATION

UNION with CHRIST

SANCTIFICATION

FAITH & REPENTANCE

OVERCOMING
Grace

REGENERATION & CALLING

OUTRAGEOUS
Grace

ATONEMENT

RESURRECTING
Grace

UNION with CHRIST
Determined before time

FOREKNOWLEDGE & PREDESTINATION

PLANNED
Grace

Appendix 3

FOR WHOM DID JESUS DIE?

TODAY, THE BELIEF THAT JESUS SACRIFICED HIS LIFE in place of his predestined people is sometimes termed "limited atonement" — a dour and misleading label that no Reformer or early Reformed pastor would have recognized! Despite some disagreements on the specifics, here's what the Reformed pastors at Dort declared together about the extent of the atonement:

> [The] death of God's Son ... is of infinite value and worth, more than sufficient to atone for the sins of the whole world.... It was God's will that Christ through the blood of the cross ... should effectively redeem from every people, tribe, nation, and language all those and only those who were chosen from eternity to salvation and given to him by the Father.... Whoever believes in Christ crucified shall not perish but have eternal life (2:3 – 5).[2]

Part of the reason why the pastors at Dort were able to find consensus on this point was because it was already a familiar doctrine for most of them. Hundreds of years prior to the gathering at Dort, a scholar named Peter the Lombard concluded that Jesus "offered himself for all as far as the sufficiency of the price is concerned, but, as far as

the effectiveness is concerned, it was only for those that are chosen."[3]
John Calvin followed this time-honored tradition when he cited with
approval the formula from earlier scholars that the Messiah "suffered
sufficiently for the whole world but efficiently only for the elect."[4]
And so a definite atonement for particular people — "planned grace,"
in our parlance — wasn't a theory invented by the sixteenth-century
Reformers! This was a truth already taught in churches throughout
Europe, North Africa, and western Asia centuries before John Calvin
was even born.

But planned grace isn't the only perspective that Christians have
taught when it comes to the extent of the atonement! Here's a simple
chart on the opposite page to help you understand five different view-
points on the atonement:

FOR WHOM DID JESUS DIE?

Hyper-Calvinism	Commercial Definite Atonement	Classic Definite Atonement	Universal Atonement	Universal Reconciliation
A heresy rejected by orthodox Christians	*Accepted by orthodox Christians*	*Accepted by orthodox Christians*	*Accepted by orthodox Christians*	*A heresy rejected by orthodox Christians*
The work of Jesus saved the elect	The work of Jesus secured the salvation of the elect by suffering in proportion to their sin	The work of Jesus secured the salvation of the elect and guaranteed the reconciliation of the world	The work of Jesus supplied salvation for everyone and guaranteed the reconciliation of the world	The work of Jesus supplied and secured the salvation of everyone and guaranteed the reconciliation of the world
		Multiple Intentions The work of Jesus supplied salvation for everyone and guaranteed the reconciliation of the world, but the Spirit applies salvation only to the elect.		
Global proclamation of the gospel is **not needed**; the elect are already justified and they will become aware of their justification whenever God chooses.	Global proclamation of the gospel is necessary; all are condemned until they personally trust Jesus, and it is through the sharing of the gospel that God calls his people to himself. Jesus suffered in proportion to the sins of the elect.	Global proclamation of the gospel is necessary; all are condemned until they personally trust Jesus, and it is through the sharing of the gospel that God calls his people to himself. The death of Jesus becomes effective in the lives of the elect when they believe.	Global proclamation of the gospel is necessary; all are condemned until they personally trust Jesus, and it is through the sharing of the gospel that people choose whether or not to believe. The death of Jesus supplied salvation for everyone.	Global proclamation of the gospel is **not needed**; everyone will eventually trust Jesus. The death of Jesus supplied and secured salvation for everyone.

Appendix 4

WHAT'S THE POINT OF PREDESTINATION?

It was pretty ornery preaching," Huckleberry Finn mused when he found himself in church one particular Sunday morning, "and had such a powerful lot to say about faith and good works and free grace and preforeordestination, and I don't know what all, that it did seem to me to be one of the roughest Sundays I had run across yet."[5] But "free grace and preforeordestination" were never meant to produce rough Sundays or "ornery preaching." Here's what the doctrine of predestination provides for the people of God, according to the Scriptures:[6]

1. **Comfort in trials**, because — if God is capable of choosing zombie rebels and turning them into beloved children — there is no hardship in all creation that he won't be able to work together for the good of those who love him (Romans 8:28 – 30).
2. **Motivation for praise**, because praise was part of God's purpose in predestining particular people for salvation (Ephesians 1:5 – 6).
3. **Encouragement for evangelism**, because sharing the gospel with unbelievers is a necessary means that God uses to bring his predestined people to faith and repentance. Paul persisted in

evangelism and church planting even during times of persecution precisely because he knew that God had already chosen particular people for salvation: "I endure everything for the sake of the elect, that they too may obtain the salvation that is in Christ Jesus" (2 Timothy 2:10).

But Christians haven't always agreed about the doctrine of predestination. In fact, Christians throughout the centuries have taken at least four different perspectives on predestination:

	Predestination based on our foreseen faith	Predestination based on our union with Christ	Predestination based on God's unconditional choice	Predestination based on God's unconditional choice with no offer of gospel to the non-elect
On what basis does God predestine people?	God foresaw the faith of those who would choose him; predestination was God's response to the faith that he foresaw in these individuals.	God predestined all who would be united to Jesus Christ through faith. Also known as corporate election.	God predestined particular individuals to have faith in Jesus Christ. Also known as unconditional election.	The outward call of the gospel does not apply to the non-elect.

| How should we respond to this view? | This Pelagian and Arminian view should be rejected because God's "knowing" of people in Scripture refers to his covenant love for them, not merely to his awareness of what they will do (Genesis 18:19; Exodus 33:17; Jeremiah 1:5). "Foreknowledge" is not God's foresight of particular facts about people's future actions, but God's choice before time to include particular people in his covenant (Romans 8:29). | This Arminian and Reformed view rightly recognizes that Christians are predestined "through Jesus Christ" and that all who believe are united with Christ (Ephesians 1:5; see also Romans 8:29; Ephesians 1:11). Alone, this view does not account adequately for the basis on which God chooses and saves particular individuals for salvation. | This Reformed view rightly recognizes that God predestined particular individuals to salvation on the basis of his own sovereign choice for his own glory, not on the basis of any human choice or work that he foresaw (John 15:16; Romans 9:6 – 29; Ephesians 1:4 – 6). God chooses to leave others to follow their own way. | This hyper-Calvinistic view should be rejected because God does not actively cause anyone to be condemned. God predestined particular persons for salvation and ordained that others would simply follow their own way (1 Peter 2:8); the condemned will be condemned because of their own personal rejection of God's way and their personal refusal to believe (John 3:18; Romans 1:18 – 32), not because God prevented their faith or actively predestined their condemnation. |

Appendix 5

WHAT ABOUT FREE WILL?

THERE'S A ROUGHNESS ALONG THE EDGES of the doctrine of overcoming grace — a difficult dilemma that may already have crossed your mind. The sentiment is usually expressed in a statement like this: "I just can't believe that God would drag people into heaven against their will, kicking and screaming!" Such reactions reveal a clear misunderstanding of how God works in people's lives. And yet, when Calvinists use words like "irresistible" and "overcoming," it's easy to see how miscues of this sort might emerge in people's minds. The concern that many people have at this point is whether God forces people to love him — which wouldn't be love at all! — or if we freely choose to love God.

Faced with the possibility that overcoming grace might reduce someone to a robot, some Christians immediately dust off their audio cassettes from the band Rush and begin wailing along with Geddy Lee: "There are those who think that life is nothing left to chance / a host of holy horrors to direct our aimless dance / ... I will choose a path that's clear / I will choose free will."[7] But do the Reformed doctrines of grace really claim that God saves people against their will? Does God direct every detail of our lives to the point that our deeds are an "aimless dance"? And, if he doesn't, where in God's overcoming grace is there space for human freedom?

First off, let's suppose for a moment that God *did* turn sin-infected rebels into his children despite their kicking and screaming. My children have spent plenty of time kicking and screaming in the pediatrician's office, quite convinced that getting a shot is the worst idea since finishing a serving of brussels sprouts and feta cheese. And yet, I choose to violate their wills for the sake of their life and health. And what about instances when someone adopts an infant from an abusive home or rescues an unconscious person from a burning building? Should adoptive parents leave a child to be abandoned and abused until she can make her own choices about her family situation? Should we wait until the person wakes up and expresses an explicit desire for life before pulling him from the structure engulfed with flames? Even we, with our limited wisdom, ignore people's wills to save their lives! So what if an infinitely wise God did bypass the free wills of hell-bound rebels and cause them to become his beloved children because he knows what they need better than they do? There are worse fates, after all, than being dragged kicking and screaming into a life of infinite love and light.

As it turns out, though, neither the New Testament nor any Reformed confession of faith declares that God saves people against their will. There is plenty of space in God's overcoming grace for human freedom and divine sovereignty, and we don't have to choose one over the other.

Did God Push You Down the Stairs?

Did you hear the one about the Calvinist who fell down five flights of stairs? He got up and said, "Well, I'm glad that's over with." It's an over-told joke and not particularly humorous. It does, however, highlight a common misperception that Calvinists believe in a God who predetermines everything to the point that no space remains for human freedom.[8] Yet that's not at all what Calvinists have historically confessed. (And, by the way, there are a lot of Calvinist jokes less clichéd than the Calvinist falling down the stairs, like the one about the Calvinist who built a baseball scoreboard. They had to remove the scoreboard from the ballpark because it kept posting the final score before the game began.)

So what *do* the Reformed confessions of faith have to say about human freedom?

Well, according to the pastors at the Synod of Dort, God does not deal with "people as if they were blocks and stones" — I'm fairly certain that, if they were penning these words today, they would write "robots" in place of "blocks and stones" — nor does the Spirit's work "coerce a reluctant will by force" (3/4:15). In another Reformed confession of faith written later in the same century, it's stated that God has given every human being the gift of "natural liberty."[9] And here's what the Abstract of Principles, penned by nineteenth-century Calvinistic Baptists, has to say about how God governs the world:

> God, from eternity, decrees or permits all things that come to pass, and perpetually upholds, directs, and governs all creatures and all events; yet so as not in any wise to be author or approver of sin nor to destroy the free will and responsibility of intelligent creatures.

"Free will and responsibility"? "Natural liberty"? A calling that refuses to "coerce a reluctant will"? So much for the caricature that Calvinists believe in a God who drags people into heaven kicking and screaming!

Who Chose Your House, Your Spouse, and Your Striped Socks?

But let's take this charge against the Reformed doctrines of grace as seriously as possible and admit that, sometimes, it *does* seem like some Reformers denied free will. Martin Luther, for example, penned a work entitled *On the Bondage of the Will* — a writing that Luther meant to dismantle the very notion of free will!

But here's the key point: What Christian theologians meant by "free will" in past centuries was far removed from what this phrase means to people today.[10] Among the Reformers and their opponents, "free will" described *a human capacity to make choices in our own power that result in progress toward salvation* — and that's what the Reformers so strongly rejected.[11] Luther's point in *On the Bondage of the Will* was that since our wills are enslaved to sin, none of us will ever choose to pursue God's way of righteousness apart from God's work of grace (John 6:65; 8:34). The pastors at Dort put it this way: "If the marvelous Maker of every good thing were not dealing with us, we would have no hope of getting up from our fall by our own free choice, by which we plunged ourselves into ruin when still standing upright" (3/4:16).

And so, the sixteenth-century debates about free will weren't about whether God fated your fall down five flights of stairs or whether you possess the liberty to choose your spouse, your house, or the striped socks you pulled out of the dryer this morning. The focus of these debates was every person's desperate need for grace. Luther clearly affirmed that human beings enjoy freedom in the things "beneath us" — in the ordinary, day-by-day choices we make.[12] And when "Calvin indicates that we are deprived of free choice, ... he certainly does not mean ... that a person is not free to choose between Merlot and Cabernet Sauvignon."[13] God is sovereign over our choices, and he has preordained each one — but God's meticulous providence is fully compatible with voluntary choices, and our selections are never coerced.[14]

ACKNOWLEDGMENTS

THE COMPANIONS WHO ACCOMPANY US ON OUR JOURNEYS can be — as Geoffrey Chaucer seems to have recognized in *The Canterbury Tales* — every bit as significant as the journeys themselves. The redemption of Anakin Skywalker required not only Luke and Leia but also Han Solo, Chewbacca, and a duo of faithful droids; Reepicheep's coracle could never have hurtled into Aslan's Country without the help of Edmund and Lucy and Eustace Clarence Scrubb; and every member of the Fellowship of the Ring was necessary to bring Frodo to the completion of his quest.

So it has been on the journey that has led to the completion of *PROOF: Finding Freedom through the Intoxicating Joy of Irresistible Grace*.

The book began as a sermon series and an in-house devotional at Sojourn Community Church. The winding pathway that led from sermon to this book required research assistance from Justin Karl, Nick Weyrens, Jacob Sweeney, Dustin Bruce, and Coleman Ford as well as additions, editing, and critique from Jared Kennedy, Amanda Edmondson, and Bobby Gilles, with Chris Bennett creating the fantastic chapter art. Kyle Noltemeyer graciously provided access to his family's farmhouse for research and writing retreats. Mike Nappa at Nappaland Literary Agency secured the perfect contract with the perfect publisher, and — despite the fact that the two of us were less than perfect when it came to some of our deadlines — Ryan Pazdur of Zondervan academic department was relentlessly supportive throughout every step of the process. In all of this, God has continued to work through the people of Sojourn Community Church to convict us, to comfort us, and to nurture our own much-needed growth in grace.

Daniel: Pounding out *PROOF* over the last couple of years has been an absolute joy, especially due to the collaborative nature of the project. There have been so many evident proofs of God's grace. Timothy Paul Jones and I took a series of retreats, filled with reflection on grace, God's Word, and *PROOF*, that were not only deep in content but rich in friendship. Jonah Sage came on the first retreats as an eager research intern. Now at the completion of *PROOF*, by God's grace, Jonah is a campus pastor at our church and my dear friend.

The catalyst for *PROOF* came when I was speaking at a Resurgence conference a few years ago. While I was sitting in a hotel lobby and contemplating how to communicate God's grace anew, I had the idea for *PROOF* as a fresh look at the doctrines of grace. I am thankful for elders at Sojourn who are always challenging me to contend for old truths boldly with freedom to contextualize creatively.

I am especially thankful for my wife, Mandy. I am a verbal processor and she is a patient and loving listener. There is likely not a word I've put on paper that wasn't processed first in the kitchen with her. I am thankful for her sensitivity to help navigate my ideas and her strength in editing and critiquing my ideas.

Timothy: The bulk of the words in this book were shaped and edited at Quills Coffee on Bardstown Road and at Starbucks Coffee Company on Frankfort Avenue in Louisville. Many thanks are due to the baristas at both cafés who continued to caffeinate me long after my presence officially qualified as loitering. What wasn't written in those two locations was developed along Ecclesall Road in Sheffield, England, as well as in the homes of Tim Chester and Steve Timmis — thanks to both of them for their hospitality to me and to my family. I remain appreciative of the supportive environment provided through the leadership of the Southern Baptist Theological Seminary; I grow more grateful each day at the undeserved providential goodness that has brought someone like me to a place like this.

Without the support of my wife, Rayann, nothing that I have written would have been possible. In the two decades since we stood between the candles and spoke our vows, there has never been an evening when I have not eagerly anticipated returning home. For that, I am ever and always thankful.

ACKNOWLEDGMENTS

Much has changed in my family since this book began. When Daniel Montgomery and I first discussed the vision that has blossomed into this book, my wife and I had two daughters and my parents seemed as healthy as they had ever been. Before I finished the first draft of this book, cancer had claimed my father's life. I thought often of him — a rural pastor who learned late in life to love the Reformed doctrines of grace — as I wrote, and I longed many times for his feedback.

Alongside that loss in our family, there has been an addition to our family as well. As I wrestled with the final chapters of *PROOF*, God unexpectedly blessed our household with a third daughter, Kylinn Rosamond Jones. Through this six-year-old who now bears my name and fills my heart, I am learning again and anew the wonder of a heavenly Father who turns sin-shattered orphans into beloved sons and daughters. "The LORD gave and the LORD has taken away; may the name of the LORD be praised" (Job 1:21).

NOTES

Chapter 1: Wake Up to Grace

1. Christian Smith with Melinda Lundquist Denton, *Soul Searching* (New York: Oxford University Press, 2005), 35, 164–65; Christian Smith with Patricia Snell, *Souls in Transition* (New York: Oxford University Press, 2009), 154–56, 285.

2. Julie Gold, "From a Distance" (Julie Gold Music, 1986), as recorded by Bette Midler, *Some People's Lives* (Atlantic Records, 1990).

3. Smith, *Soul Searching*, 167.

4. Greg Forster, *The Joy of Calvinism* (Wheaton, IL: Crossway, 2012), 93.

5. Some have suggested that full-fledged monotheism emerged late in Israel's history and that Israel during the time of Moses saw Yahweh not as the sole deity but as the deity for Israel among or above other deities (for a contemporary summary of this perspective, see Mark Biddle, *Deuteronomy* [Macon: Smyth and Helwys, 2003], 87–90). However, although Israelites did turn to other deities at various times, such actions represented deliberate rejection of Israel's constitutive covenant which, even in the time of Moses, identified deities other than Yahweh as ineffective nonentities (see Jeffrey Tigay, *Deuteronomy: The JPS Torah Commentary*, vol. 5 [Philadelphia: Jewish Publication Society, 1996], 433–35).

6. J. M. Boice and Philip Ryken, *The Doctrines of Grace*, reprint ed. (Wheaton, IL: Crossway, 2009), 18.

7. C. H. Spurgeon, "Divine Sovereignty" (May 4, 1856).

8. *"Hominis ingenium perpetuam, ut ita loquar, esse idolorum fabricam"* (John Calvin, *Institutio Christianae Religionis*, 1:11:8). *Fabrica* referred in ancient times to the workshop of a Roman legion, where weapons and tools were manufactured and maintained, and eventually came to refer to any place of production. Although often rendered "factory" in this quotation from Calvin, the mechanized nature of the modern factory diminishes the implication in *fabrica* of a deliberate crafting of idolatrous

allegiances. Calvin's point was not that human beings manufacture a series of identical deities in mass quantities, but that these idols are carefully constructed and perpetually produced in ever-evolving varieties.

9. Moralistic Therapeutic Deism—the system that we have described, drawing from Christian Smith's imagery, as belief in a butler-and-therapist deity—is prevalent not only among professed Christians but also among persons with other faith commitments and with no specific religious commitments (Smith, *Soul Searching*, 163).

10. "Our Ministry," *http://www.joelosteen.com*; Joel Osteen, *Become a Better You* (New York: Free Press, 2007), xiv, 5, 41, 301–2, 308.

11. Joel Osteen, *Your Best Life Now* (New York: Hachette, 2004), 192.

12. Martin Luther, "*Tertia Disputatio: Alia Ratio Iustificandi Hominis Coram Deo*," *Quinque Disputationes*, thesis 6.

13. Robert Farrar Capon, *The Astonished Heart* (Grand Rapids, MI: Eerdmans, 1996), 105.

14. Robert Farrar Capon, *The Mystery of Christ . . . and Why We Don't Get It* (Grand Rapids, MI: Eerdmans, 1993), 62.

15. Dietrich Bonhoeffer, "*Die teure Gnade*," *Nachfolge*, *http://www.zeitzubeten.org*.

16. J. I. Packer with Jean Watson, *In God's Presence* (New York: Doubleday, 2000), 10.

17. Paul F. M. Zahl, *Grace in Practice* (Grand Rapids, MI: Eerdmans, 2007), Kindle ed., location 491.

18. Jared Wilson, *Gospel Wakefulness* (Wheaton, IL: Crossway, 2011).

19. In 1740 the daily ration was reduced from a pint per day to a tot, or one-eighth of a pint (Tom Colls, "What Did They Do with the Drunken Sailor?" [July 30, 2010], *http://news.bbc.co.uk*).

20. Bankole Johnson and Gabrielle Marzani-Nissen, "Alcohol: Clinical Aspects," in *Addiction Medicine: Science and Practice*, ed. Bankole Johnson (Dordrecht: Springer, 2011), 1:284.

21. The use of this metaphor should not be construed in any way as an encouragement for Christians to consume alcoholic beverages. The idea of rejoicing and conviviality connected to wine is a biblical metaphor in which the imagery of intoxication is employed to depict joy without any encouragement toward actual inebriation (see, e.g., Zechariah 10:7). The Scriptures consistently condemn drunkenness as a sin (Habakkuk 2:15; Romans 13:13; Galatians 5:21) without prohibiting moderate or medicinal consumption of inebriating substances (Psalm 104:15; Isaiah 25:6; John 2:1–10; 1 Timothy 3:8; 5:23). Some Christians see voluntary abstention from alcoholic beverages as the wisest position for believers in Jesus Christ, while others take the view that alcoholic beverages may be

consumed with caution and in moderation. For the sake of avoiding the temptation to abuse alcohol, churches or Christian organizations may validly require members to abstain from inebriating beverages; voluntary release of this Christian freedom does not necessarily imply that moderate consumption of inebriating beverages is sinful or unwise. Regarding issues such as this one, Paul wrote, "Accept the one whose faith is weak, without quarreling over disputable matters.... Each of them should be fully convinced in their own mind" (Romans 14:1, 5). In other words, non-abstaining individuals or groups should receive those whose consciences compel them to abstain without question or quarrel on the basis of the finished work of Jesus Christ, and vice versa. Both groups should be convinced of their own perspective on the issue without demanding agreement on this issue from the other.

22. Mike Cosper, *Rhythms of Grace* (Wheaton, IL: Crossway, 2013), Kindle ed., location 2642.

23. This aspect of the metaphor is derived in part from Michael Horton, *Putting Amazing Back into Grace* (Grand Rapids, MI: Baker, 2011), Kindle ed., location 2062–77.

24. The noun χάρις ("grace") derives from the verb χαίρω ("I rejoice, I am glad"). "The basis of the usage [of χάρις, "grace"] is the relation to χαίρω. Χάρις is what delights.... It is joyous being, 'charm,' understood not in terms of the beautiful but of the element of the delightful in the beautiful" (Hans Conzelmann, "χάρις, χαρίζομαι, χαριτόω, ἀχάριστος," in *Theological Dictionary of the New Testament*, volume 9, ed. Gerhart Kittel, et al., trans. Geoffrey Bromiley [Grand Rapids: Eerdmans, 1964] 372-373).

25. Based in part on definition found in John Piper, *The Pleasures of God* (Sisters: Multnomah, 1991) 203.

26. In the Septuagint – the Greek translation of the Hebrew Scriptures— forms of the Greek χαίρω ("I rejoice") translate the Hebrew חמשׂ in both of these texts: "ἐσθίοντες καὶ πίνοντες καὶ χαίροντες" (1 Kings 4:20=3 Kingdoms 2:46a) and "χαρήσεται ἡ καρδία αὐτῶν ὡς ἐν οἴνῳ" (Zechariah 10:7). In the larger context of both texts, the rejoicing appears among references to God's covenant faithfulness. Covenantal language appears in Zechariah 10:6 ("because I have compassion on them"), and 1 Kings 4:20 alludes to the covenant promises in Genesis 22:17.

27. Grace "connotes favor, usually by a superior to an inferior.... 'Grace' as a characteristic of God grounds divine-human relations in God's generous initiative and sustaining faithfulness culminating in the powerful, restorative activity of God on behalf of humanity" (Joel Green, "Grace," in *New Dictionary of Biblical Theology* [Downers Grove: InterVarsity, 2001] 524-525). Χάρις describes benevolence from the stronger to the

weaker not only in Jewish and Christian texts but also in extra-biblical texts where the term describes the benevolence of a ruler toward his subjects. For a typical example of χάρις as the favor of a ruler, see "τοῦ θεοῦ Κλαυδίου χάριτι" in an edict of Tiberius Julius Alexander ("Edictum Praefecti Aegypti Tiberii Iulii Alexandri," in *Roman Law Library*, ed. Alexandr Koptev and Yves Lassard: http://www.justinien.net).

28. Joel Green, "Grace," in *New Dictionary of Biblical Theology* (Downers Grove: InterVarsity, 2001) 524.

29. In the New Testament, word-pairs such as "grace and truth" (χάριτος καὶ ἀληθείας, John 1:14) evoke Hebrew word-pairs such as חסד (*hesed*) and תמא (*emet*). See Peter J. Gentry and Stephen J. Wellum, *Kingdom through Covenant* (Wheaton: Crossway, 2012) 141, 609.

Chapter 2: Planned Grace

1. Chrysaora quinquecirrha apparently hook up along the Florida panhandle during certain weeks each summer to produce the next generation of sea nettle jellies. The jellyfish repellent at the diving supply store is only moderately effective, and calamine lotion is the most soothing of the available solutions for pain relief. Trust my family on this one [TPJ].

2. Harold Kushner, *When Bad Things Happen to Good People* (New York: Schocken, 1981), 134.

3. Merle Haggard, "Mama Tried," from the album *Mama Tried* (Capitol, 1968).

4. Clark Pinnock et al., *The Openness of God* (Downers Grove, IL: InterVarsity, 1994), 29–30; Clark Pinnock, "God's Sovereignty in Today's World," *Theology Today* 15 (1996): 19–20. The distinction between Harold Kushner's perspective and open theism is that, for Kushner as well as some process theologians, God is limited by his very nature, whereas, for open theists, God voluntarily chose self-limitation of knowledge when he created the world and, as such, knows all possibilities simultaneously without necessarily knowing or determining which realities his creatures and his cosmos will produce. In the end, from an open theist perspective, the infinite creativity of God and the defeat of Satan through the cross and empty tomb will result in the establishment of God's eternal kingdom, the annihilation of rebellion, and the renewal of the cosmos. Even as we find the case for open theism unconvincing, the most robust case for open theism may be found in Gregory Boyd's bivalentist omniscience perspective in which God over-knows the future, being fully aware at every moment of every possibility and of every possible response to every possibility. For critiques of open theism, see Richard Mayhue, "The Impossibility of *God of the Possible*," *Master's Seminary Journal* 12 (Fall 2001):

203 – 20; John Piper et al., *Beyond the Bounds* (Wheaton, IL: Crossway, 2003); Thomas Schreiner and Bruce Ware, eds., *Still Sovereign* (Grand Rapids, MI: Baker, 2000); Bruce Ware, *God's Lesser Glory* (Wheaton, IL: Crossway, 2000); and R. K. McGregor Wright, *No Place for Sovereignty* (Downers Grove, IL: InterVarsity, 1996). In open theism, God guides the cosmos toward the end he has determined by responding creatively and redemptively to the actions of his creation, but God does not know which courses of action will be taken until the choices and events in the created order actually occur. From an open theist perspective, when God allowed Adolf Hitler to be born, God did not know for certain that Hitler would oversee the murder of millions of people; all God knew was the myriad of possibilities that Hitler might actualize. See Gregory Boyd, *The God of the Possible* (Grand Rapids, MI: Baker, 2000), 98 – 99.

5. For the apostle John as author of Revelation, see Timothy Paul Jones et al., *Rose Guide to End Times Prophecy* (Torrance, CA: Rose, 2011), 224 – 26. In Revelation 13:8, it is possible that "from the creation of the world" (απο καταβολης κόσμου) should be linked to the omission of names from the book of life instead of the slaughter of the Lamb. This would turn the pretemporal determination indicated in the text into a statement of reprobation instead of a statement of redemption; however, it seems quite unlikely that the concluding phrase "from the creation of the world" was intended to be linked to "not written" (ου γεγραπται) since a total of twelve words in the Greek sentence stand between the prepositional phrase and the verb (G. K. Beale, *The Book of Revelation* [Grand Rapids, MI: Eerdmans, 1999], 702; Grant Osborne, *Revelation* [Grand Rapids, MI: Baker Academic, 2002], 503).

6. The language here is based on the imagery of Timothy George, *Amazing Grace*, rev. ed. (Wheaton, IL: Crossway, 2011), 91.

7. The idea of a "maverick molecule" is taken from R. C. Sproul, *Not a Chance* (Grand Rapids, MI: Baker, 1994), 3.

8. Jerry Bridges, *Trusting God Even When Life Hurts* (Colorado Springs: NavPress, 1988, 2008), 12.

9. Tim Keller, "Questions of Suffering," Redeemer Presbyterian Church podcast for August 1, 2013.

10. The two views of the atonement summarized here are penal substitution and *Christus Victor*. Other views of the atonement throughout church history have included: (1) Recapitulation: According to Irenaeus of Lyons, Jesus lived the perfect life that every human being ought to have lived and thus reversed the curse brought through the sin of Adam. The weakness of the recapitulation perspective is that it does not account adequately for how the benefits of Jesus' death are applied to believers.

(2) Ransom: According to Origen of Alexandria, Gregory of Nyssa, and John of Damascus, Satan had usurped God's ownership of humanity. Jesus offered his life to Satan in return for Satan's relinquishment of his ownership of humanity. By means of the resurrection, Satan was tricked and God regained his rightful ownership of humanity. In the ransom theory, the death of Jesus purchased humanity, and his resurrection defeated Satan. The weakness of the ransom theory is that it may ascribe too much dominion to Satan and it does not account adequately for how the benefits of Jesus' death are applied to believers. (3) Satisfaction: According to Anselm of Canterbury, humanity robbed God's honor by failing to offer him appropriate honor and by defiling his domain. Jesus, through his death, paid a price greater than the value of what humanity stole. In the satisfaction view, Jesus restored God's honor. The weakness of this view is that, while perhaps helpful as a metaphor for penal substitution, it is a metaphor rooted more in the medieval feudal system than in Scripture. (4) Moral influence: According to Peter Abelard, the death of Jesus revealed God's deep love for humanity, and this example of selfless love should influence people to turn from their sins and to love God and others. The failure of the moral influence view is both that the death of Jesus was unnecessary and that his death accomplished nothing objective. (5) Governmental: According to Hugo Grotius, God as governor of the universe can establish and relax laws at his pleasure. Because of God's love for humanity, God relaxed the penalty for sin and accepted the death of Jesus as a payment equivalent to what humanity deserved. Jesus did not die in place of people; he satisfied God's law by suffering a penalty equivalent to what people deserve. God, in light of this equivalent suffering, chose to forgive those who trust in Jesus. The failure of this view is that the death of Jesus was not necessary, so the Father would have inflicted sufferings on his Son that were not needed to save his people. For references to primary source materials, see Gregg Allison, *Historical Theology* (Grand Rapids, MI: Zondervan, 2012), 390–404.

11. Dominion over the earth and animals had been given to primal humanity as vice-regents of God's creation (Genesis 1:28–30), but Adam and Eve abdicated their rightful exercise of this role by submitting to a beast who questioned the wisdom and integrity of God (Genesis 3:4–6). Whatever dominion Satan gained on the earth was temporary (Genesis 3:15; Romans 16:20) and subservient to God's sovereignty (Job 1:6—2:6). It is possible that Matthew 4:8–9 and Luke 4:5–7 refer to satanic dominion over earthly kingdoms, but, given the perspective of Jesus and his first-century followers that Satan is the source of lies (John 8:44), it seems more likely that Satan's words to Jesus were partial truths

at best. At the same time, from such texts as John 13:27 and 1 Corinthians 2:6 – 8, it seems clear that God allowed Satan and his minions to have some influence in the plot to kill Jesus. During the earthly ministry of Jesus, the demons recognized Jesus, but they were uncertain why he was sent (Mark 1:23 – 24; 3:11; 5:7). The outcome of Jesus' execution apparently remained a mystery to powers of darkness until after his death (Ephesians 3:8 – 12). Only after the resurrection did it become fully clear that the plot to defeat Jesus through death had resulted in Satan's defeat and that Satan's time was now limited (Revelation 12:12). This understanding of the atonement — sometimes termed *Christus Victor* — was the primary perspective among Christians for nearly a millennium. This is not to imply that ancient and early medieval Christians did not believe in penal substitution (penal substitution is, e.g., implied in the Epistle to Diognetus and more explicitly affirmed in the writings of Augustine of Hippo); it means only that for several hundred years, penal substitution was not the position most emphasized among Christians. Both the reconciliation of the cosmos through the devil's defeat and the redemption of the elect through sacrificial substitution are biblical perspectives on the atonement, and neither view negates the other (see Colossians 2:13 – 15, where the application of the atonement by means of regeneration results not only in triumph over powers of darkness but also in release from sin and removal of legal charges). See Michael Horton, *Lord and Servant* (Louisville, KY: Westminster John Knox, 2005), 243 – 57; J. I. Packer, "What Did the Cross Achieve?" in J. I. Packer and Mark Dever, *In My Place Condemned He Stood* (Wheaton, IL: Crossway, 2008); and Sinclair Ferguson, "Christus Victor et Propitiator," in *For the Fame of God's Name*, ed. Justin Taylor and Samuel Storms (Wheaton, IL: Crossway, 2010). For *Christus Victor* as initial promise of atonement and penal substitution as necessary and integral means for Christ's victorious removal of resistance to God's reign of peace, see Graham Cole, *God the Peacemaker* (Downers Grove, IL: InterVarsity, 2009). Regarding Christ's work as cosmic victory over the kingdom of Satan, see Tremper Longman III and Daniel Reid, *God Is a Warrior* (Grand Rapids, MI: Zondervan, 1995).

12. The phrasing in Ephesians particularly reflects the context in western Asia Minor in which church members had once relied on magical rituals to gain the favor of cosmic powers and authorities, which Paul identified as demonic (see Peter O'Brien, *The Letter to the Ephesians* [Leicester: Apollos, 1999], 136 – 44, for a balanced appropriation of C. E. Arnold, *Ephesians: Power and Magic* [Cambridge: Cambridge University Press, 1989]). How precisely the death of Jesus defeated the devil is not

explicitly spelled out in Scripture. Some early theologians speculated that the devil bartered his dominion for the death of the Son of God; as a result, when Christ was raised in glory, the devil lost both his limited dominion over the earth and his triumph over the Son of God (see, e.g., Rufinus, *Commentary on the Apostles' Creed*, 16). Most probable, in light of the primacy placed on penal substitution throughout the Scriptures, is that the defeat of the devil occurred by means of penal substitution. In the Epistle to Diognetus, the reality of Christ's ransom is mingled with belief in penal substitution (*Epistle to Diognetus*, 9). Hilary of Poitiers similarly brings together victory over darkness and vicarious atonement (Hilary of Poitiers, *Sancti Hilarii Pictaviensis Episcopi: De Trinitate: Praefatio, Libri I – VII*, ed. Pierre Smulders, *Corpus Christianorum Series Latina* [Turnhout, Belgium: Brepols, 1979], 14 – 15). Augustine of Hippo claimed that God paid this ransom to himself, while Anselm of Canterbury saw the price as a penalty paid to restore God's honor. The biblical authors, however, simply affirmed that a ransom was owed and paid without deeming it necessary to identify the precise recipient of the payment. The focus of the biblical authors, particularly Paul, was on humanity's enslavement to sin and on the freedom from slavery that Christ's payment of the ransom effected. See Frank Thielman, *Ephesians* (Grand Rapids, MI: Baker, 2010), 58 – 60.

13. Thomas Schreiner, "The Penal Substitution View," in *The Nature of the Atonement*, ed. Paul Eddy and James Beilby (Downers Grove, IL: InterVarsity, 2006), 68.

14. R. C. Sproul, *The Righteous Shall Live by Faith* (Wheaton, IL: Crossway, 2009), 55; John R. W. Stott, *The Cross of Christ*, 20th anniversary ed. (Downers Grove, IL: InterVarsity, 2006), 153.

15. Alice Cooper (Vincent Furnier) and Bob Marlette, "I Just Wanna Be God," *Dragontown* (Spitfire, 2001).

16. Martin Luther, "The Freedom of a Christian (1520)" in *Martin Luther's Basic Theological Writings*, ed. Timothy F. Lull (Minneapolis: Fortress, 1989), 603.

17. Ibid., 604.

18. "The death of Christ pays for all the sins of all people. But not one individual has his own account settled until he believes. If he never believes, then even though the price has been fully paid, his sins will not be forgiven" (Charles Caldwell Ryrie, *Basic Theology* [Chicago: Moody, 1986, 1999], 373). The Arminian position in the Quartodeciman Controversy that culminated at the Synod of Dort was that "the price of the redemption which Christ offered to God his Father is not only in itself and by itself sufficient to redeem the whole human race but was also paid for all

people, every individual, according to the decree, will, and grace of God the Father" (*Acta* 1:116, as translated in Lee Gatiss, *For Us and for Our Salvation* [London: Latimer, 2012]).

19. Shai Linne, "Mission Accomplished," *The Atonement* (Lamp Mode, 2008); C. H. Spurgeon, "The Mission of the Son of Man" (July 18, 1858). For further explication of this same point, see Francis Turretin, *Institutes of Elenctic Theology*, ed. James T. Dennison Jr., trans. George Musgrave Giger (Phillipsburg, NJ: P&R, 1993), 2:467.

20. "Christ's death does not save either actually or potentially; rather it makes all men savable" (Lewis Sperry Chafer, "For Whom Did Christ Die?" *Bibliotheca Sacra* 137 [October 1980]: 325). However, in such texts as Luke 22:19–20; John 11:50–52; Romans 5:8; 1 Corinthians 11:24; and Galatians 3:13, υπερ clearly portrays the death of Christ as a sacrificial substitution *in place of* people, not merely *for the sake of* a possibility. Additionally — following John Owen in his classic text *Salus Electorum, Sanguis Jesu, or The Death of Death in the Death of Christ* — a ransom cannot, by its very nature, purchase a possibility. Jesus did not pay a price to ransom a possible population or a type of person; he ransomed actual people. See John Owen, *Salus Electorum, Sanguis Jesu*, 3rd ed. (Falkirk: Johnston, 1799), 227–29. Richard Baxter contended that Owen opened the way for a lowering of God's standard. Owen answered this charge in his later text *On the Death of Christ* by demonstrating that God did not lower his standard of holiness by accepting the death of Christ in place of the death of the elect. The penalty due to the elect was not a particular degree of suffering but death itself, and Jesus did die the death of the elect in place of the elect. This death purchased not only redemption but also the gift of faith by which elect sinners enter into the new covenant.

21. None of the texts cited in this section specifically states that Jesus died for the elect *to the exclusion of* the non-elect. As such, these texts alone cannot constitute conclusive proof of particular atonement. However, given that Scripture emphasizes the death of Jesus for "his people," "for the sheep" (who are designated as "sheep" even before they respond to the gospel, John 10:16), and for persons "from" every people-group with no mention of atonement on behalf of those who do not persist in faith (Revelation 5:8–10), it is reasonable to infer the strong likelihood that the atonement does not extend to the non-elect. One text that might reasonably lead one to conclude otherwise is 2 Peter 2:1. However, the allusion in 2 Peter 2:1 to Deuteronomy 32:6 suggests that "bought them" should be taken in light of the Old Testament context, as a reference to the false teachers' origin in the community that has been bought by God ("among the people," "among you"). Additionally, read in light of

Deuteronomy 32:6, "sovereign Lord" or "Master" in 2 Peter 2:1 refers not to Jesus but to God as Father and Creator. As such, this text might be taken (1) as a phenomenological reference to the false teachers' falsely professed place in the community of the redeemed ("the Master whom they professed to have bought them"), (2) as a non-soteriological reference to Jewish false teachers who were part of God's old covenant people ("the Master who purchased them in the old covenant"), or (3) as a non-soteriological reference to God's rightful lordship over all creation ("the Master who as Creator rightfully owns them"). As an additional point of interest, when the verb translated "bought" appears in a soteriological context in the New Testament, it is typically accompanied by "price" (ὀέἰΡὸ) or by some other clear reference in the immediate context to the death of Christ; no such reference may be found in 2 Peter 2:1. Even so, 2 Peter 2:1 remains the most difficult text to reconcile with the clear witness to particular atonement that pervades the rest of Scripture. For further discussion and a defense of the phenomenological view, which we take as the preferable reading of the text, see Thomas Schreiner, *First, Second Peter, Jude* (Nashville: Broadman and Holman, 2003), 328 – 31, and Thomas Schreiner, " 'Problematic Texts' for Definite Atonement in the Pastoral and General Epistles," in *From Heaven He Came and Sought Her*, ed. David Gibson and Jonathan Gibson (Wheaton, IL: Crossway, 2013), 369 – 93.

22. Shai Linne, "Mission Accomplished," *The Atonement* (Lamp Mode, 2008).
23. The Old Covenant high priest interceded and offered sacrifices for particular people, not for everyone, and not for hypothetical populations. Likewise, as the sole and perfect New Covenant high priest, Jesus sacrificed himself and served as high priest for particular people. The priestly proof for definite atonement confirms the trinitarian proof. For more on the priestly argument for definite atonement, see Stephen Wellum, "The New Covenant Work of Christ," in *From Heaven He Came and Sought Her*, Gibson and Gibson (Wheaton, IL: Crossway, 2013), 511 – 34.
24. An unlimited atonement sets the Son against the Father and Spirit. In such a scenario, the Father chooses a particular people, and he only sets the seal of the Spirit on believers, but the Son dies to redeem everyone. Robert Letham, who labels limited atonement "effective atonement" and unlimited atonement "provisional atonement," sounds the alarm. "The doctrine of the Trinity requires ... effective atonement.... This is by far the most serious problem with provisional atonement. It introduces disorder into the doctrine of God. The Father and the Holy Spirit have different goals from the Son." Robert Letham, *Work of Christ* (Downers Grove, IL: InterVarsity, 1993), 237.

25. Corrie ten Boom, *I Stand at the Door and Knock* (Grand Rapids, MI: Zondervan, 2008), 155.

26. D. A. Carson, *The Gospel According to John* (Leicester: Apollos, 1991), 295. At least three overlapping meanings for κοσμος may be identified in the New Testament: (1) drawing from the function of κοσμος in Greco-Roman culture, "world" may describe the order of human society as the context for human history; (2) "world" may function as a dynamic equivalent for Hebraic descriptions of the whole created order (e.g., "the heavens and the earth"); and (3) "world" may point to the fallen human social order, including both Jews and Gentiles, that forms the context for salvation history; in this final sense, those who believe are in the world yet not part of the world. For this meaning, which predominates John's writings in particular, see Carson, *Gospel According to John*, 122 – 25, 236 – 38, 295, 525. In no instance in Scripture does "world" refer explicitly to every individual human being; "world" functions either contextually and impersonally as a reference to the created order or corporately and distributively as a reference to all types of people; it may be universal in a locational sense (all the created order) and in a qualitative sense (all types of persons), but never in a quantitative sense (every individual). For the sense of all types of persons, see, e.g., the placement of "the Savior of the world" (John 4:42) between a pericope demonstrating the extension of God's grace to the Samaritans (John 4:1 – 41) and another in which "the Galileans welcomed" Jesus (John 4:45). Other texts throughout the New Testament, particularly in John's Gospel, are impossible to reconcile with the idea that "world" requires inclusion of every individual who has ever lived, but when "world" is seen as fallen human society encompassing both Jews and Gentiles, these same texts are far more comprehensible. So, e.g., "I am not praying for the world" — for that which remains engaged with the fallen world order, in which Jews and Gentiles alike persist in their rejection of God — "but for those you have given me" — for those called out from the world — "for they are yours" (John 17:9). For further discussion of Christ's work for the world and of the intent of "world," see David Jackman, *The Message of John's Letters* (Leicester: InterVarsity, 1988), 47; R. B. Kuiper, *For Whom Did Christ Die?* reprint ed. (Eugene, OR: Wipf and Stock, 2003), 30 – 34; Gary Long, *Definite Atonement* (Nutley, NJ: Presbyterian and Reformed, 1976), 106 – 19.

27. The context of John 12:32 corroborates the interpretation of "all people" not as every individual throughout human history but as a reference to Jews and Gentiles. An encounter with Greeks who wished "to see Jesus" immediately precedes this declaration (John 12:20 – 22), and the segment

succeeding these words describes the persistent unbelief of the Jewish people (John 12:37 – 43).

28. For a classic exposition of John 3:16 that identifies "world" as an array of ethnic identities, see James Haldane, "Examination of John 3:16 and 17," *Doctrine of the Atonement,* reprint ed. (Choteau, MT: Old Paths Gospel, 1999). In this section in particular, critiques and suggestions from David Schrock were helpful.

29. For Jesus as representative of Israel — the one righteous remnant of Israel and thus the true and new Israel — see, e.g., Graeme Goldsworthy, *According to Plan* (Downers Grove, IL: InterVarsity, 1991), 204 – 6; Tremper Longman III and Raymond B. Dillard, "Isaiah," in *An Introduction to the Old Testament,* 2nd ed. (Grand Rapids, MI: Zondervan, 2006), 315; N. T. Wright, "Jesus, Israel, and the Cross," *Society of Biblical Literature Seminar Papers,* ed. K. H. Richards (Chico, CA: Scholars Press, 1985), 75 – 95.

30. Analogy alludes to Michael Horton, *Putting Amazing Back into Grace,* rev. ed. (Grand Rapids, MI: Baker, 2011), Kindle ed., location 1790. For examples, see Johanna Ginsberg, "Jewish Gymnast Recalls Olympic Mitzva," *New Jersey Jewish News* (June 5, 2013). In this article, "the worldwide reaction was hardly straightforward," and she performed "in front of the whole world."

Chapter 3: Resurrecting Grace

1. Bob Dylan and Tim Drummond, "Saved," *Saved* (Columbia, 1980).

2. The Louisville Zombie Attack began in 2005 as a zombie-themed birthday party; the party grew from fewer than one hundred people the first year to more than 15,000 in recent years. The unintended coordination with Michael Jackson's birthday was fitting, given his contribution to the popularization of zombies through the music video *Michael Jackson's Thriller* (Vestron, 1983). The popular fictional form of zombies should be distinguished from *zombi, zonbi, nzambi,* and *nzumbe* — human bodies, in certain African and Caribbean traditions, that were thought to be prevented from experiencing new life after death or that were reanimated through sorcery (perhaps of a pharmacological nature) (see Wade Davis, *Passage of Darkness* [Chapel Hill: University of North Carolina Press, 1988]; L. P. Mars, "The Story of Zombi in Haiti," *Man* 1945. : 38 – 40, accessed at *www2.webster.edu/~corbetre/haiti/voodoo/mars-zombi.htm*; Amy Wilentz, "A Zombie Is a Slave Forever" [October 30, 2012], *http://www.nytimes.com*). George Romero's 1968 film *Night of the Living Dead* shaped the contemporary fictional conceptualization of the zombie; this zombie is typically a single reanimated corpse (hence Frankenstein's

amalgamation, pieced together from multiple corpses, is not a zombie) with a will that is subservient to a particular person, power, or appetite — though, even in such Romero films as *Day of the Dead*, zombies may possess varying degrees of intelligence and empathy (June Pulliam, "The Zombie," in *Icons of Horror and the Supernatural*, ed. S. T. Joshi [Westport, CT: Greenwood, 2007], 2:724 – 34; Thomas Weaver, *Return of the B Science Fiction and Horror Movie Makers* [Jefferson, NC: McFarland, 1999], 307). Daniel O'Bannon's 1985 film *The Return of the Living Dead* is set in Louisville and likely originated the concept of zombies hungering specifically for brain tissue — a motif that has resurfaced more frequently in zombie humor and satire than in serious zombie fiction (see, e.g., Eric Spitznagel, "Who Says Zombies Eat Brains?" [May 27, 2010], *http://www.vanityfair.com*).

3. Robin Becker, *Brains* (New York: HarperCollins, 2010), 36.
4. Seth Grahame-Smith, *Pride and Prejudice and Zombies* (Philadelphia: Quirk, 2009), 1.
5. Chuck Klosterman, "My Zombie, Myself" (December 3, 2010), *http://www.nytimes.com*.
6. Ibid.
7. For exegetical evidence for a covenant of divine faithfulness and love in the garden of Eden, see Peter Gentry and Stephen Wellum, *Kingdom through Covenant* (Wheaton, IL: Crossway, 2012), 211 – 21. See specifically Hosea 6:7.
8. David Cote et al., *Wicked: The Grimmerie* (New York: Hyperion, 2005), 140.
9. The Smashing Pumpkins, "Tales of a Scorched Earth," *Mellon Collie and the Infinite Sadness: Twilight to Starlight* (Virgin, 1995).
10. The phrase "ἐφ' ᾧ πάντες ἥμαρτον" (Romans 5:12) suggests not only that every person chooses to sin but also that — through one man's sinful act ("ἐφ' ᾧ πάντες ἥμαρτον") — every human being became spiritually dead and alienated from God (Thomas Schreiner, *Romans* [Grand Rapids, MI: Baker, 1998], 275 – 76). Augustine of Hippo, quite likely relying on a faulty Latin rendering of this text, read more into Romans 5:12 than the text itself can sustain, arguing that all humanity was present in Adam and participated in his sin such that Adam's sin is rightly imputed to every human being prior to any act of sin (Michael Azokoul, "Peccatum Originale," *Patristic and Byzantine Review* 3 1984. : 43; David Weaver, "From Paul to Augustine," *St. Vladimir's Seminary Quarterly* 27 1983. : 203). Augustine's contention may indeed be true, and Romans 5:12 does not contradict such a possibility; however, Romans 5:12 does not require acceptance of the imputation of Adam's guilt to every human being prior

to human action. The imputation of Adam's guilt is sustained, independent of any theory of seminal presence in Adam, not only from Romans 5:12 but also from the larger context of Romans 5, particularly verses 16, 18, and 19 — Adam and Christ being placed in parallel representative roles, in which many "were made sinners" through one transgression and in which condemnation (in Adam) and righteousness (in Christ) are imputed to human beings apart from any human work — as well as from such texts as Hebrews 7:9 – 10, wherein a later individual may have the actions of a representative progenitor imputed to him (not in a sense in which children would bear fathers' sins — see Ezekiel 18:20 — but in the sense that a progenitor may be designated as a representative). The precise means by which Adam's sinful act is imputed and Adam's sinful nature is imparted to humanity has been a subject of long-standing debate; this debate has been intertwined with discussions of the origin of the human soul. In terms of impartation of a sinful nature and imputation of actual guilt from Adam, the *realist view* (held, e.g., by W. G. T. Shedd) asserts that every human being was ontologically present in Adam in undifferentiated form, hence all humanity fell in Adam; the *federalist view* (held, e.g., by Charles Hodge) sees Adam as the divinely designated head of all humanity, hence all humanity fell representatively in Adam. In terms of the origin of the soul, *traducianism* (held, e.g., by Tertullian) sees the formation of a new human soul as a divinely designed aspect of the human process of reproduction in which spiritual substance is passed from the father and becomes differentiated into individual children; *creationism* (held, e.g., by Jerome) attributes the formation of each new human soul to a direct divine act that accompanies human conception. Traducianism and creationism are mutually exclusive, while realism and federalism are not mutually exclusive. A traducian could be a realist or a federalist, but a creationist cannot be a realist. G. C. Berkouwer rightly pointed out that both traducianism and creationism assume some degree of dualism, such that the spiritual aspect of human nature derives from some source or process separate from that by which the body comes into existence (*Man: The Image of God* [Grand Rapids, MI: Eerdmans, 1962], 279 – 309). For a classic treatment of the various positions, see chapter 7 in A. A. Hodge, *The Atonement: The Nature of the Atonement* (Philadelphia: Presbyterian Board of Education, 1867). Our position is that resolving the debate between traducianism and creationism is unnecessary and perhaps impossible; that guilt has been imputed to humanity by means of Adam as the head and source of the human race; and that a sinful nature is imparted by means of Adam as the one through whom all nature, including human nature, was perverted and disordered. Even as we accept imputed guilt prior to any human action as both biblical and historically venerable, it should be noted that Reformed soteriology could remain fully coherent with or without imputation of guilt prior to human action. It would be possible for Adam's guilt to be imputed at the time when individuals first approve their sinful nature and for Christ's righteousness to be imputed when, through God's choice and work, an individual is united with Christ. There are similarities between this perspective and the viewpoint posited by Millard Erickson known as conditional imputation, but with the distinction that imputation of righteousness is divinely ratified rather than, as in Erickson's treatment of imputation, humanly ratified (see Millard Erickson, *Christian Theology*, 2nd ed. [Grand Rapids, MI: Baker, 1998], 656). Nevertheless, the whole of Romans 5 taken in context seems most congruent with imputation of Adamic guilt prior to any human action.

11. Andrew Peterson, "Day by Day," *Light for the Lost Boy* (Centricity, 2012).

12. John Wycliffe, *Writings of the Reverend and Learned John Wickliff* (London: Religious Tract Society, 1831), 42; M. S. Royce, *A Series of Brief Historical Sketches of the Church of England and of the Protestant Episcopal Church in the United States* (New York: General Protestant Episcopal Sunday School Union, 1860), 84; George Stokes, *Lives of the British Reformers* (Philadelphia: Presbyterian Board, 1842), 42.

13. The language here is adapted from Michael Horton, *Putting Amazing Back into Grace*, rev. ed. (Grand Rapids, MI: Baker, 2011), Kindle ed., location 900.

14. The greater promise referenced here is the consummate covenant foretold by Jeremiah and fulfilled in Jesus Christ ("new covenant," Jeremiah 31:31; "grace and truth" = "steadfast love and covenant faithfulness," John 1:17; "better covenant," Hebrews 8:6). God's covenants of loyal love form the backbone of his plan to save his chosen people (Peter Gentry and Stephen Wellum, *Kingdom through Covenant* [Wheaton, IL: Crossway, 2012], chapters 1, 2, 3, and 7).

15. Russell Moore, *Tempted and Tried* (Wheaton, IL: Crossway, 2011), Kindle ed., location 1817.

16. "Man is entirely, perfectly and unspeakably different from a mere machine, in that he has reason and understanding, and has a faculty of will, and so is capable of volition and choice; and in that his will is guided by the dictates or views of his understanding; and in that his external actions and behavior and in many respects also his thoughts, and the exercises of his mind, are subject to his will; so that he has liberty to act according to his choice, and do what he pleases; and by means of these things is capable of moral habits and moral acts" (Jonathan Edwards,

The Freedom of the Will, ed. A. S. Kaufman [Indianapolis: Bobbs-Merrill, 1969], 212). Human freedom or liberty consists of power, opportunity, or advantage to do as one pleases. Human beings freely choose that which they most desire, given the possibilities known and available to them. Thus, faced with the possibility of losing one's life to a thief, an individual exercises liberty to choose to freely give up a wallet because that individual values continued earthly existence more highly than personal property. What Edwards denied was that freedom of the will entailed self-determining power of a sort that enables human beings to make choices free from the constraints of their natures. In spiritually dead humanity, the desire for autonomy from God will always be stronger than any desire to submit to God. Hence, no human being will ever choose faith in Jesus until God has made that person spiritually alive. Put another way, human beings possess natural ability to choose Christ, but lack the moral ability to do so. The theological term for this aspect of humanity's fallen condition is "total inability." Jonathan Edwards's observation recognizes the biblical truth that conversion is the fruit of regeneration, not the cause, while simultaneously affirming and upholding human free agency. It is a misconstrual of Reformed theology to claim that Calvinism denies human freedom in the sense of denying humanity's capacity to make choices as responsible free agents. Human beings are by nature free agents with the capacity to choose in a manner that is not divinely coerced. In most instances, when Reformed theologians have denied free will, the point has not been that God's sovereignty eliminates humanity's capacity to make authentic choices, but that human nature is inclined toward sin in such a way that human beings will never choose in their own power to follow Jesus or even to prepare to receive God's grace. For a concise and helpful discussion, see Greg Forster, *The Joy of Calvinism* (Wheaton, IL: Crossway, 2012), Kindle ed., location 369 – 444.

17. Translation by author [TPJ] from *The Greek New Testament: Society of Biblical Literature Edition*, *www.sblgnt.com*. Rendering the present participial form of εἰμί in Ephesians 2:1 as a past-tense verb, as it has been translated in many standard versions and as I have done here, smoothes the English construction but may obscure the ongoing reality of death in the recipients' lives prior to regeneration.

18. Aaron Aupperlee, " 'I Know This Is Horrible,' Says Friend Who Kept Jackson Man's Body for Months" (July 12, 2012), *http://www.mlive.com*; Aaron Aupperlee, "Forgery Charges against Linda Chase Bring Closure, Frustration to Family of Man Kept More Than 18 Months after Death" (July 26, 2012), *http://www.mlive.com*; James Eng, "911 Call That Led to Body Left for 18 Months" (July 12, 2012), *http://www.nbcnews.com*.

19. The primary point of "dead in your transgressions and sins" is most likely that transgressions and sins are *the sphere of* the person's state of death (that is to say, "dead *in the context of* your transgressions and sins"). The grammatical construction would allow for transgressions as the context of death or as the cause of death (Clinton Arnold, *Ephesians* [Grand Rapids, MI: Zondervan, 2010], 130; Andrew Lincoln, *Ephesians* [Dallas: Word, 1990], 93); however, the imagery of walking around (περιεπατήσατε) in transgressions and sins fits better with sin as the context for the former way of life rather than with personal sins as the cause of death. For sphere as a sense of the dative case in this text, see Harold Hoehner, *Ephesians* (Grand Rapids, MI: Baker, 2002), 308.

20. Two centuries before Paul visited Ephesus, the poet Antipater of Sidon said, regarding the temple in Ephesus, "I have set eyes on the wall of lofty Babylon on which is a road for chariots, and the statue of Zeus by the Alpheus, and the hanging gardens, and the Colossus of the Sun, and the huge labor of the high pyramids, and the vast tomb of Mausolus; but when I saw the house of Artemis that mounted to the clouds, those other marvels lost their brilliancy, and I said, 'Behold, apart from Olympus, the Sun never looked on anything so grand'" (*Greek Anthology*, 9:58; see Robert Gundry, *The Old Is Better* [Tübingen: Mohr Siebeck, 2005], 229). Estimates for the population of first-century Ephesus have ranged as high as a half million; the bulk of recent scholarship has, however, placed the population of the city itself closer to 200,000. For estimates of the population of Ephesus, see Richard Strelan, *Paul, Artemis, and the Jews in Ephesus* (Berlin: Walter de Gruyter, 1996), 43. A population of 250,000 would have placed Ephesus among the four most populous cities in the Roman Empire. (Comparatively, according to the United States Census Bureau, the 2010 population of Orlando was 238,304, *http://www.census .gov.*) The two authors of this book are fully aware of the questions — both textual and historical — related to whether the church in Ephesus was the intended destination of the letter now known as "Ephesians." However, even if Ephesians was an encyclical letter, Ephesus was almost certainly one of the destinations; additionally, the city of Ephesus influenced all of western Asia Minor, so examination of circumstances in Ephesus remains helpful for understanding the context of the letter, even if Ephesus might not have been the sole or final destination. Arguments for non-Pauline authorship of Ephesians have been examined and found to be wholly unconvincing and unworthy of serious consideration. For a summary defense of Ephesian destination and Pauline authorship of this letter, see "Introduction to Ephesians" in Clinton Arnold, *Ephesians* (Grand Rapids, MI: Zondervan, 2010).

NOTES

21. For athletic and musical competitions during the month of Artemision, see Jerome Murphy-O'Connor, *St. Paul's Ephesus* (Collegeville, MN: Liturgical, 2008), 175–76, 199. For references to shrines of the temple and figures of Artemis, see Paul Trebilco, "Asia," in *The Book of Acts in Its Graeco-Roman Setting*, ed. D. W. J. Gill and Conrad Gempf (Grand Rapids, MI: Eerdmans, 1994), 2:336–42. No silver shrines of Artemis have been found, but their existence is attested in Acts 19, and this attestation seems plausible given the silver statuettes of Artemis that were carried in parades in Ephesus as well as the shrines made from other materials that have been discovered. For magical practices in Ephesus even among Jewish populations, see Arnold, *Ephesians*, 34–38. For mingling of devotion to Artemis with magical practices, see Hoehner, *Ephesians*, 86. For Paul's battle against "wild beasts" as a struggle against demonic magical and spiritual powers that were perceived as dominating people's lives in Ephesus, see Guy Williams, "An Apocalyptic and Magical Interpretation of Paul's 'Beast Fight' in Ephesus," *Journal of Theological Studies* 57 (2006): 42–56.

22. This entire passage provides a delightful glimpse into Martin Luther's vivid imagery and rhythms of speech: "Als ein Barbier ihm die Haare abschnitt und den Bart abnahm, daß die Erbsünde im Menschen wäre, gleichwie eines Mannes Bart, welcher, ob er wohl heute abgeschnitten würde, daß einer gar glatt ums Maul wäre, dennoch wüchse ihm der Bart des Morgens wieder. Solches Wachsen der Haare und des Bartes höre nicht auf so lang ein Mensch lebt, wenn man aber mit der Schaufel zuschlägt, so hört es auf" (Sinnreiche Tischreden den hauptstücken christlicher lehre verfaßt [Leipzig: Reiger, 1836], 1:341).

23. God alone is capable of creating, and all that God creates is good. Powers of evil exist and expand not by creating evil but only by corrupting that which is good; evil exists only as a disordering or distortion of that which is beautiful and good; therefore, beauty and goodness remain present, albeit in disordered and distorted form, even in the most depraved human soul. Thomas Aquinas, citing Augustine of Hippo's declaration against Julian of Eclanum "*non fuit omnino unde oriri posset malum, nisi ex bono*" (*Contra Julianum*, 1:9), identified the nature of evil as the absence of natural and rightful good in an act or desire; this absence results from the separation of the good act or desire from its divinely designed disposition and purpose (Thomas Aquinas, *Summa Theologiae*, p. 1: q. 49: art. 1).

24. Horton, *Putting Amazing Back into Grace*, location 738. See also James Montgomery Boice and Philip Ryken, *The Doctrines of Grace*, reprint ed. (Wheaton, IL: Crossway, 2009), 30. Total inability (deprivation of desire for God's reign in one's life and for God's remedy for sin) and total depravity (pervasiveness of sin throughout every aspect of human existence) are two

aspects of the impartation of the effects of Adam's sin to human nature. The impartation and imputation of Adam's sin are two components of the doctrine of original sin. In imputation, God charges Adam's sin to humanity's account; in impartation, Adam's fallen nature is inherited by humanity, inclining every aspect of human life toward sin and depriving humanity of desire for God's remedy for sin and reign over humanity.

25. C. H. Spurgeon, "Honest Dealing with God" (June 20, 1875).

26. Though we are treating the two primary clauses in Ephesians 2:3 separately, the και ("and," "even") in the second clause positions the two clauses as parallel declarations with the first clause emphasizing the external experience of rebellion and the second clause moving to the internal source and deserved result. The phrase "sons of disobedience" in 2:2 (RSV) suggests chosen and active patterns of sin befitting the greater maturity of "sons," while "children of wrath" in 2:3 (RSV) (obscured by the paraphrase "deserving of" in the NIV) seems to imply wrath due to a passive reception of sinfulness on the basis of one's ancestry. Φυσις ("nature") may point to (1) lineal descent (see Galatians 2:15), (2) natural quality or identity (see Romans 11:21 – 24), or (3) the intended practice of the created world (see Romans 1:26). The third sense clearly does not fit here; the first or second senses would produce similar practical implications, though the first sense seems best to fit the context. Φυσις in the dative case most naturally refers to the condition into which someone was born. Οργής ("of wrath," genitive of οργή) should probably be taken as a genitive of destination ("children headed for wrath"), though the phrase might also be read as a description of that which is deserved ("children deserving of wrath"); the implication and application of these two possibilities would be nearly identical. See Hoehner, *Ephesians*, 322 – 23; Frank Thielman, *Ephesians* (Grand Rapids, MI: Baker, 2010), 127.

27. Translation by author [TPJ] from *The Greek New Testament: Society of Biblical Literature Edition*, www.sblgnt.com. Markus Barth, while overemphasizing the metaphor of a cosmic lawsuit, rightly recognized the verb ἐνδεικνυμι as a reference to the provision of evidence, through the church, of God's kindness toward all types of people, particularly the Gentiles (*Ephesians*, ed. W. F. Albright and D. N. Freedman [Garden City, NY: Doubleday, 1974], 238 – 42) — hence the translation here "he might prove."

28. Regeneration as a divine response to a human decision is a heretical assertion characteristic of semi-Pelagianism and Pelagianism. Regeneration as a divine act and result of prevenient grace that makes faith and repentance possible (and which thus, in some sense, precedes faith and repentance) but which remains dependent in its culmination on a human decision not to resist is characteristic of classical Arminianism;

although we firmly disagree with Arminianism, Arminian soteriology stands within the boundaries of orthodoxy and should be seen as distinct from every form of Pelagianism. For a classical Arminian perspective on regeneration and faith, see Roger Olson, *Arminian Theology* (Downers Grove, IL: InterVarsity, 2009), 36 – 37, 163 – 67.

29. Language alludes to James K. A. Smith, *Letters to a Young Calvinist* (Grand Rapids, MI: Brazos, 2010), 26.

30. Adapted from John Calvin, *Commentarius Epistolam ad Timotheam I*, 2:3 – 4; John Calvin, *Concerning the Eternal Predestination of God* (London: Clarke, 1961), 138.

31. Lady Gaga, "Born This Way," *Born This Way* (Interscope, 2011).

32. Joel Osteen, *Your Best Life Now* (New York: Hachette, 2004), chapter 2; Jean Twenge and Keith Campbell, *The Narcissism Epidemic* (New York: Free, 2009), 246 – 48.

33. Seventy-four percent of American adults and 52 percent of American evangelicals agree that "when people are born, they are neither good nor evil" ("Americans Draw Theological Beliefs from Diverse Points of View" [October 8, 2002], *http://www.barna.org*).

34. J. Cole with James Fauntleroy, "Born Sinner," *Born Sinner* (Roc Nation, 2013).

35. For sympathetic overviews of the life and thought of Pelagius, see John Ferguson, *Pelagius* (Cambridge: Cambridge University Press, 1956), and Gerald Bonner, "How Pelagian Was Pelagius?" *Studia Patristica* (1966): 350 – 58. Even Augustine admitted that Pelagius was a pious individual who had made progress in godly living (Augustine of Hippo, *Epistola*, 138).

36. According to Pelagians, everyone possesses a God-given capacity to choose the right way or the wrong way; when an individual makes the right choice, God responds by giving grace. See Pelagius, *Pro Libero Arbitrio*, as quoted in Augustine of Hippo, *De Gratia Christi*, 19 (18). The relevant section in context in *De Gratia Christi* reads, "Habemus autem … possibilitatem utriusque partis a Deo insitam, velut quamdam, ut ita dicam, radicem fructiferam atque fecundam, quae ex voluntate hominis diversa gignat et pariat, et quae possit ad proprii cultoris arbitrium, vel nitere flore virtutum, vel sentibus horrere vitiorum." Celestius and other followers of Pelagius seem to have proceeded further than Pelagius himself, claiming that Adam's sin damaged only his own nature, that Adam's sin did not directly affect the human race as a whole, and that infants are born in the same moral state as Adam prior to the primal sin (Augustine of Hippo, *De Gestis Pelagii*, 23 11, and *De Peccato Originali*, 3, 14 13.) Pelagius disavowed these teachings as distortions of his thinking, albeit insincerely, according to Augustine.

37. Augustine, *De Gestis Pelagii*, 20.
38. Augustine of Hippo, *De Dono Perseverantiae*, 38.
39. Gregg Allison, *Historical Theology* (Grand Rapids, MI: Zondervan, 2011), 350.
40. Rush, "Free Will," *Permanent Waves* (Mercury, 1980).
41. John Wesley, *Working Out Our Own Salvation*, in *The Works of John Wesley* (Grand Rapids, MI: Zondervan, 1958), 6:512.
42. Bruce Springsteen, "Dancing in the Dark," *Born in the U.S.A* (Columbia, 1984).
43. Arthur Bennett, ed., "Regeneration," *The Valley of Vision: A Collection of Puritan Prayers and Devotions* (Edinburgh: Banner of Truth Trust, 1975), 84 – 85.
44. John Calvin, *Institutio Christianae Religionis*, 3.13.2. Coleman Ford contributed original research to this sidebar.

Chapter 4: Outrageous Grace

1. William Cowper and John Newton, "41. Faith's Review and Expectation, 1 Chronicles 17:16, 17," *Olney Hymns: In Three Parts* (London: Nelson and Sons, 1855), 58.
2. Johnny Cash, interview with Bill Moyers, *Amazing Grace with Bill Moyers* (Public Affairs Television, 1990).
3. During a storm at sea in 1748, John Newton began to question his earlier unbelief. According to Newton's own account, "The tenth (that is, in the present style, the twenty-first) day of March, is a day much to be remembered by me, and I have never suffered it to pass wholly unnoticed since the year 1748. On that day the Lord sent from on high, and delivered me." By the time Newton disembarked in Ireland on April 8, he "had a satisfactory evidence … of the truth of the gospel … and its exact suitableness to answer all [his] needs." In 1748 and 1749, Newton served as first mate on a slaving vessel. During that voyage, he became desperately ill; during this illness, he "was enabled to hope and believe in a crucified Saviour. The burden was removed." It was not until 1750 that John Newton became captain of a slaving vessel; he commanded three voyages before suffering a stroke in 1754 that ended his seafaring career. See John Newton, Letters 8 – 13, "An Authentic Narrative," *The Works of the Reverend John Newton: Volume 1* (New York: Robert Carter, 1847), 96 – 109. The lyrics that later became "Amazing Grace" were penned in 1772 for a New Year's Day worship service in 1773. No less a publication than the *New York Times* has erred on the chronology of this story: "Some listeners detected an allusion to a passage in 'Amazing Grace,' the

hymn written by a slave trader turned minister and abolitionist, John Newton, after he survived an Atlantic storm" (Elisabeth Bumiller, "The President Makes Danger His Campaign Theme," *New York Times* (January 25, 2004), *http://www.nytimes.com.*

4. Newton, Letter 13, "Authentic Narrative," 108.

5. For descriptions of the Middle Passage, see John Newton, "Thoughts on the African Slave Trade," *The Works of the Reverend John Newton: Volume 4* (New Haven: Nathan Whiting, 1826), 530–34; Olaudah Equiano, *The Interesting Narrative of the Life of Olaudah Equiano, or Gustavus Vassa, The African* (London: Olaudah Equiano, 1789, 1794), chapter 2; Hugh Thomas, *The Slave Trade* (New York: Simon and Schuster, 1997), 409–48.

6. Steven Mintz, *African-American Voices*, 4th ed. (West Sussex: Wiley, 2009), 10. Arguably, the founding sin of slavery stained the emerging United States with "a national birth defect" ("Rice Hits U.S. 'Birth Defect,'" *http://www.washingtontimes.com* [March 28, 2008]) that contributed to the later loss of more than a half-million lives in the American Civil War, followed by generations of racial segregation and discrimination. For the American Civil War as judgment on rebellion against Great Britain and on the subsequent expansion of slavery, see Steven Keillor, *This Rebellious House* (Downers Grove, IL: InterVarsity, 1996), 43–80, 149–50.

7. The neuter pronoun translated "this" or "it" (τοῦτο) in "this is the gift" cannot refer to "faith" because πίστεως is feminine, nor to "grace" since χάριτι is also feminine, nor to "[having been] saved" since σεσωσμένοι is masculine. "This" refers back to the whole divine work of salvation described in Ephesians 2:1–7 and, while inclusive of faith, is not denotative of faith. Still, since "this" describes the whole work of salvation, faith — as well as regeneration, union with Christ, and all other benefits in Ephesians 2:1–7 — may rightly be described as a divine gift.

8. Quotations from Synod of Dort drawn from *Canones Synod: Dordechtanae*, in *Creeds of Christendom* vol. 3, ed. P. Schaff (New York: Harper, 1884).

9. Translation by author [TPJ] from *The Greek New Testament: Society of Biblical Literature Edition*, www.sblgnt.com.

10. According to Jakob Arminius, faith — a gift given through the work of God's Spirit when an individual does not resist prevenient grace — is not only the foundation for justification but also a condition for election. The basis of predestination was not God's unconditional choice, but his foresight of an individual's willingness not to resist grace and of subsequent choices to remain in grace. God's predestinating decree was, Arminius argued, "to save and to damn certain particular [*sekere bysondere*] persons;

[this] decree depends on [*steunt op*] the foreknowledge of God, by which he has known from eternity which persons … through his prevenient grace would [*souden*] believe" (*Declaration of Sentiments*, in *The Works of James Arminius*, trans. James and William Nichols [Grand Rapids, MI: Baker, 1986], 1:653 – 54). For a balanced portrayal of the life and theology of Jakob Arminius, see Keith Stanglin, *Arminius on the Assurance of Salvation* (Leiden, Netherlands: Brill, 2007), and Keith Stanglin and Thomas McCall, *Jacob Arminius* (Oxford: Oxford University Press, 2012).

11. For further discussion, see S. M. Baugh, "The Meaning of 'Foreknowledge,'" in *Still Sovereign*, ed. Thomas Schreiner and Bruce Ware (Grand Rapids, MI: Baker, 2000), 183 – 200; Thomas Schreiner, *Romans* (Grand Rapids, MI: Baker, 1998), 452.

12. Quoted in Michele Scott, *Praying Through Your Adoption* (Enumclaw, WA: WinePress, 2011), 30.

13. Thomas Watson, "Of Adoption," in *A Body of Practical Divinity Consisting of Above One Hundred Seventy-Six Sermons on the Lesser Catechism Composed by the Reverend Assembly of Divines at Westminster* (London: Parkhurst, 1692), 139.

14. Basil Manly Jr., *Abstract of Principles* (Southern Baptist Theological Seminary, 1858), article 5.

15. I [TPJ] have in several seasons of life seriously struggled with Reformed soteriology. Each time, I have ended up researching, translating, and exegeting Romans 9 again — and, each time, I have found myself convinced anew that only a Reformed reading adequately takes into account this full text and its context. Paul's reference to his willingness to be damned for the sake of his fellow Israelites (Romans 9:1 – 5) precludes limiting the implications of the text to God's temporal blessings on the Jewish people. And, while the text certainly includes corporate election, it is both as individuals and as a group that persons participate in God's promises; as such, there is no adequate exegetical foundation for excluding individual election from this text, especially in light of Paul's references to individual election in Romans 10. For more on this text, see Thomas Schreiner, "Does Romans 9 Teach Individual Election unto Salvation?" *Journal of the Evangelical Theological Society*, 36 (March 1993): 25 – 40.

16. John Calvin, *Institutio Christianae Religionis*, 1:6:3; 3:21:5.

17. This usage of "scandal" derives from the response of the disciples to Jesus' condemnation of religious leaders for their reliance on keeping human commands and principles to justify themselves before God. According to the disciples, this teaching "offended" or "scandalized" the Pharisees ("οἱ Φαρισαῖοι ἀκούσαντες τὸν λόγον ἐσκανδαλίσθησαν," Matthew 15:12). Nominal followers of Jesus found it similarly scandalous when Jesus

declared that persons are made right with God by receiving Jesus as one would receive food and drink — and that even this receiving is initiated and enabled by the work of God, not by any human choice or response (John 6:44, 61). The New Testament uses of σκανδαλον and σκανδαλιζω are rooted in a range of Old Testament descriptions of rejecting God's way (see Revelation 2:14 and Numbers 25:1), of exploitative treatment that failed to seek the welfare of those less capable (see Romans 14:13 and Leviticus 19:14), as well as of God's eschatological judgment of those unfaithful to him (see Matthew 14:31 and Zephaniah 1:3). "Scandalized" in Matthew 15:12 likely echoes 13:57 and centers on the Pharisees' offense at (and resulting rejection of) God's way while alluding to God's coming judgment on them due to their rejection of the Messiah.

18. James Proctor, "Hymn 64," in *Songs of Love and Mercy for the Young* (London: Morgan and Scott, n.d.), 38 – 39.

19. Robert Farrar Capon, *Between Noon and Three* (Grand Rapids, MI: Eerdmans, 1997), 292.

20. The pronoun τούτο in Ephesians 2:8 – 9 refers to the whole divine work of salvation and — while inclusive of faith — does not denote faith.

21. Tullian Tchividjian, *One-Way Love* (Colorado Springs: Cook, 2013), Kindle ed., location 658.

22. Paraphrased from P. F. M. Zahl, *Grace in Practice* (Grand Rapids, MI: Eerdmans, 2007), Kindle ed., location 53.

23. In addition to (1) driving the elect toward the gospel, the law also (2) restrains the unrighteousness of unbelievers (1 Timothy 1:9 – 10) and (3) provides moral guidelines that believers pursue through the power of the Holy Spirit (Romans 8:4; 13:10), not as an attempt to earn God's favor but as a pattern of life rooted in the new covenant by which God has brought together undeserving sinners from every nation on the basis of the blood of Jesus Christ. The first two uses of the law are designated as *usus politicus sive civilis* and *usus elenchticus sive paedagogicus*. The third use of law, as a continuing norm for Christian life (*usus didacticus sive normativus*) is not accepted by all Reformed theologians.

24. Tchividjian, *One-Way Love*, Kindle ed.

25. Ralph Erskine, *The Sermons and Practical Works of Ralph Erksine* (Glasgow: Smith, 1778), 10:283, as quoted in Jason Meyer, *The End of the Law* (Nashville: B&H, 2010), 2.

26. Walter Marshall, *The Gospel Mystery of Sanctification.* (Eugene, OR: Wipf and Stock, 2004), 117.

27. William D. Hendricks, *Exit Interviews: Revealing Stories of Why People Are Leaving the Church* (Chicago: Moody Press, 1993).

28. Robert Farrar Capon, *Between Noon and Three*, 41.

29. See Martin Luther's exposition of Psalm 117 in *Luther's Works*, 14, 37, as well as *Finem commentarii in XV. Psalmos graduum*, 1532–33, in *Martin Luther's Werke, Weimarer Ausgabe*, 40/3, 352, 3. Though Martin Luther did not originate the phrase commonly attributed to him regarding justification — "articulus stantis et cadentis ecclesiae," "article of the church's standing and stumbling" — the underlying concept may be clearly found in the writings noted above.

30. Brian Vickers, *Justification by Grace through Faith* (Phillipsburg, NJ: P&R, 2013), 183.

31. Ibid., 158.

32. Imputation of Christ's righteousness occurs *by means of* union with Christ, with Christ himself present in the believer's faith performing the works of Christ through the believer. See Constantine Campbell, *Paul and Union with Christ* (Grand Rapids, MI: Zondervan, 2012), 399–401; Mark Seifrid, *Christ Our Righteousness* (Downers Grove, IL: InterVarsity, 2000), 149.

Chapter 5: Overcoming Grace

1. Robert Webster and Elizabeth Walker, "Influenza," *American Scientist* 91 (March–April 2003): 122.

2. Fatima Dawood et al., "Estimated Global Mortality Associated with the First 12 Months of 2009 Pandemic Influenza," *Infectious Diseases* 12 (September 2012): 687: "Globally there were 201,200 respiratory deaths ... with an additional 83,300 cardiovascular deaths ... associated with 2009 pandemic influenza A H1N1." More than half of these deaths occurred in Africa and southeast Asia.

3. In the words of Augustine of Hippo in *De Correptione et Gratia*, 12 (33), humanity before the fall was "able not to sin, able not to die, and able not to forsake what is good" ("potuit enim non peccare primus homo, potuit non mori, potuit bonum non deserere").

4. Post-fall, humanity is unable not to sin, unable not to die, and unable not to forsake what is good (Augustine, *De Correptione et Gratia*). Redeemed and glorified humanity will be in a greater state even than primal humanity: unable to sin, unable to die, and unable to forsake what is good ("novissima erit multo maior, non posse peccare ... novissima erit multo maior, non posse mori ... novissima erit felicitas perseverantiae, bonum non posse deserere") (Augustine, *De Correptione et Gratia*). The imagery used throughout this chapter of a diseased will and residual sinful nature is rooted in Augustine of Hippo, *Enchiridion de Fide*, 31 (118): even in the believer, "the disease is not yet fully cured" ("nondum tota infirmitate sanata").

NOTES

5. Timothy George, *Amazing Grace: God's Pursuit, Our Response*, 2nd ed. (Wheaton, IL: Crossway, 2011), 86.
6. R. C. Sproul, *Chosen by God*, rev. ed. (Wheaton, IL: Tyndale, 1994), 55.
7. For a contemporary example of this analogy, see *navfusion.com/gospel*. The sentiment identifying God as "a gentleman" appears to have originated in the early eighteenth century with Lord Anthony Ashley Cooper, third earl of Shaftesbury, as part of his overall attempt to downplay concepts of wrath and judgment in perceptions of God (H. E. Barnes, *World Politics in Modern Civilization* [New York: Knopf, 1930], 72). For a diverse sample of contemporary expressions of this same sentiment selected from a plethora of possible examples, see John and Katherine Ford, *When Evil Reigns* (Mustang, OK: Tate, 2010), 263; Greg Hoffman, *The Forest from the Trees* (Bloomington, IN: CrossBooks, 2011), 74; Anne Graham Lotz, *God's Story*, rev. ed. (Nashville: Nelson, 2009), xxxiv.
8. *The Baptist Faith and Message* (Nashville: BSSB/LifeWay, 2000), article 4.
9. *Westminster Confession of Faith and Catechisms* (Lawrenceville: PCA, 2007), 10:1.
10. Robert Palmer, "Simply Irresistible," *Heavy Nova* (EMI, 1988).
11. For implication of ποίημα as inaugurated new creation, see Psalms 91:4 and 142:5 in Septuagint (P. T. O'Brien, *The Letter to the Ephesians* (Grand Rapids, MI: Eerdmans, 1999), 178–79.
12. Ελκυω functions in a parallel passage in John 12:32 similarly to how the term functions in 6:44: "And I, when I am lifted up from the earth, will draw all people to myself." It is through the work of Jesus on the cross ("I am lifted up") that the Father works transformatively and effectively to bring sinners to himself. Ben Witherington III reads this drawing as a "certain sort of spiritual magnetism" exhibited by Jesus (*John's Wisdom* [Louisville, KY: WJK, 1995], 225), but this understanding of the verb ελκυω is simply not sustainable in light of other usages throughout the New Testament (John 21:6, 11; Acts 16:19). The point of "all people" in John 12:32 is not a resistible "spiritual magnetism" that extends to each individual throughout the earth. It is a transformative and effective drawing of particular persons from all nations without regard for ethnicity or social class. John demonstrated that his usage of "all" was qualitative ("all types of people") rather than quantitative ("every individual person") by situating John 12:32 between episodes in which the Greeks sought to see Jesus (John 12:20–22) and in which many Jewish people rejected Jesus (John 12:34–43). See D. A. Carson, *The Gospel According to John* (Grand Rapids, MI: Eerdmans, 1991), 293.
13. J. W. Stallings, *The Gospel of John*, ed. Robert Picirilli (Nashville: Randall, 1989), 103–104.

14. While agreeing with R. C. Sproul's ultimate conclusions regarding the doctrine of effectual or irresistible grace, it should be noted that Sproul overstates his lexical case when dealing with ἑλκυω (rendered "draw" in most English translations) by overemphasizing the potential implication of "drag" in John 6 (R. C. Sproul, *Chosen by God*, rev. ed. [Wheaton, IL: Tyndale, 1994], 52–54). Dragging of an inert or resistant object would not, for example, fit the usage of this same word in Eubulus, *Fragments* (Cambridge: Cambridge University Press, 1983), fragment 77, where starving people are said to be drawn to bread ("Μαγνητις γαρ λίθος ως ἑλκει τους πεινωντας"). At the same time, against interpretations that attempt to limit this drawing to mere winsome persuasion, the drawing implied in ἑλκυω is clearly more than an attempt to convince. It is an effective drawing—perhaps even an irresistible attraction—in which the object is helpless, but this helplessness does *not* necessitate that the object has no role whatsoever in the movement toward the one drawing.

15. Translation by author [TPJ] from *The Greek New Testament: Society of Biblical Literature Edition*, www.sblgnt.com. The added words "before the foundation of the world" pick up the intended timeframe of προ from Ephesians 1:4, reflected in the προ- prefix of προητπιμασεν.

16. "Although we in ourselves are sinners, Christ—the new person—is present within faith, performing his works" (Mark Seifrid, *Christ, Our Righteousness* [Downers Grove, IL: InterVarsity, 2000], 149). The believer's good works are the means by which Christ's presence in the believer's faith becomes apparent and actualized.

17. Our presentation of union with Christ draws from Constantine Campbell's four descriptive concepts: union, participation, incorporation, and identification (*Paul and Union with Christ* [Grand Rapids, MI: Zondervan, 2012], 407–20). As Campbell admits, the term "union" may be expressed, with some explication, in terms of identification and incorporation (413). Theologian Louis Berkhof provided this classic definition of union with Christ, which also frames our presentation: "that intimate, vital, and spiritual union between Christ and his people, in virtue of which he is the source of their life and strength, of their blessedness and salvation" (*Systematic Theology*, 6th ed. [Edinburgh: Banner of Truth, 1959], 449).

18. John Murray, *Redemption: Accomplished and Applied* (Grand Rapids, MI: Eerdmans, 1955), 161.

19. Faith is a condition not only of justification but also of adoption and union with Christ (Galatians 3:26; Ephesians 1:13; 3:17). John Calvin's exegesis led him to the conclusion that union with Christ is a consequence of faith ("Etsi autem verum est, hoc fide nos consequi") and that the Holy Spirit is the bond of this union ("Huc summa redit, Spiritum sanctum

vinculum esse, quo nos sibi efficaciter devincit Christus") (John Calvin, *Institutio Christianae Religionis*, 3:1:1).

20. For God the Father regarding and responding to believers as he does Jesus, see, e.g., Robert Letham, *Union with Christ* (Phillipsburg, NJ: P&R, 2011), 51 – 55; David Broughton Knox, *Justification by Faith* (London: Church Book Room, 1959), 6; Lane Tipton, "Union with Christ and Justification," in *Justified in Christ*, ed. K. S. Oliphint (Fearn, Ross-Shire: Mentor, 2007), 25.

21. Anthony Hoekema, *Saved by Grace* (Grand Rapids, MI: Eerdmans, 1989), 57.

22. "Before time began, in one and the same decree, Christ was chosen to be the redeemer and the church was chosen to be redeemed in him" (Herman Bavinck, *Reformed Dogmatics*, vol. 2, *God and Creation* [Grand Rapids, MI: Baker Academic, 2004], 401 – 5). God's election of those who would be redeemed was dependent on his election of Christ for the work of redemption. "God did not choose us because Christ died for us, but Christ died for us because God chose us in him" (Robert Letham, summarizing Hieronymus Zanchius, in *Union with Christ* [Phillipsburg, NJ: P&R, 2011], 68).

23. Murray, *Redemption: Accomplished and Applied*, 162.

24. Thomas Goodwin, *An Exposition of Ephesians, Chapter 1 to 2:10*, reprint ed. (Evansville, IN: Sovereign Grace, 1958), 74 – 75.

25. There is a distinction at this point between classical covenantal theology and progressive covenantal (or new covenant) theology. According to classical covenantalism, a single covenant of grace, centered in the work of Jesus Christ, extends from God's provision of grace after humanity's primal sin until the end of time. As a result, old covenant believers are understood to have experienced union with Christ and the indwelling of the Spirit even though Christ had not yet been enfleshed, crucified, or raised from the dead. Put another way, every experience in the order of salvation (*ordo salutis*), including the experience of union with Christ and of the indwelling of the Spirit as the bond of this union, has remained unchanged throughout the history of salvation (*historia salutis*). With classical covenantalists, progressive covenantalists (as well as some progressive dispensationalists) affirm that old covenant believers experienced regeneration and, through faith in a Messiah yet to come, the imputed righteousness of the Messiah Jesus. Unlike classical covenantalists, progressive covenantalists (as well as dispensationalists, though with different assumptions and implications in some instances) recognize not one single covenant of grace but a multiplicity of grace-conveying covenants and covenant renewals in the Old Testament. Until

the incarnation, death, and resurrection of Jesus Christ, old covenant believers — some of whom were alive during the time of Jesus, but most of whom were long deceased by the time Jesus arrived — awaited certain new covenant experiences that depended on Christ's incarnation and obedience to God the Father. New covenant experiences that were contingent on the incarnation, death, and resurrection of Christ include union with Christ and the indwelling of the Holy Spirit (see John 14:16–20; 15:26; 16:7; Romans 7:4; Galatians 2:20; Ephesians 2:6; Colossians 2:12; 3:1). This is not to say that old covenant believers were not in some sense united to Christ; it is to say that union with Christ in the new covenant sense includes experiential aspects that are dependent on knowledge of the obedient life, death, and resurrection of Jesus Christ and on participation by means of the indwelling Holy Spirit. Although differing with regard to the experiences of soteriological realities among old covenant believers, classical covenantalists, progressive covenantalists, progressive dispensationalists, and even modified dispensationalists in the Reformed tradition are generally able to find agreement on the nature and conditions of union with Christ in the new covenant, though perhaps not on the precise placement of union in relation to justification and sanctification. For further discussion of this distinction between classical covenantal and progressive covenantal theology, see Peter Gentry and Stephen Wellum, *Kingdom through Covenant* (Wheaton, IL: Crossway, 2012), 113–33, 684–85. For the indwelling Holy Spirit as a distinctly new covenant phenomenon, see James Hamilton, *God's Indwelling Presence* (Nashville: B&H, 2006).

26. The believer's justification and union with Christ depend on Christ's union with human nature through the incarnation. "He is substituted *for* us, because he is one *with* us" (Hugh Martin, *The Atonement* [Edinburgh: Lyon and Gemmell, 1877], 38). This point was put most succinctly by Gregory of Nazianzus in a letter to Cledonius during the fourth-century Apollinarian controversy: "το γαρ απροσληπτον, αθεραπευτον" ("For whatever [aspect of human nature] [Christ] did not take on himself, he did not heal," *Epistole* 101). Karl Barth extended the implications of Christ's union with human nature and contended that every human being is, by means of the incarnation, an objective participant in Christ. For Barth, since Christ is the perfect expression of human nature and since no human being exists apart from Christ, every human is already objectively in Christ; by means of faith that engenders obedience, persons become subjective participants in union with Christ (Adam Neder, *Participation in Christ* [Louisville, KY: WJK, 2009]). The present subjective participation of the Christian in Christ is rooted in the eternally

preexisting participation of the Father and Son in one another (Karl Barth, *Die Kirchliche Dogmatik*, 4:3:2). Although Barth's claim of objective participation of every human in Christ is exegetically unsustainable, his articulation of objective and subjective aspects of participation as well as his recognition of the rootedness of union with Christ in the eternal relationship of the Trinity are helpful. Christ indeed participated in human nature, but human beings participate in his nature only through subjective, personal appropriation of his righteousness through faith.

27. Augustine of Hippo, "Psalm 81, Deus Stetit in Synagoga Deorum," Mainz Sermon 13:1.

28. This union entails not only forensic change in status but also participative change that results in transformation. The sinner's spirit — previously deadened to divine truth but now enlivened to yearn for God and for holiness — participates, through communion with the Holy Spirit, in the very life of the Triune God without becoming consubstantial with or absorbed into the being of God. For union as transformative and participatory without resulting in ontological deification or in mystical absorption into the divine essence, see, e.g., John Calvin, *Institutio Christianae Religionis*, 1:15:5; John Calvin, *Commentarii*, 2 Peter 1:4.

29. John Calvin and Reformed theologians in the century after him presented (1) initial imputation of righteousness (justification) and (2) ongoing growth in righteousness (sanctification) as distinguishable but ultimately inseparable graces. For discussion, see J. Todd Billings, *Union with Christ* (Grand Rapids, MI: Baker, 2011), Kindle ed., location 600 – 644. Calvin summarized the *duplex gratia* or twofold grace of God in this way: "Christ was given to us by God's generosity, to be grasped and possessed by us in faith. By partaking of him, we principally receive a twofold grace [*duplicem gratiam*]: namely, that being reconciled to God through Christ's blamelessness, we may have in heaven instead of a Judge a gracious Father, and secondly, that sanctified by Christ's Spirit we may cultivate blamelessness and purity of life" (*Institutio Christianae Religionis*, 3:11:1). See also *Institutio Christianae Religionis*, 3:11:6, and *Commentarii*, 1 Corinthians 1:30. Of these two graces, Calvin clearly saw justification as primary and foundational: the gift of a life of repentance is placed second ("quae secunda est gratia") in relation to the gift of justification, which stands as the principal hinge on which religion turns ("praecipuus esse sustinendae religionis cardo," *Institutio Christianae Religionis*, 3:11:1). Beginning in the eighteenth century and particularly in the nineteenth century, these two aspects began to be perceived and presented separately. The emphasis in theological treatments of union with Christ shifted to the imputative aspect; increasingly conflated with justification,

union with Christ was deemphasized in Reformed theology. See William Evans, *Imputation and Impartation* (Eugene, OR: Wipf and Stock, 2008), 111 – 12. In the twentieth century, John Murray declared union with Christ to be the most central and basic truth in God's soteriological work. See John Murray, *Redemption: Accomplished and Applied* (Grand Rapids, MI: Eerdmans, 1955), 201. Richard Gaffin went even further, seeing union with Christ as so central that the links in the golden chain of the *ordo salutis* become irrelevant; each link in the *ordo salutis* is, according to Gaffin, simply an aspect or corollary of union; baptism provides the sign and seal of this union. See Richard Gaffin, *By Faith, Not by Sight* (Waynesboro: Paternoster, 2006), particularly chapter 2, and Richard Gaffin, *The Centrality of the Resurrection* (Grand Rapids, MI: Baker, 1978). Michael Horton's work has retained the *ordo salutis* and treated union with Christ primarily as an expression of the incorporative aspect of each stage in the *ordo salutis,* with justification by faith functioning as the foundation for sanctification. See Michael Horton, *Covenant and Salvation* (Louisville, KY: WJK, 2007), 131 – 51, as well as chapters 17 through 21 in *The Christian Faith* (Grand Rapids, MI: Zondervan, 2011). We have retained the *ordo salutis* as a helpful tool for considering the unique elements of different aspects in the Christian experience and have treated sanctification simultaneously as *a gift that results from union* and as *a progressive experience that is grounded in justification.*

30. William Willimon and Stanley Hauerwas, *Lord, Teach Us* (Nashville: Abingdon, 1996), 28 – 29, 77, 108.

31. Augustine of Hippo, *Confessions*, 3:1; 4:4; 8:7.

Chapter 6: Forever Grace

1. Stephen Brindle, "Perseverance of the Saints," *The Perseverance Mixtape*, *http://believinstephen.bandcamp.com.*

2. William Secker, *The Nonsuch Professor in His Meridian Splendor* (Chicago: Revell, n.d.), 196.

3. A seal (1) prevented tampering and thus implied protection on contents and (2) denoted ownership. Seals also indicated (3) genuineness or (4) authenticity. See Harold Hoehner, *Ephesians* (Grand Rapids, MI: Baker, 2002), 238.

4. Jared Wilson, *Gospel Deeps* (Wheaton, IL: Crossway, 2012), 50.

5. Robert Peterson, *Our Secure Salvation* (Phillipsburg, NJ: P&R, 2009), 38–39.

6. Thomas Schreiner and Ardel Caneday, *The Race Set Before Us* (Downers Grove, IL: InterVarsity, 2001), 67.

7. Ibid., 264.
8. Robert A. Peterson, *Our Secure Salvation: Preservation and Apostasy* (Phillipsburg, NJ: P&R, 2009), 201.
9. Steve Brown, *A Scandalous Freedom* (New York: Howard, 2004), 246.
10. Douglas Wilson, *Easy Chairs, Hard Words* (Moscow: Canon, 1991), 24.
11. Thomas Schreiner, *New Testament Theology* (Grand Rapids, MI: Baker, 2008), 568.
12. Dallas Willard, "Live Life to the Full," *Christian Herald* (April 14, 2001), *www.dwillard.org.*
13. Schreiner and Caneday, *The Race,* 49–50.
14. Thomas Schreiner, *Run to Win the Prize* (Wheaton, IL: Crossway, 2010), 72–73.
15. This discussion has been substantively shaped by Peter Gentry and Stephen Wellum, *Kingdom through Covenant* (Wheaton, IL: Crossway, 2012), 140–41.
16. Michael Horton, *Putting the Amazing Back into Grace* (Grand Rapids, MI: Baker, 2002), 183.

Chapter 7: Living Proof

1. From the perspective of certain strains of late medieval theology, people were to focus on "doing what [was] in [them]" (see, e.g., *facienti quod in se est,* in Gabriel Biel, *Collectorium circa Quatuor Libros Sententiarum,* ed. Wilfrid Werbeck and Udo Hofmann [Tübingen: Mohr Siebeck, 1984], 2:27:1:3). Righteous choices and actions performed by persons in relationship with God were understood to be prompted by grace. From the perspective of those with nominalist tendencies who placed more explicit emphasis on the formula "do what is in you," God could save people by any means that did not conflict with his nature, but he had chosen to save people by rewarding believers' efforts to do right, even though these human efforts were not actually sufficient to merit God's favor (Euan Cameron, *The European Reformation* [Oxford: Oxford University Press, 1991], Kindle ed., location 1186–1224; Gerhard Forde, *On Being a Theologian of the Cross* [Grand Rapids, MI: Eerdmans, 1997], Kindle ed., location 606). Martin Luther's struggle, viewed within the framework of medieval nominalism, was whether he could ever do enough beyond the sacraments to merit God's favor. Even such scholastic luminaries as Thomas Aquinas saw salvation to some degree in terms of becoming righteous by acting righteously and meritoriously in response to grace ("ad primum ergo dicendum quod homo sua voluntate facit opera meritoria vitae aeternae; sed, sicut

Augustinus dicit, ad hoc exigitur quod voluntas hominis praeparetur a Deo per gratin," Thomas Aquinas, *Summa Theologiae*, p. 1 of p. 2: q. 109: art. 5). Recommendations from Shawn Wright and Gregg Allison were particularly helpful in this section.

2. A Roman Catholic theologian from Spain estimated that the typical Christian would spend between one and two millennia in purgatory. Pope Sixtus V granted an indulgence of 11,000 years if people recited a particular prayer. William Tyndale described purgatory as a fiction in which, according to Roman Catholic prelates, Christians would spend seven years for every unconfessed sin (Steven Greenblatt, *Hamlet in Purgatory* [Princeton: Princeton University Press, 2001], 35, 70).

3. Quotations from Martin Luther adapted from Roland Bainton, *Here I Stand* (Peabody, MA: Hendrickson, 1950, 1977), 26, 35 – 36, 41.

4. Steven Lawson, *Pillars of Grace* (Lake Mary, FL: Reformation Trust, 2011), Kindle ed., location 5121 – 22.

5. For discussions of Martin Luther's *Turmerlebnis* on the toilet, see Heiko Oberman, *The Reformation* (New York: T&T Clark, 1994), 95 – 103, and Steven Ozment, *The Age of Reform (1250 – 1550)* (New Haven: Yale, 1980), 230.

6. Alister McGrath, *In the Beginning* (New York: Random House, 2008), 46.

7. In Roman Catholic theology, sinners were not perceived to be *declared* righteous on the basis of righteousness outside themselves; they were understood to *become* righteous by means of grace-enabled works of merit. *Iustitia Christi* — the benefits of Christ's righteousness — could be received in a sinner's lifetime, but *iustitia Dei* — God's legal declaration of righteousness — could not be received until final glorification. Martin Luther's recognition of the applied reality of the passive righteousness of God in Christ was a recognition that *iustitia Dei* and *iustitia Christi* are received simultaneously, with the perfect righteousness of Christ being imputed to believers by means of union with Christ, resulting in acquittal before God prior to glorification; this imputation of righteousness occurs in this life by grace through faith (Heiko Oberman, *The Dawn of the Reformation* [Edinburgh: T&T Clark, 1986], 96, 119 – 20).

8. Martin Luther, *Praefatio methodica totius scripturae in epistolam Pauli ad Romanos*.

9. Preserved Smith, ed., *Luther's Correspondence and Other Contemporary Letters* (Philadelphia: LPS, 1913), 1:34, quoted in Gregg Allison, *Historical Theology* (Grand Rapids, MI: Zondervan, 2011), 510.

10. Robert Farrar Capon, *Between Noon and Three* (Grand Rapids, MI: Eerdmans, 1997), 109.

11. Ibid., 109 – 10.

12. One of Jakob Hermanszoon's teachers, Theodore Beza, had developed theological foundations that later developed into supralapsarianism, the view that God's decree of salvation and reprobation logically and conceptually preceded humanity's fall into sin. Beza's visual presentation in *Tabula Praedestinationes* was perceived by some to imply that God works actively and equally both in salvation and reprobation. Franciscus Gomarus, a supralapsarian, became a chief opponent of Jakob Hermanszoon and his followers. In the end, the Synod of Dort did not affirm supralapsarianism — the majority of delegates at the synod favored the infralapsarian position, that God's decree of salvation and reprobation took into account humanity's fall into sin — but neither did the wording of the Canons of Dort reject the supralapsarian position. For further discussion, see J. V. Fesko, "Lapsarian Diversity at the Synod of Dort," in *Drawn into Controversie*, ed. Michael A. G. Haykin and Mark Jones (Oakville, CT: Vandenhoeck and Ruprecht, 2011), 99 – 123. By 1608, Hermanszoon (Arminius), having rejected both supralapsarianism and infralapsarianism, had settled on a position that perceived God's eternal decrees as a response to foreseen human deeds and choices: "A thing does not come to pass because it is foreknown or foretold, but it is foreknown or foretold because it is yet to be" (R. A. Muller, *God, Creation, and Providence in the Thought of Jacob Arminius* [Grand Rapids, MI: Baker, 1991], 161).

13. Arminius agreed, with qualifications, that "'faith is not peculiar to the elect,' and, 'some believers finally decline from the faith.'" He also stated that the reception of saving grace is "both of divine grace and of the human will" (Arminius, *The Apology of James Arminius against Certain Theological Articles Extensively Distributed*, articles 1 – 2, 28). According to the Arminian Remonstrance, God helps "those who are incorporated into Christ" and "keeps them from falling," but this help depends on the disposition and deeds of the Christian; this help comes to Christians only if "they are ready for the conflict, and desire [Christ's] help, and are not inactive" (*Articuli Arminiani sive Remonstratia*, article 5). At the same time, the Remonstrance leaves open the question of whether Christians may fully and finally forfeit their salvation. Even as we reject Arminian soteriology, it is important to note that neither Arminius nor the Remonstrants were soteriological heretics; they did not embrace Pelagianism or even semi-Pelagianism. Pelagianism asserts that persons are capable of doing and choosing good without divine enablement, and grace is thus reduced to the human capacity for good; for Pelagians, a person's nature is not sinful, only the person's actions. Semi-Pelagianism contends that God may assist the individual's initial choice to follow God, but after that point,

it is up to the individual to continue the process of salvation; in addition, semi-Pelagianism downplays or denies humanity's inherited sinful nature and imputed guilt. "In A.D. 431 Pelagianism was condemned in Ephesus ... because it affirmed natural and moral human ability to do God's will apart from the special operation of divine grace. Arminius rejected this teaching, and so do all of his followers. Semi-Pelagianism was condemned by the Second Council of Orange in A.D. 529 because it affirmed human ability to exercise a good will toward God apart from special assistance of divine grace; it places the initiative on the human side, but Scripture places it on the divine side. Arminius also rejected semi-Pelagianism" (Roger Olson, *Arminian Theology* [Downers Grove, IL: InterVarsity, 2006], 81). In Reformed theology, justification is a monergistic work of God to which the newly regenerated individual freely responds with saving faith; sanctification is a synergistic process that includes both divine and human effort. Arminianism is thoroughly synergistic, requiring human choices and divine enablement both in the initiation and in the continuation of salvation. Nevertheless, Arminian and Reformed theologians stand together in their rejection of every form of Pelagianism.

14. R. K. McGregor Wright, *No Place for Sovereignty* (Downers Grove, IL: InterVarsity, 1997), 143.

15. The Canons of Dort responded to the five Arminian articles under four headings, combining the responses to the third and fourth articles — the articles that addressed the extent of human corruption and the manner of conversion — under a single heading ("Tertium et Quartum Doctrinæ Caput, de Hominis Corruptione, et Conversione ad Deum ejusque Modo," *Creeds of Christendom*, vol. 3, ed. Philip Schaff [New York: Harper and Brothers, 1884]). In one sense, then, the Synod of Dort issued only four responses; however, these canons included explicit responses to the third and the fourth articles of the Remonstrance; as such, one can still reasonably refer to five points from the synod.

16. By this, we do not mean that the Canons of Dort repeated precisely what the sixteenth-century Reformers taught. The canons clearly reflect theological developments that occurred throughout the preceding century. Still, the Canons of Dort represent faithful development on the same trajectory as the Reformation, with particular attention having been given to developing theological assertions by means of faithful exposition of the Scriptures. From the Reformers to the Synod of Dort, there was continuity, but there was also development, and neither negates the other. For discussions of the larger issues of continuity and discontinuity in the centuries that separate Calvin from Calvinists, see Richard Muller, *Calvin and the Reformed Tradition* (Grand Rapids, MI: Baker, 2012),

Kindle ed., location 602 – 25, and Carl Trueman, "The Reception of Calvin," in *Histories and Fallacies* (Wheaton, IL: Crossway, 2010), Kindle ed., location 2910 – 3018.

17. Some of the earliest English Baptists held to the Reformed doctrines of grace ("Christ … suffered all those things by which God … might reconcile his elect only" [article 17, London Baptist Confession of Faith]), as did the Orthodox Patriarch Cyril Loukaris (Michael Horton, *For Calvinism* [Grand Rapids, MI: Zondervan, 2011], Kindle ed., location 155; John Meyendorff, *The Orthodox Church* [Yonkers, NY: St. Vladimir's Seminary Press, 1981], 83 – 84). The Synod of Dort never intended their five-point summary to function independently; they meant the five points to serve as a soteriological clarification, supplementing the Belgic Confession and the Heidelberg Catechism. Richard Muller suggests that "it would be a major error — both historically and doctrinally — if the five points of Calvinism were understood as the sole or even the absolutely primary basis for identifying someone as holding Calvinistic or Reformed faith" ("How Many Points?" *Calvin Theological Journal* 28 1993: 426). From the perspective of the Synod of Dort, Muller is undoubtedly correct. However, in the centuries after Dort, the five points did indeed take on a life of their own, separate from their original context, in which they became a primary basis for summarizing Reformed soteriology. One consequence (almost certainly unintended) of this separation of a five-point soteriological clarification from the more comprehensive Reformed confession and catechism was that the Canons of Dort provided a summation of one aspect of Reformed theology — the soteriological aspect — that was no longer inextricably bound to any particular church or movement. This isolated soteriological summation was able to be imported into a variety of other contexts — credo-Baptist churches, for example — where neither the Belgic Confession nor the Heidelberg Catechism could have been embraced in their entirety. In this way, the reductionism that was forced, in some sense, by the necessity of responding to the Arminian Remonstrance became the very factor that ensured the resilience of the Reformed doctrines of grace by making them accessible and transferable beyond their initial confessional context.

18. Quotations from the Canons of Dort are translated from *Canones Synodi Dordrechtanae*, in *Creeds of Christendom*, vol. 3, ed. Philip Schaff (New York: Harper and Brothers, 1884).

19. Steven Lawson, *Pillars of Grace* (Lake Mary, FL: Reformation Trust, 2011), Kindle ed., location 6362; T. H. L. Parker, *John Calvin* (Louisville, KY: WJK, 2007), 191; H. J. Selderhuis, *John Calvin*, ed. Albert Gootjes (Downers Grove, IL: InterVarsity, 2009), 258. The stone engraved with

the name of John Calvin in Cimetière de Plainpalais is a memorial, not a burial site; no one knows the precise location of Calvin's remains.

20. Sixteenth-century correspondence makes it clear that fellow Reformers felt no compulsion to defer to John Calvin's opinions. Martin Bucer and Peter Martyr Vermigli freely critiqued Calvin. Vermigli in particular seems to have contributed as much to the early shaping of Reformed theology as Calvin. For documentation, see Richard Muller, *Calvin and the Reformed Tradition* (Grand Rapids, MI: Baker, 2012), Kindle ed., location 360–400, 790, 997. The term "Calvinist" emerged in the mid–sixteenth century among Calvin's opponents to describe Calvin's view of the Lord's Supper (Michael S. Horton, *For Calvinism* [Grand Rapids, MI: Zondervan, 2011], Kindle ed., location 204). In the seventeenth century, "Calvinist" persisted as a pejorative term utilized by opponents. See, e.g., Peter Heylin, *Ecclesia Vindicita, or The Church of England Justified* (London: Clark, 1681), 525, 605, 633. It was in the eighteenth and nineteenth centuries that persons who embraced Reformed soteriology also began to embrace the epithet "Calvinist." See, e.g., Andrew Fuller, *The Complete Works of the Reverend Andrew Fuller*, reprint ed. (Harrisonburg, VA: Sprinkle, 1988), 1:77: "I reckon strict Calvinism to be my own system." Though Fuller was a Baptist and his view of Christ's atoning work was perceived at times to be out of alignment with others in his day whose soteriology was Reformed, Fuller found it expedient to describe himself as a Calvinist.

21. See W. B. Knight, *Considerations on the Subject of Calvinism* (London: Longman et al., 1822); *The Trial of the Reverend David Swing before the Presbytery of Chicago* (Chicago: Jansen, McClurg, 1874), 36; Robert Lewis Dabney, *The Five Points of Calvinism* (Richmond: Presbyterian Committee, 1895).

22. According to an article from 1913, a certain "Dr. McAfee" of Brooklyn used the TULIP acrostic to summarize the five points of Calvinism "in a popular lecture" delivered around 1905 to the Presbyterian Union of Newark (William Vail, "The Five Points of Calvinism Historically Considered," *The Outlook*, 104 1913. : 394–95). This individual was almost certainly Cleland McAfee, pastor of Lafayette Avenue Presbyterian Church and later professor of didactic and polemic theology at McCormick Theological Seminary in Chicago as well as director of the Presbyterian Board of Foreign Missions. This is the first known usage of TULIP; it appears that the mnemonic device was the creation of Cleland McAfee. In 1903, while a pastor at Park College Presbyterian Church in Missouri, Cleland McAfee wrote the music and lyrics for "There Is a Place of Quiet Rest (Near to the Heart of God)" after his brother and sister-in-law lost both of their daughters to diphtheria within twenty-

four hours; McAfee sang the hymn with a choir in the yard of the quarantined home. For more on McAfee, see "Brooklyn Likely to Lose Great Church Leader," *New York Observer* (May 2, 1912), 548; C. Michael Hawn, "'Near to the Heart of God' Arises from Tragic Loss," *United Methodist Reporter*, http://www.umportal.org.

23. By the time Loraine Boettner published *The Reformed Doctrine of Predestination* (Grand Rapids, MI: Eerdmans, 1932), the terminology for this point had shifted from "universal sovereignty" to "unconditional election." It is uncertain from where Boettner derived his awareness of TULIP. Both Boettner and Cleland McAfee, the apparent originator of TULIP, were Presbyterians from Missouri, though from different areas and in time periods that barely overlapped.

24. Walich Ziwertsz, a Dutch Protestant, was cultivating tulips in Amsterdam in 1573; botanist Carolus Clusius took a position at the University of Leiden around 1593 and popularized tulips in the Low Countries. By the 1630s, the popularity of particularly rare tulips led to a "tulip bubble" in which tulip bulbs were grossly overvalued, resulting in significant financial losses for investors (Mike Dash, *Tulipomania* [London: Gollancz, 1999], 54–60).

25. A broad range of writers and theologians arrived at similar conclusions regarding TULIP; see, e.g., Greg Forster, *The Joy of Calvinism* (Wheaton, IL: Crossway, 2012), 165–67; Richard Muller, *Calvin and the Reformed Tradition* (Grand Rapids, MI: Baker, 2012), Kindle ed., location 1055–1135; James K. A. Smith, *Letters to a Young Calvinist* (Grand Rapids, MI: Brazos, 2010), 14. Forster proposes this alternative acrostic: (1) wholly defiled, (2) unconditional choice, (3) personal salvation, (4) supernatural transformation, and (5) in faith persevering. "This gives us the handy mnemonic WUPSI, pronounced 'whoopsie'—as in, 'Whoopsie, we just realized that TULIP is giving everyone heinously false ideas of what Calvinism is all about.' Perhaps it's not as memorable as TULIP, but it has other virtues to make up for that."

26. "Ever since the appearance of Loraine Boettner's magisterial *The Reformed Doctrine of Predestination*, it has been customary to refer to the five points according to the acrostic TULIP" (David Steele and Curtis Thomas with Lance Quinn, *The Five Points of Calvinism*, rev. ed. [Phillipsburg, NJ: P&R, 2004], xiv). The common perception is that "Calvinists produced the TULIP acronym at the Synod of Dort in 1618 and 1619 in response to the followers of Arminius" (Collin Hansen, *Young, Restless, and Reformed* [Wheaton, IL: Crossway, 2008], 38)—when in fact the synod produced no acronym at all; they wouldn't have used the English word "tulip" even if they had created the acronym (the Dutch word for the bulbous flower

in question is *tulp* not "tulip"), and no one at the synod would likely have claimed the title "Calvinist" as a soteriological label.

27. Kate Shellnut, "Church Stereotypes, According to Google: What Millions and Millions of Searches Reveal about Internet Users' Perceptions," *Christianity Today Online* (October 17, 2013), *http://www.christianity-today.com/ct/2013/october-web-only/church-stereotypes-according-to-google.html*.

28. John Piper, "Why Are Calvinists So Negative?" *Desiring God* (May 21, 2008), *http://www.desiringgod.org/resource-library/ask-pastor-john/why-are-calvinists-so-negative*.

29. Greg Dutcher, *Killing Calvinism* (Toronto: Cruciform, 2012), 14.

30. Reggie Joiner, *Think Orange: Imagine the Impact When Church and Family Collide* ... (Colorado Springs: David C. Cook, 2009), 38.

31. Though these five statements do accurately express central emphases of the Reformation, we find no evidence to suggest that anyone presented these five statements as a settled group until the twentieth century. *Sola fide*, *sola gratia*, and *sola Scriptura* may be found in various locations in the writings of the Reformers, though not as a closed or settled cluster of three. *Sola Scriptura* served as the formal principle of the Reformation, while *sola fide* was seen as the material principle. Publications from the 400th anniversary of the Reformation do refer to these three principles as a settled group (Theodore Engelder, "The Three Principles of the Reformation," *Four Hundred Years*, ed. W. H. T. Dau [St. Louis: Concordia, 1916], 97–109). The two additional principles — *solo Christo* and *soli Deo gloria* — were apparently added to the existing three to form a group of five later in the twentieth century, though *soli Deo gloria* had been in use even before the Reformation, derived from the Vulgate rendering of 1 Timothy 1:17. It may be that *sola fide* was seen as the material cause, *sola Scriptura* as the formal cause, *sola gratia* as the efficient cause, *solo Christo* as the instrumental cause, and *soli Deo gloria* as the final cause. This would provide a Protestant response to the five causes of justification as declared by the Roman Catholic Council of Trent, wherein Christ's death is the meritorious cause, God's justice the formal cause, God's mercy the efficient cause, our baptism the instrumental cause, and God's glory the final cause. More likely, however, *solo Christo* and *soli Deo gloria* simply emerged, first among German theologians, then among British and American Reformed theologians, alongside the existing three to highlight the Reformers' perceived centeredness in the sufficiency of Christ and the glory of God. Discussions with Tom Nettles were helpful in exploring the origins of the five *solae*.

32. Wayne Grudem, *Systematic Theology* (Grand Rapids, MI: Zondervan, 1994, 2000), chapters 4, 6 – 8.
33. Canons of Dort, 3/4:3.
34. Grudem, *Systematic Theology*, 149.
35. Søren Kierkegaard, *Philosophical Fragments*, 2nd ed. (Princeton: Princeton University Press, 1962), 46.
36. Grudem, *Systematic Theology*, 219.
37. Ernest Reisinger and Matthew Allen, *Beyond Five Points*, (Cape Coral, FL: Founders, 2002), 199.
38. Belden Lane, *Ravished by Beauty* (New York: Oxford University Press, 2011), Kindle ed.

Appendices

1. Churches of the Southern Baptist Convention have historically affirmed the perseverance of every believer, but have not always agreed on the extent of the atonement, the radicality of human corruption, the unconditionality of predestination, or the irresistibility of the Holy Spirit's regenerating work. Consequently, the Baptist Faith and Message — a doctrinal statement that summarizes truths held in common among congregations affiliated with the Southern Baptist Convention — allows for Reformed soteriology while never explicitly affirming or requiring acceptance of any tenet of Reformed theology other than the final perseverance of believers. The Abstract of Principles of the Southern Baptist Theological Seminary affirms three of the five points from Dort, but leaves open the issues of the resistibility of grace and extent of the atonement. In 2013 a Calvinism Advisory Committee, appointed by the president of the Southern Baptist Convention Executive Committee, issued a statement entitled "Truth, Trust, and Testimony in a Time of Tension." In this statement, representatives from Reformed and non-Reformed perspectives on salvation clearly and joyfully reaffirmed the capacity and commitment of Reformed and non-Reformed Southern Baptists to cooperate for the sake of global missions.

2. Another way of articulating this question is by considering whether impetration — that which the death of Jesus accomplished — is (1) less extensive than application (atonement pays the price for every individual, even for those who will never believe), (2) categorically different from application (atonement does not purchase persons but obtains the possibility of salvation for all who persist in faith), or (3) coextensive with application (atonement secures the salvation of the elect). The discussions at the time of the Synod of Dort did not, however, center on

impetration, but on intention: What did God intend the death of Christ to accomplish? For further consideration of this discussion, see R. A. Muller, *Calvin and the Reformed Tradition* (Grand Rapids, MI: Baker, 2012), Kindle ed., location 1358–1403. Moises Amyraut argued that, since Jesus was fully human, his atonement must necessarily extend to all humanity, contingent on fulfillment of the condition of faith; this is God's revealed will—but God has another will as well. God's hidden will has to do with the precise identities of those who will, through God's gracious work, fulfill the condition of faith. Amyraut erred not only by moving from Christ's participation in human nature to universal impetration of redemption but also by splitting God's single will, accomplished through duplex means, into two separate wills. For further discussion of the views of Amyraut, see Amar Djaballah, "Controversy on Universal Grace," in *From Heaven He Came and Sought Her*, ed. David Gibson and Jonathan Gibson (Wheaton, IL: Crossway, 2013), 163–98. Due to limited space, we have intentionally not directly addressed the multiple-intentions view of the atonement (sometimes known as "definite indefinite atonement" or "unlimited limited atonement"). Both the classic sufficient-efficient formula and the multiple-intentions viewpoint take seriously the universal aspects of Christ's work while maintaining the biblical emphasis on soteriological particularity. What we have termed "planned grace" includes the multiple-intentions view, and several leaders at Sojourn Community Church hold varying forms of the multiple-intentions view. For a summary of multi-intentioned atonement, see Gregg Allison, *Historical Theology* (Grand Rapids, MI: Zondervan, 2012), 407–8.

3. Peter the Lombard, *Libri Sententiarum Quatuor*, in *Patrologiae Cursus Completus, Series Latina*, ed. J.-P. Migne (Paris: Lutetiae Parisiorum, 1845), 3:20:5.

4. John Calvin, *Commentarius in Epistolas Catholicas: Epistolas Ioannis*, in *Ioannis Calvini Opera Quae Supersunt Omnia*, vol. 55, ed. G. Baum et al. (Brunswick: Schwetschke, 1863), 1 John 2:2. In the sufficiency-efficiency formula, Peter the Lombard did not invent a new perspective on the atonement; he named and articulated more clearly an existing stream of thinking. A theological strand may be identified at least as early as Prosper of Aquitaine that explicitly proclaimed God's intent in Christ to secure the salvation of the elect while simultaneously affirming the sufficiency of this redemption for the whole world, with no apparent sense that one of these truths must be conformed to the other. (Gottschalk of Orbais appears to have been one of the first theologians to affirm explicitly the Father's intent to secure the salvation of the elect

and only the elect to the exclusion of all others through the sufferings
of his Son, but Gottschalk does not seem to have upheld any form of
universal sufficiency. However, since Gottschalk's works do not include
any single comprehensive statement of his views on predestination, it is
difficult to determine his precise perspective on universal sufficiency. For
summaries of Gottschalk's predestinarian views, see J. V. Fesko, *Diversity
within the Reformed Tradition* [Greenville: Reformed, 2001], 32; Francis
X. Gumerlock, "Gottschalk of Orbais," in *Kerux* [December 2007]:
17 – 34. For the works of Gottschalk, see Victor Genke and Francis X.
Gumerlock, eds. and trans., *Gottschalk and a Medieval Predestination Controversy* [Milwaukee: Marquette University Press, 2010], 54.)
Until the emergence of nominalism, most medieval Roman Catholic
theologians followed Peter the Lombard in embracing some form of the
sufficiency-efficiency formula. Immediately after John Calvin's affirma-
tion of the sufficiency-efficiency formula, John Calvin denied its ap-
plicability to 1 John 2:2 without denying the validity of the formula itself.
Calvin's more nuanced view moved beyond the sufficiency-efficiency
formula, but did not contradict it. In Calvin's thinking, God has one will
with a twofold character, not two separate wills: God intends particularly
to save the elect (the precise workings of this aspect of his will remain
hidden), but the means by which he accomplishes the salvation of the
elect is the universal and indiscriminate proclamation of the gospel (this
aspect of his will is openly commanded and communicated in Scripture)
(John Calvin, *Institutio Christianae Religionis*, 1:18:3). As a result, Calvin
seems to have been satisfied to state both that Christ expiated the sins of
the world — that is to say, the sins of all types of people — and that God's
intention was to save particular persons by means of Christ's sacrificial
substitution. For a clear example of this pattern, see Calvin's sermons on
1 Timothy 2, particularly his interpretation of verses 3 – 6, in *Sermons sur
La Premiere Epitre a Timothee*, in *Ioannis Calvini Opera Quae Supersunt
Omnia*, vol. 53, ed. G. Baum et al. (Brunswick: Schwetschke, 1863). Prior
to the Synod of Dort, very few followed Theodore Beza in rejecting the
sufficiency-efficiency formula (W. Robert Godfrey, "Reformed Thought
on the Extent of the Atonement to 1618," *Westminster Theological Journal*
37 1975. : 142 – 50). In the aftermath of the Quartodeciman Controversy,
scholars such as Johannes Piscator and Herman Witsius did reject or
radically modify the sufficiency-efficiency formula, but most Reformed
theologians of the seventeenth century still seem to have maintained
some form of particular efficiency coupled with universal sufficiency.

5. Mark Twain, *The Adventures of Huckleberry Finn* (London: CRW, 2004),
135 – 36.

6. These benefits of the doctrine of predestination are based in part on Wayne Grudem, *Systematic Theology* (Grand Rapids, MI: Zondervan, 2000), 672–73.

7. Geddy Lee, Alex Lifeson, and Neal Peart, "Freewill," *Permanent Waves* (Mercury, 1980).

8. The Reformed view of God's government of human affairs is not causally deterministic but *compatibilistic*, understanding Scripture to teach both comprehensive divine sovereignty and human free agency with neither of these twin truths contradicting the other. For complementary but distinct presentations of compatibilism, see D. A. Carson, *Divine Sovereignty and Human Responsibility* (Eugene, OR: Wipf and Stock, 2002); Donald A. Carson, "The Mystery of Providence," *How Long, O Lord?* (Grand Rapids, MI: Baker, 1990), 199–228; Bruce A. Ware, *God's Greater Glory* (Wheaton, IL: Crossway, 2004); Bruce A. Ware, "The Compatibility of Determinism and Human Freedom," *Whomever He Wills* (Cape Coral, FL: Founders, 2012), ePub ed., location 6246–6666.

9. *Westminster Confession of Faith*, 3:1; see also 9:1.

10. Abstract of Principles, article 4.

11. For function of "free will" in sixteenth-century and earlier debates, see Greg Forster, *The Joy of Calvinism* (Wheaton, IL: Crossway, 2012), 30–32.

12. In *On the Bondage of the Will*, Martin Luther defined and rejected free will as that "power in the human will, by which, a man may apply himself to those things which lead unto eternal salvation" (see *De Servo Arbitrio* 41–43). This definition of free will derives from Desiderius Erasmus, *De Libero Arbitrio Diatribe sive Collatio*, to which Luther's work was a response.

13. On this point, Gerhard Forde accurately summarizes Luther's thought: "There is a large arena in which we do pretty much as we will. Luther called this arena the things 'beneath us (*inferioris*),' that is, those things over which we have dominion because nothing actually stops us. He also speaks of 'means and possessions (*facultatibus et possessionibus*),' which one has a right to use or not, things one can do or not do as one pleases. Luther means that we decide what to do with our money and goods, to come and to go, take what jobs we wish, choose our friends, and so on" (*Theology Is for Proclamation* [Philadelphia: Fortress, 1990], 44–45).

14. Richard Muller, foreword to Dewey Hoitenga, *John Calvin and the Will* (Grand Rapids, MI: Baker, 1997), 7. In *Institutio Christianae Religionis*, 2:2:6–8 in particular, John Calvin clearly affirmed human capacity to make free choices in a manner that is compatible with divine sovereignty while rejecting *libero arbitrio* as the most appropriate phrase to describe this capacity.

SCRIPTURE INDEX

217

Philippians